GENDER AND THE POETICS OF RECEPTION IN POE'S CIRCLE

Poe is frequently portrayed as an isolated idiosyncratic genius who was unwilling or unable to adapt himself to the cultural conditions of his time. Eliza Richards revises this portrayal through an exploration of his collaborations and rivalries with his female contemporaries. Richards demonstrates that he staged his performance of tortured isolation in the salons and ephemeral publications of New York City in conjunction with prominent women poets whose work he both emulated and sought to surpass. She introduces and interprets the work of three important and largely forgotten women poets: Frances Sargent Osgood, Sarah Helen Whitman, and Elizabeth Oakes Smith. Richards re-evaluates the work of these writers, and of nineteenth-century lyric practices more generally, by examining poems in the context of their circulation and reception within nineteenth-century print culture. This book will be of interest to scholars of American print culture as well as specialists of nineteenth-century literature and poetry.

ELIZA RICHARDS is Assistant Professor of English at Boston University. She has published essays in *Arizona Quarterly*, *The Yale Journal of Criticism*, and *Poe Studies*.

Recent books in this series

GENDER AND THE POETICS OF RECEPTION IN POE'S CIRCLE

ELIZA RICHARDS

Boston University

CAMBRIDGE
UNIVERSITY PRESS

CAMBRIDGE UNIVERSITY PRESS
Cambridge, New York, Melbourne, Madrid, Cape Town, Singapore,
São Paulo, Delhi, Dubai, Tokyo, Mexico City

Cambridge University Press
The Edinburgh Building, Cambridge CB2 8RU, UK

Published in the United States of America by Cambridge University Press, New York

www.cambridge.org
Information on this title: www.cambridge.org/9780521174398

First published 2004
First paperback edition 2010

A catalogue record for this publication is available from the British Library

Library of Congress Cataloguing-in-Publication Data
Richards, Eliza.
Gender and the poetics of reception in Poe's circle / Eliza Richards.
p.   cm. – (Cambridge studies in American literature and culture: 144)
Based on author's thesis (doctoral) – University of Michigan, 1997.
Includes bibliographical references and index.
ISBN 0 521 83281 0
1. American poetry – New York (State) – New York – History and criticism.   2. Poe, Edgar Allan,
1809–1849 – Homes and haunts – New York (State) – New York.   3. Smith, Elizabeth Oakes Prince,
1806–1893 – Criticism and interpretation.   4. Osgood, Frances Sargent Locke, 1811–1850 – Criticism
and interpretation.   5. Whitman, Sarah Helen, 1803–1878 – Criticism and interpretation.   6. Poets,
American – Homes and haunts – New York (State) – New York.   7. Women and literature – United
States – History – 19th century.   8. American poetry – Women authors – History and criticism.
9. American poetry – 19th century – History and criticism.   10. Poe, edgar Allan,
1809–1849 – Friends and associates.   11. New York (N.Y.) – Intellectual life – 19th century.
12. Poe, Edgar Allan, 1809–1849 – Contemporaries.   13. Authorship – Sex differences. I. Title.
II. Series.
PS255.N5R53   2004
811'.30997471 – dc22   2003069737

ISBN 978-0-521-83281-6 Hardback
ISBN 978-0-521-17439-8 Paperback

In memory of Ann, and for Raúl.

Helen thy beauty is to me
Like those Nicéan barks of yore . . .

Poe, "To Helen"

The face was my lover's face. Do you know those white, water-lily magnolias? I suppose I thought the words he said. He said "Helen thy beauty." Is poetry enchantment? Have people forgotten what poetry is?

H. D., *Paint it Today*

Contents

Illustrations

Acknowledgments

I'm as sorry as I am certain that I cannot name all those who have provided myriad forms of support over the years it has taken to write a dissertation and transform it into this book. I'm indebted to all my teachers at the University of Michigan, and especially to the members of my dissertation committee for their careful attention to this project in its earlier stages. Carroll Smith-Rosenberg graciously agreed to sign on late in the process, asked important questions about methodology and scope, and offered important research suggestions. David Scobey read chapter drafts with the fullest enthusiasm and unstintingly shared his historical expertise. Julie Ellison's innovative intellectual energy was positively contagious; she encouraged me to pursue promising, unlikely lines of inquiry. Rei Terada's insightful, challenging marginal meditations initiated an ongoing conversation that has immeasurably benefited both me and my work. Kerry Larson's wise, rigorous mentoring began long before he agreed to direct my dissertation; his standards of excellence have continued to serve as my benchmark for the value and integrity of academic labor.

My Americanist reading group at the University of Michigan – Maria Bergstrom, Alix Casteel, Mike Niklaus, Dottie Webb, and David Westbrook – provided a lively forum for discussing chapter drafts. Yopie Prins' intellectual generosity has inspired me and sustained my work. Susan Rosenbaum has helped unfailingly at crucial moments, offering clear and concise evaluations of my writing, often under demanding time constraints. The readers at Cambridge University Press, anonymous at the time but now revealed to me as Caroline Levander and Virginia Jackson, offered thoughtful, incisive suggestions that have made this a better book. For reading and discussing work in progress and offering valuable criticism, my thanks go to David Anthony, Paula Bennett, Bill Brown, Bonnie Costello, Bridget Ford, Susan Stanford Friedman (especially for drawing my attention to H.D.'s Poe dream), Teresa Goddu, June Howard, Mary Kelley, Janice Knight, Laura Korobkin, Mary Loeffelholz, Chris Lukasik, Jack Matthews,

Meredith McGill, Susan Mizruchi, Jolynn Parker, Anita Patterson, Adela
Pinch, Christopher Ricks, John Paul Riquelme, Karen Sànchez-Eppler,
Jani Scandura, Jim Sidbury, Patricia Meyer Spacks, and Nick Yablon. I
benefited from the discussions of chapters at the University of Michigan's
Institute for the Humanities, the University of Chicago's Early American
Seminar, the 1997 graduate seminar on nineteenth-century women's poetry
at the University of Michigan, and Boston University's Humanities Foundation; thanks to all participants. The Nineteenth-Century American Women
Writers Group has provided a congenial setting for exchanging ideas with
other feminist scholars; I am grateful to all who have attended our gatherings
over the years. My thanks go also to the talented undergraduate students
in my poetry classes at Boston University; my ideas have developed in
dialogue with them. Kristin Smith worked through the page proofs with
cheerful efficiency and care; I deeply appreciate her help at a crucial time.

The faculty in the English Department at Boston University have supported the development of my work, and I'm grateful for their warm colle-
giality. For their extraordinary generosity, I'd particularly like to thank Bill
Carroll, Bonnie Costello, Laura Korobkin, Chris Lukasik, Jack Matthews,
Jim Siemon, and James Winn. I'm also grateful for the enthusiastic support
of Dean Jeffrey Henderson and Dean Susan Jackson. The College of Arts
and Sciences generously provided funds for the illustrations. I had the pleasure and privilege of spending the 2002–2003 academic year at the American
Antiquarian Society on a National Endowment for the Humanities
Fellowship. The release from teaching helped me to complete the revi-
sions on *Gender and the poetics of reception in Poe's circle* even while I was
conducting research on my next project. I'm grateful for the fellowship
of Karsten Fitz, Bridget Ford, Bob Gross, Jim Sidbury, and Nick Yablon;
thanks also to Heike Fitz, Sarah Fitz, and Caroline Sloat.

A number of institutions have generously provided funding for research
and writing. A Mellon Foundation Dissertation Grant provided a much-
needed year of support. The Rackham Graduate School at the University
of Michigan provided a semester of support as well as grants for travel to
archives. I benefited greatly from the year I spent as a Graduate Fellow at the
University of Michigan's Institute for the Humanities. Warm thanks go to
the Institute's helpful staff: Betsy Nisbet, Linnea Perlman, Mary Price, and
Eliza Woodford. As a Harper-Schmidt Postdoctoral Fellow at the University
of Chicago, I worked with gifted undergraduates and was afforded substantial time and resources to pursue my scholarship. Boston University's
Humanities Foundation provided a semester's release from teaching at a
crucial time.

This book could not have been written without access to archival materials, and I am grateful to a number of institutions for permission to quote from their holdings. I have quoted from the Elizabeth Oakes Smith Papers (#38-707), Special Collections, University of Virginia Library and the Elizabeth Oakes Prince Smith Papers, Manuscripts and Archives Division, The New York Public Library, Astor, Lenox and Tilden Foundations. The Frances Sargent Locke Osgood Papers are used by permission of the Houghton Library, Harvard University. Letters from George Eveleth to Sarah Helen Whitman are quoted by courtesy of the Lilly Library, Indiana University, Bloomington, Indiana. The Sarah Helen Whitman Papers and a memoir by William Whitman Bailey in the Hay Manuscripts are used courtesy of the Brown University Library. Thanks to the Brown University Library and to the American Antiquarian Society for their kind permission to reproduce images from their holdings as illustrations. I am grateful for the expert help of Mark Brown and Jean Rainwater at the John Hay Library. At the American Antiquarian Society, Joanne Chaison, Tom Knowles, Marie Lamoureux, and Jennifer Moore provided generous help as I was working on the final stages of manuscript preparation.

Portions of chapter 1 were published in an earlier version as "'The Poetess' and Poe's Performance of the Feminine" in *Arizona Quarterly* 55: 2 (Summer 1999). A portion of chapter 3 was published in an earlier version as "Lyric Telegraphy: Women Poets, Spiritualist Poetics, and the 'Phantom Voice' of Poe" in *The Yale Journal of Criticism* 12: 2 (1999); I'm grateful to these journals for their permission to reprint materials here.

My mother, Ann Forbes Greenough Richards, generously helped me to pursue goals that were not as readily available to her; she died before she could see the completion of the project. Raúl Miguel Aguilar provided loving support and understanding through every stage of the process; I dedicate this book to them.

Note on Texts Used

I have done my best to track down the full citations for newspaper and magazine clippings that I first encountered in library special collections. Occasionally, however, I was unable to locate the clipping's source; in these cases, I give as much information as possible.

Abbreviations

PIL   Lizzie Doten, *Poems From the Inner Life* (Boston: William White and Co., 1864).

PL   *The Poe Log: A Documentary Life of Edgar Allan Poe, 1809–1849* (Boston: G. K. Hall and Co., 1987).

PW   *The Poetical Writings of Elizabeth Oakes Smith* (NY: J. S. Redfield, 1845).

RWE   *Ralph Waldo Emerson.* Ed. Richard Poirier (New York: Oxford University Press, 1990).

SHWP   Sarah Helen Whitman, *Poems* (Boston: Houghton, Osgood, and Co., 1979).

SP   John Grier Varner, *Sarah Helen Whitman: Seeress of Providence* (Ph.D. Diss. University of Virginia, 1940).

Archives

Virginia   Elizabeth Oakes Smith Papers (308–707), Special Collections, University of Virginia Library.

Brown   Sarah Helen Whitman Papers (MS 79.11), Brown University Library.

Houghton   Frances Sargent Osgood Papers (bMS Am). Houghton Library, Harvard University.

Lilly   Sarah Helen Whitman Papers, Lilly Library, Indiana University, Bloomington, IN.

NYPL   The Elizabeth Oakes Smith Papers, Manuscripts and Archives Division, The New York Public Library.

Introduction

POE'S CIRCLE

In 1845, at the height of his career, Edgar Allan Poe asked popular "poetess" Frances Sargent Osgood to write a poem "equal to my reputation" that he could present at the Boston Lyceum (*EAP* 286). The request presumes Osgood's ability to emulate his work so closely that her poem could pass as his own. The mimic powers of poetesses intrigued Poe, and he was not above imitating them. That Elizabeth Barrett's "Lady Geraldine's Courtship" was a rhythmic prototype for "The Raven" is commonly known, but there are many other unacknowledged occasions when women's poems inform his work. Soliciting his attention, poetesses also imitated Poe, writing tributes in the style of "Israfel" and "The Raven." While this fluid exchange of copies renders the project of identifying an original questionable at best, critics have persistently credited Poe with the powers of innovation and the force of genius, even in recent studies that place him within the context of antebellum mass and print culture. The "poetess" tradition, on the other hand, has long been associated with the generic repetition of feminine forms that silence women's attempts to speak as anyone in particular. This study of a male genius figure who impersonates women poets, and women poets who personify mimesis, offers a way to understand the collusion of genius and mimicry in the nineteenth-century lyric and its legacies. I aim to show that seemingly opposed poetic modes are inseparable aspects of a process of cultural transmission; that men's and women's literary traditions are overlapping and interdependent, though not identical; that the gendering of poetic practices is far more fluid and complex than has been previously portrayed; and that the poetics of creation are inseparable from the poetics of reception.

This project returns to the scene of Poe's creation, the literary salons and ephemeral publications of New York City, where he publicly staged his performance of tortured isolation in collaboration with prominent

I

women poets – Frances Sargent Osgood, Sarah Helen Whitman, and Elizabeth Oakes Smith – whose work he both emulated and sought to surpass.[1] Drawing extensively on archival research, I re-evaluate the work of this circle of writers, and of nineteenth-century lyric practices more generally, by interpreting poems in terms of their circulation within social networks in a period when the "whole tendency of the age is Magazine-ward," in the words of Poe (*ER* 1414).[2] All four writers succeeded in an antebellum literary culture that valued poets as performance artists and celebrities as well as geniuses. While salons and genteel periodicals portrayed authorship as the domain of uniquely gifted individuals, they also fueled the rise of a celebrity culture that placed "geniuses" and "poetesses" in close conversation. Publications such as *The Home Journal, Godey's Lady's Book*, and *Graham's Magazine* both published the poems, sketches, and stories of the New York literati and reported on their social activities. Literary gossip conveyed scenarios of intimate exchange among authors through ever-expanding, increasingly impersonal print networks.[3] These depictions encouraged readers to interpret poems as acts in interpersonal dramas that mediated spiritual, erotic, and conversational exchanges among poets, rather than as autonomous expressions of individual thought and feeling. Readers imitated these intimate models of public exchange when imagining their relation to writers they had never met: they wrote fan letters, offered proposals of marriage, confided secrets, and composed tributes in the style of their favorite poets. This contagious quality of the poet's work built literary reputation, for the greater the number of imitators, the farther-flung the poet's inspirational "presence."[4]

While all four poets earned significant measures of celebrity, in large part due to their dramatic collaborations, "Poe" has come to stand as the sign of the poet to which the poetesses' practices are ascribed, and this study inquires into the riddle of remembered and forgotten names. The reflexive intimacy of their exchanges makes it impossible to extricate genius from mimicry, or expression from quotation, in any of these authors' work. Poe's readings of poetesses became the poems he wrote; and poetesses' readings of Poe became the poems they wrote. In reading poetesses, then, Poe wrote himself, and in reading Poe, poetesses wrote themselves. While the process was fully transactional, however, the results were not symmetrical. For in writing themselves, poetesses wrote Poe into cultural memory, whereas in writing himself, Poe wrote poetesses into the dustbins of history. Because gendered understandings of poetry in the antebellum period and beyond have attributed distinct practices and capacities to male and female poets, Osgood, Whitman, and Oakes Smith circulated as literary commodities and consumers regardless of how much poetry they produced; and Poe circulated as a literary producer regardless of how much women's poetry he consumed, or how extensively he commodified himself. This is not to say that readers have conspired to bury talented poetesses, but rather that the terms of reception so shaped the terms of poetic production that the poetesses had to render their work ephemeral, even against their will, because existing conditions required it.

In spite of the asymmetry of these exchanges and their legacy, writing as one's "self" under these conditions meant writing as the other. For this reason, celebrating these writers for being "themselves," or condemning them for not being able to find or transmit their "true voices" misses the point in a way that fundamentally misreads nineteenth-century poetic culture. By championing particular voices as authentic, we rescue individual figures at the expense of understanding a literary culture in which voice is not easily attributable. Paradoxically, the search for authentic women's voices has rendered the cultural work of poetesses largely illegible, and has significantly limited readings of Poe and other nineteenth-century American poets.[5]

I will argue that Osgood, Whitman, and Oakes Smith have been forgotten not, or not only, because twentieth-century critics have discriminated against women's voices, nor because a modernist sensibility has supplanted an earlier sentimental aesthetic that the critic must recover and render comprehensible. Rather, the uncanny affinity between poetesses and lyric media marked them as vehicles of cultural transmission. Instead of inscribing their future reception under their proper names, the poetesses grounded their "fictions of form" in ephemerality, self-dissolution, and ventriloquy.[6] While erasing the author's signature, these disappearing or indecipherable forms nevertheless served as powerful transmitters of ideas. Indeed, the practices of poetesses became so wholly identified with the genre of poetry that their influence lives on anonymously, not as canonical poetry's opposite, but as its generic underpinning.[7] Poe stood among the women writers as one who sought to harness their receptive powers and upstage their popular success by performing a more authentic relation to feminine traditions of mediumship, one that was at once more estranged and more derivative. By establishing his imitation of the feminine as superior to women's own impersonations, Poe's literary survival comes at the expense of his female contemporaries, but their work nevertheless lives on in his name.[8] While this *is* a book on Poe, then, I understand "Poe" to be a reversal or mirroring of the type of the poetess; he is a figure to which the transactions among a circle of poets is ascribed, and through which poetic conventions of romantic exchange survive in a crystallized form.

Although Poe criticism frequently centers on the figure of the dead woman, ubiquitous in his poetry and fiction, and although Poe biographies explore in sometimes fanciful detail his personal relationships with women – his marriage to his tubercular young cousin Virginia; the possibility of a scandalous affair with Frances Sargent Osgood; his fleeting engagement to Sarah Helen Whitman; his friendship with Elizabeth Oakes Smith – the crucial impact of women's writing practices on his own has received minimal attention.[9] This oversight is surprising considering the extent of Poe's interactions with women poets, who appeared frequently in both the journals that he edited and those to which he contributed, who hosted the salons that he attended, and who inspired his romantic interest on more than one occasion. Many of Poe's later reviews, moreover, were devoted to women's poetry. The persistence with which this large body of criticism is dismissed as mere flattery suggests that Poe's place in the canon depends upon a negation of his connections with poetesses, a negation that foregrounds his physical attraction to women writers at the expense of his interest in their words. I argue, to the contrary, that in Poe's poetry the force of erotic attraction towards women's bodies stands in for and suppresses a stronger attraction and reaction to their mimic strategies of poetic embodiment. Replicating and extending this logic, traditions of Poe criticism deny women's influence and sacrifice Poe's feminine-identified poetry to his prose in order to maintain his tenuous canonical status. Examining this tradition of critical advocacy helps to explain the erasure of these once prominent women poets from cultural memory.

I am less interested in exposing the peculiar contradictions of a particular male author's engagements with a collection of poetesses than in elucidating the complex gendering of American romantic lyricism in the nineteenth century. Though feminine receptivity was a crucial trait in delineations of male genius – a trait associated most powerfully with the lyric in the late eighteenth and early nineteenth century – the influx of women poets onto the American literary scene in the early part of the nineteenth century caused male poets defensively to redefine ideas of creative process.[10] If the "feminine" was a key component of genius, and women had a greater concentration of it, then how could men retain a claim to poetic primacy? On the other hand, the resemblance between profiles of romantic genius and of ideal womanhood emboldened women to identify a renewed sense of poetic vocation. The following chapters demonstrate the ways in which male writers worked to codify and thus to stabilize the relations between gender and poetics to their advantage. By contrast, the poetesses took up postures towards the feminization of the poetics of reception that were simultaneously more direct and more oblique. Because most studies of nineteenth-century American women's poetry have charted a separate women's tradition, the cultural dissemination and appropriation of their work has fallen outside of the scope of these earlier projects. Myra Jehlen's warning that feminist critics "have been, perhaps, too successful in constructing an alternative footing" so that "our female intellectual community . . . becomes increasingly cut off even as it expands" remains trenchant particularly for the study of nineteenth-century women's poetry.[11] Here I track the ways that the work of poetesses is overtly dismissed by, but nevertheless implicitly informs, canonical literary tradition.

Poe's circle of poetesses serves as a particularly useful place to explore these processes of cultural transmission because, as Jonathan Elmer has argued, Poe's work foregrounds to an unusual degree the inextricable relation of individual and mass forms of expression. His oscillation between the two poles has generated a reception history in which critics have pronounced Poe's work both wonderful and horrible, original and derivative, sublime and ridiculous. Because Poe is such an equivocal figure, the critical labor invested in making him into an autonomous, self-enclosed genius is more defensive, more extensive, and therefore more easily traced than other canonical writers.[12] Writing on Poe's "unauthorized" circulation in his time, Meredith McGill argues that "there remains a potent instability between the underinscription of the author's name in antebellum periodicals and the overproduction of the apparatus of attribution in twentieth-century criticism, an imbalance that works more as an engine for attribution than as a spur to thinking about the difference between these two literary regimes."[13] Poe criticism is by now so well established that the difference made by reintroducing his circle of poetesses is immediately and dramatically evident. These women writers were so closely associated with mass culture that extricating Poe in order to stabilize his literary authority necessarily entails erasing his connections to them. But the labor is never permanently successful. Poe's connections to poetesses are so obvious and extensive that they perennially arise and must be repeatedly discredited in critical acts that mimic Poe's own response to his female peers. Analyzing the production and reception of poetry within his circle allows me to trace the ways that interpersonal exchanges and cultural transactions come to be received as internal processes of gifted individuals. The model of literary and cultural production that emerges is inter-subjective and interactive and cannot be fully attributed to anyone in particular.

LYRIC CIRCULATION: MEDIUMS AND MEDIA

Recent studies of gender and sentiment in nineteenth-century American literature and culture have largely anchored their claims in readings of the novel and other narrative forms. I argue that poetry played a crucial but neglected role in engendering personality and sociability in the period. In contrast to the novel, lyric was associated with the capacity for unmediated personal expression. Its brevity also lent it a superior ability to circulate broadly through epistolary and print networks. While the novel carried, constituted, and influenced a range of competing social discourses, it did not serve as an active medium of social exchange in the same way as poetry.[14] Poetry served as a communicative form that enabled the exchange of ideas among individuals, within social groups, and between arenas coded as private and public.

Reading lyric in terms of its circulation, then, has the potential to expand and revise understandings of the function, location, and limitations of gendered forms of literary expression in the nineteenth-century public sphere.[15] Lauren Berlant has argued that women's sentimental fiction created a "a safe feminine space, a textual habitus" through which women could both acquiesce to and critique the patriarchal public sphere that dictated and constrained their forms of expression.[16] Berlant's analysis of "the female complaint," characterized by "a collaboration between the commodity form and the stereotype on behalf of a feminine counter-politics," has crucially informed this study, which traces the ways that gendered conventions both limit and enable gender critique in poetic form (432–433). When attending to lyric, however, I find that delineating a female counter-public sphere is largely impossible. Instead I assert that poetesses – in connection with Poe and other male poets – *constituted* a lyric public sphere through exchanges in which gendered poetic convention is distinct from the author's gender. The circulation of lyric in print renders gender conventions mobile, flexible, and transferable in a way that the corporeal presence of the author disallows. Because the relation between men's and women's poems is reciprocally imitative, it is impossible to separate out strains of male and female poetic practice. In fact, the constant traffic between gendered forms and values ensures that antebellum fictions of segregated genres – which hold that the author's sex determines the contours and content of lyric expression – operate in the service of gender exchange. Because there is no separate feminine "textual habitus," there is no distinct ground from which to launch a counter-cultural critique.

There is moreover no way to recover or represent historically particular women or men within the public economy of forms that are only generically personal. Berlant identifies a "counterstrain" of sentimentality, developed by writers such as Harriet Beecher Stowe and Fanny Fern, "which aimed critically to distinguish 'women' in their particularity from 'woman' in her generic purity" (434). The idea that women might find a way to represent their historical particularity in the printed lyric, however, extends the logic that Berlant critiques, for nineteenth-century conventions of reception coded women's lyric writings as embodied vocal expression. Most nineteenth-century poetesses are today found lacking because they did not achieve the impossible: they could not make print speak as if it were a living woman's voice. In other words, a literal reception of generic conventions of female presence has erased the generic contributions of historically particular women poets. Though speaking in print is impossible, women's generic writings are not void of expression, nor are they entirely identical with the writings of men, nor are they politically or aesthetically neutral. The poetess' lyric is an involuntary mode of transport for multivalent cultural messages, which is nevertheless marked, albeit indirectly, by individual agency.

Because the cultural field of nineteenth-century lyric is less familiar than that of the novel, it is worth reviewing some of the ways in which poetry circulated through genteel social spaces – especially the salon and the magazine – in the service of conflicting but mutually constitutive impulses of democratic exchange and social discrimination. Occupying a place at the threshold between domestic and public urban arenas, the literary salons that sprang up in American cities in the 1830s and reached their peak in the '40s and '50s were key locations for the performance and dissemination of intimate models of lyric transaction (fig. 1). An extension of parlor gatherings, which had long provided family circles with inexpensive home entertainment, literary salons promoted interchange among a larger, more impersonal group of distinguished guests.[17] In a lecture entitled "The Salon in America," writer and reformer Julia Ward Howe identifies three main uses for the institution: "to make people better friends"; "to enlarge individual minds by the interchange of thought and expression with other minds"; and to employ "certain sorts and degrees of talent which would not be available either for professional, business, or educational work, but which, appropriately combined and used, can forward the severe labors included under these heads, by the instrumentality of sympathy, enjoyment, and good taste."[18] According to Howe, the gatherings render boundaries between individuals and social sectors permeable, promoting the circulation and

Fig. 1: "The Soirée." Unsigned. *Godey's Lady's Book*, vol. 30 (January–June 1845).

reception of ideas even as they reinforce the contours and limits of white, middle-class gentility. In this setting, as people become intellectually receptive and socially adhesive, individual knowledge becomes the semi-public property of a broader, but still exclusive, or "discriminating" (Howe's word), community.

Howe casts the American salon as a key component of a democratic system of "power and social recognition" that is fluid, metamorphic, and diffused. Whereas she imagines European systems to be static, stable, and centralized, she claims that "in our own broad land, power and light have no such inevitable abiding place, but may emanate from an endless variety of points and personalities" (129). Because America's "boundaries should be elastic, capable even of indefinite expansion," its survival and growth depend on maintaining the proper circulation of "intelligence and sympathy" through myriad, node-like "centres," "each subordinated to the governing harmony of the universe, but each working to keep together the social atoms that belong together" (120). Howe does not wish to dispense with "social discrimination"; rather, the salon affords a decentralized form of social control that organizes the circulation of thoughts and feelings through highly permeable identic boundaries, but nevertheless wards off the indiscriminate mixing and cultural homogenization – the massing – that could result: "'What then!' will you say, 'shall society become an agrarian mob?' By no means. Its great domain is everywhere crossed by boundaries. All of us have our proper limits, and should keep them, when we have once learned them" (119). According to John Kasson, "established codes of behavior have often served in unacknowledged ways as checks against a fully democratic order and in support of special interests, institutions of privilege, and structures of domination."[19] Howe's comments suggest that salons were one arena where polite standards of behavior were instituted and practiced as a form of social control.

Because salons operated in the service of cultural transmission, it is not surprising that poetesses frequently hosted salons and personified their aims and principles. Prominent antebellum hostesses included Ann Lynch, Elizabeth Oakes Smith, Lydia Sigourney, Stella Lewis, Emma Embury, and the Cary sisters.[20] The salon hostess was supposed to elicit the creative facets of guests and blend disparate individuals into a harmonious, cohesive group. According to A. C. Bloor, who published a memoir of Lynch:

the woman of society forms and maintains the salon which gathers within its walls the cream of her entourage, and forms an exchange not for the coarser – if essential – commodities of the field and the mine, but for those gifts of intellect, breeding, and courtesy which, to the highly trained man or woman, are such essential elements to happiness, and which so largely contribute to refine and sweeten everyday life.[21]

A version of the commodities trader, the hostess traffics in cultural rather than material goods. She "forms an exchange" that promotes civility by circulating ineffable "gifts" through the medium of her home and, even more intimately, her bodily presence.

Participants appreciated salons and their hostesses for promoting cosmopolitan cultural exchange within the bounds of "fashionable society." Oakes Smith recalls: "I had my well-attended receptions like Dr. Dewey, and many others, but those of Miss Ann C. Lynch . . . became of wide celebrity. She had all the tact of a French woman – was an author of no small merit – was personally pretty, with a glow and repartee quite charming" (*HL* 270). Emerson hailed Lynch's New York salon, which figures as one of the backdrops for this study, as the "house of the expanding doors."[22] Lynch's doors expanded to include visitors that literary history has sifted into distinct categories: Bronson Alcott, William Cullen Bryant, the Cary sisters, Emerson, Margaret Fuller, Henry Wadsworth Longfellow, Herman Melville, Elizabeth Oakes Smith, Frances Sargent Osgood, Poe, R. H. Stoddard, Bayard Taylor, H. T. Tuckerman, Sarah Helen Whitman, and N. P. Willis. Foreign visitors included the violinist Ole Bull, the Swedish novelist Frederika Bremer, and the actress Fanny Kemble. Guests recited poetry, played musical instruments, donned costumes, exchanged valentines, and discussed the current political and cultural scene at home and abroad. They cultivated personalities as art forms; fashionable self-presentation was a notable achievement, and conversation had as much aesthetic value as poetry.[23]

Fostering the interplay between hermetic self-enclosure and public display, Lynch's salon provided a place where "isolated" genius and promiscuous popularity mingled in a contingent, mutually constitutive, and even interchangeable relation. Famously alienated later in his career, the young "Melville, with his cigar and his Spanish eyes, talked Typee and Omoo just as you find the flow of his delightful mind on paper." Promoting a poetess' genius, "Poe led a lively discussion on the worth of Elizabeth Oakes Smith's narrative poem, 'The Sinless Child,' insisting that it was one of the best long poems in the language."[24] Oakes Smith recalled a valentine party when Margaret Fuller – singled out today as an exceptional, iconoclastic female intellectual, and criticized by other women in her time for her sense of superiority – expressed frustration at Frances Osgood's talent for attracting admirers:

I remember Mrs. Osgood and I ran up to the dressing room with our hands full of tributes; Fannie had more than us all. As we neared the landing I heard a very heavy sigh, almost a groan, and, looking up, saw Miss Fuller looking over the balustrade. Putting my hand on her arm, I said: "You do not care for trifles like these; your one was better than all others." "It leaves me alone as I always am," was the reply.[25]

In Oakes Smith's strategic description – one that arguably contests Fuller's claim to genius in order to advance her own – Osgood's triumph of seduction sets Fuller's solitary intellectual suffering in relief. Osgood's success at trifles trumps, in this moment, Fuller's ascetic singularity, her "one." Both are social performances – the hands full of tributes, the heavy sigh of loneliness – that accrue meaning through dramatic contrast. Wanting valentines, Fuller publicly displays her tortured isolation at the balustrade in a bid for sympathy. Her lack claims the compensatory attention that Oakes Smith bestows. Fuller had a right to be disappointed, for these trifles commanded a public readership; on such occasions valentines were published in the *Home Journal* and elsewhere, confirming that Osgood and other popular poetesses had a circulatory power that Fuller did not harness (*EAP* 348–349).

Salons actively conflated privacy and publicity with the aid of the many figures in the publishing industry who were regular attendants. Prominent editors like Rufus Griswold (*Graham's Magazine*), Poe (*The Broadway Journal*), N. P. Willis (*The Home Journal*), Horace Greeley (*New York Tribune*), and Hiram Fuller (*The Mirror*) frequented salons and cultivated relationships with the writers they published in their pages. Literary hostesses were sometimes editors as well as poetesses: Emma Embury, Lydia Sigourney, Sarah Helen Whitman, and Elizabeth Oakes Smith all had editing experience. By reporting on the happenings among the invitation-only crowd, and by publishing poems exchanged among salon attendants, magazine writers and editors produced fantasies of intimacy in public media, and salon-goers in turn crafted personal intimacies through public display.[26] Howe stresses the irony that the salon's "severe restriction of membership" results in "an un-limited extension of reputation," attributing this effect to a desire for self-promotion: "We wish it to exclude the general public, but we dreadfully desire that it shall be talked about and envied by the general public" (117–118).

The lyric poem was a prime vehicle for the convergence of privacy and publicity in salons and the periodical press. Though the novel has long held a central place in American literary and cultural studies, it is less often noted that "the mid-century was the great era of poetry," characterized by a massive circulation of lyric that constituted a full-blown economy of emotional exchange.[27] More novels may have been printed in book form, but poems, because of their compactness, were more adaptable for publication in rapidly multiplying ephemeral print media. Literary historian William Charvat notes that "the rise of the American magazine was . . . crucial in the development of American poetry."[28] Not bulky enough to flesh out books easily, lyric poetry's slightness made it perfect filler, "not only because an editor must cover all his white space with type, but because magazine-buyers, geared to brevity, read and run" (102). By the mid-1820s the "periodical became the primary outlet for poets," and magazine editors were paying for their contributions (102). By the forties, the combination of increasingly professional editing practices, sound commercial management, and improvements in the national transit system put the poet in a position "to communicate directly with all literate levels of society in all populated regions. No truly popular American poetry could be produced until this phenomenon had occurred" (102–103). During this time American poetry became a profession. In the 1830s, celebrities were largely

Fig. 2: "I've Thought of Something." An inspired woman writes an "Ode" in the middle of the night while her husband holds a crying child. Painting by R. N. Buss; engraved by Alfred Jones. *The Literary Emporium: A Compendium of Religious, Literary, and Philosophical Knowledge*. Vols. 1 and 2 (NY: J. K. Wellman, 1845). Poe's "The Raven" is in the same volume.

European – Byron and Hemans were particularly marketable names – while contributions from American poets were often printed anonymously. By the early 1840s, however, the names of American poets and poetesses were prominently displayed in the table of contents of *Godey's* and on the cover of *Graham's* – two of the magazines that came closest to having a national circulation in the period (fig. 3).[29] Editors courted well-known American poets, trying to convince them to write exclusively for one journal or at least to contribute regularly, and American poets were the first to make substantial sums of money.[30]

Charvat gives the American magazine a crucial role in the development of American poetry, and yet he neglects to note that white, middle-class women poets rose to prominence on the magazine wave. Fred Lewis Pattee maintains that "the American literary 'female' as seen in the 1830s and the 1840s, was a writer of verse" (fig. 2).[31] According to Nina Baym, between

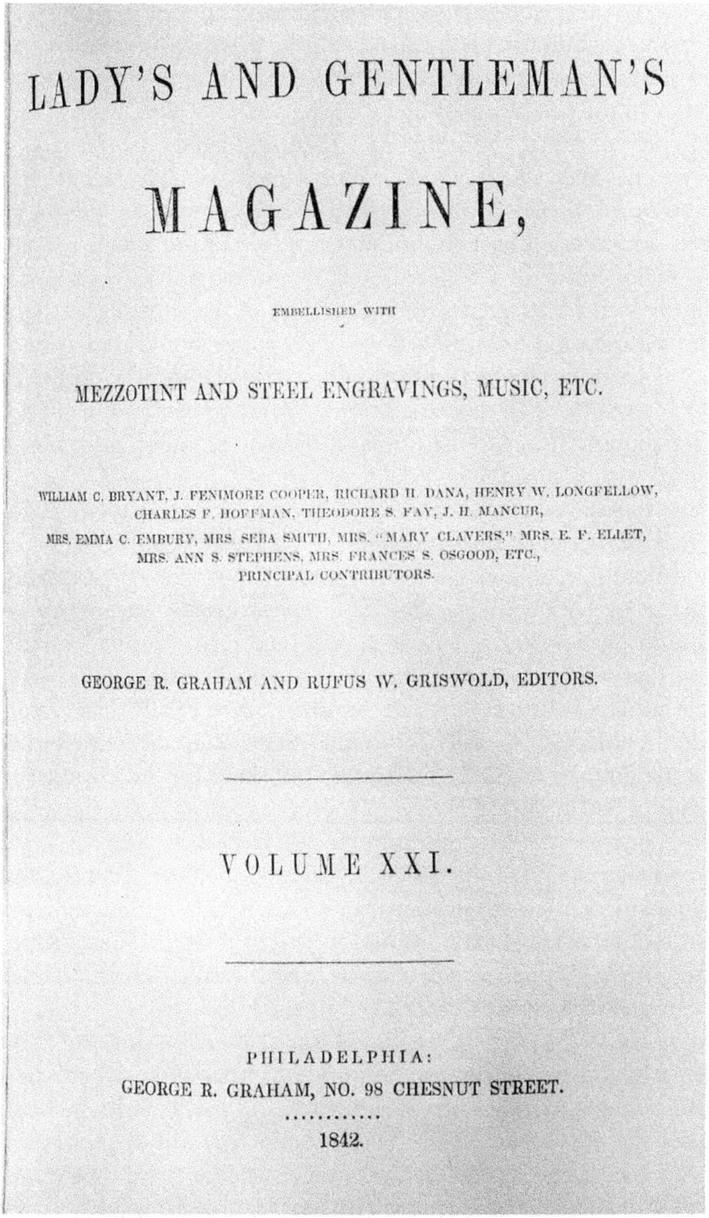

LADY'S AND GENTLEMAN'S

MAGAZINE,

EMBELLISHED WITH

MEZZOTINT AND STEEL ENGRAVINGS, MUSIC, ETC.

WILLIAM C. BRYANT, J. FENIMORE COOPER, RICHARD H. DANA, HENRY W. LONGFELLOW,
CHARLES F. HOFFMAN, THEODORE S. FAY, J. H. MANCUR,
MRS. EMMA C. EMBURY, MRS. SEBA SMITH, MRS. "MARY CLAVERS," MRS. E. F. ELLET,
MRS. ANN S. STEPHENS, MRS. FRANCES S. OSGOOD, ETC.,
PRINCIPAL CONTRIBUTORS.

GEORGE R. GRAHAM AND RUFUS W. GRISWOLD, EDITORS.

VOLUME XXI.

PHILADELPHIA:
GEORGE R. GRAHAM, NO. 98 CHESNUT STREET.
. . . .
1842.

Fig. 3: Title page, *Graham's Magazine*, vol. 21 (1842).

1800 and 1850 at least eighty women published books of poems, and more than double that number published poems in newspapers and magazines.[32] Poetry anthologies issued at the beginning and the end of the forties register a shift in the gendering of literary geography. In 1842, Rufus Griswold edited and published the influential *Poets and Poetry of America*, which included both men and women writers at a ratio of eight to one. In 1848, he published *The Female Poets of America* as a companion volume to the original, and reissued his first anthology purged of the female contingent. Many, if not most, of the poems in the anthology had been published previously in the newspapers and magazines of the time. Capitalizing on a lucrative trend that minoritized women's poetry but also made it a specialized field, three separate editors published anthologies within a year, all of which went through several editions. Women poets proliferated along with serial publications to the point where they required, or needed to be contained within, a gendered book and genre of their own.[33]

While magazines served as a venue for poetesses, poetesses promoted the circulation of magazines. *Graham's* listed Lydia Sigourney and Frances Osgood alongside William Cullen Bryant and Longfellow on its cover page, and under Poe's editorship the *Broadway Journal* usually featured a woman's poem in the lead position.[34] Women poets and magazines had a symbiotic relation that often caused contemporary commentators to fuse them into a single entity. Of Elizabeth Oakes Smith's poetry, H. T. Tuckerman says, "We doubt not, that many of her sweet fancies and holy aspirations, winged by the periodical press over our broad land, have carried comfort to the desponding and bright glimpses to the perverted."[35] A surrogate for the angelic poet, the magazine sprouts her wings; at the same time, Oakes Smith voices the sentiments of this ethereal, airborne medium. Poems animated the literary marketplace by imprinting periodical pages with sentiments that humanized – and feminized – its reproductive processes. Poetesses personified the media through which they circulated, while the media absorbed the identity of the personalities they trafficked in.

Just as Howe and others attributed to the literary salon the ability to discipline, channel, and harmonize unruly democratic social and political currents, commentators assigned to poetry, and particularly the poetry of poetesses, the capacity to infuse the new democracy with spiritual purpose. Alexis de Tocqueville and other European visitors worried their American hosts by deeming democracy distinctly hostile to Poetry, which, according to Tocqueville (who sounds like Poe in this regard), is "the search after, and the delineation of, the Ideal."[36] He baldly states that "the Americans have no poets," for in democracies, "the imagination is not extinct, but its chief function is to devise what may be useful and to represent what is real" (74, 71). Even while complaining about this evaluation, American intellectuals echoed the fear that America was a soulless marketplace driven by greed. Emerson laments "this multitude of vagabonds, hungry for eloquence, hungry for poetry, starving for symbols, perishing for want of electricity to vitalize this too much pasture, and in the long delay of indemnifying themselves with the false wine of alcohol, of politics, or of money."[37]

In a period and a place frequently associated with the ascendancy of both prose and the prosaic, poetry promised to inject the Ideal, to use Tocqueville's word, or "transcendency," to use Emerson's, into the actual. In a poem entitled "The Fountain – A Night Rhapsody," published in *Graham's* in 1843, G. G. Foster identifies the attraction of poetic sentiment in the time of its imagined demise:[38]

> Methinks, the novelty of printing metre
> In this rhyme-hating, prose-emitting age,
> Should win my Muse a welcome. Therefore greet her.

Foster argues that because the age has become increasingly preoccupied with prosaic mechanical reproduction, or the mechanical reproduction of prose, there is an increasing need to inject the mundane with poetry. "The dull race of man, sweet fancy sick, grow clods apace," yet poetry can lead readers to "some green and sunny nook each heart / Holds still within itself." Foster's poem enacts the process he advocates, beginning with his pedestrian greeting and ending, after many "labyrinthine lines," at the fountain of the title, which provides "immortal beauty, far apart / From the rude janglings of the ruder day." Foster proposes that poetry enables readers to imagine inner reserves while they are immersed in the business of everyday life. Those reserves are admittedly fantastic, but they are also emphatically public, assembled from clichés of poetic discourse. Foster's poem suggests that genteel readers and writers imagined poetry in the same way that Howe imagined the literary salon: as a medium through which to cultivate an aristocracy of fantasy within the democracy that would intangibly distinguish them from both the laboring class and the acquisitive middle class. Elizabeth Oakes Smith declares:

In our country of general knowledge amongst the people, the grades of culture are unnoticed, and our differences are known to exist more in the power to express ourselves, than by any claims to rank either by wealth or learning. Hence it is that we turn to poetry for expression, and in this find a recognition otherwise denied us, and this is natural and instinctive with us. (*HL* 314)

Poetesses played a privileged role in cultivating ineffable forms of social distinction, for like poems, women were imagined to be receptacles of emotion untainted by worldly concerns. According to what Laura Wendorff calls the nineteenth-century "Poetess Ideal," white, middle-class women were cast as natural producers of amateur verse.[39] Anthologist Caroline May remarked in the preface to *The American Female Poets* that "poetry, which is the language of the affections, has been freely employed among us to express the emotions of woman's heart" (v). We are to understand the word "express" here literally. Women poets were portrayed as fonts of unmediated emotion, nightingales or creatures with harp-like hearts who could not help but sing. Their poems were cast as identical offspring, incarnations of the poetess' intimate feelings. The relation between gender and genre was so intimate that it was common to compliment a middle-class American antebellum woman by calling her a poem. Hawthorne gushes to Sophia Peabody in December 1839:

Dearest, I wish your husband had the gift of making rhymes; for methinks there is poetry in his head and heart since he has been in love with you. You are a Poem, my Dove. Of what sort, then? Epic? – mercy on me, – no! A sonnet? – no; for that is too labored and artificial. My Dove is a sort of sweet, simple, gay, pathetic ballad.[40]

For Hawthorne, a poem is the distilled essence of womanhood, while a woman's resemblance to a poem bestows upon her the capacity for emanating a potent sentimental purity.

While Hawthorne's "dearest" is his own private poem, playing through head and heart, the melody is not her own, but her culture's: she is not a lyric, but a ballad, and as such, has no author or origin. At her most authentically personal, Sophia-the-poem is most purely popular. While women were supposed both to emanate and transmit intimate feelings, those feelings were coded as both deeply personal and fully generic. Precisely for this reason the womanhood of poems had the potential to surpass that of women themselves. Poems could be more spiritual (for they were not flesh and blood), more inaccessible (for when desiring the lyric speaker, to whom did one turn?), more chaste (for who could violate a page?), and more beautiful (for poems could more fully embody cultural ideals of womanhood).

Because women's poems promised to deliver this distilled essence of femininity, antebellum literati speculated whether they might remedy the lack that Tocqueville identified. Griswold writes, "It has been suggested by foreign critics, that our citizens are too much devoted to business and politics to feel interest in pursuits which adorn but do not profit, and which beautify existence but do not consolidate power: feminine genius is perhaps designed to retrieve our public character in this respect."[41] Poetesses proffered a soul to a nation that feared it lacked one: "we are . . . struck with the number of youthful female voices that soften and enrich the tumult of enterprise, and action, by the interblended music of a calmer and loftier sphere" (8). Poetesses' ability to "adorn," "beautify," and spiritualize capitalist "existence" depended upon their ability to appear immune to "the tumult of enterprise" even as they immersed themselves in it. Alicia Ostriker remarks that "as culture during the first half of the nineteenth century came to signify uplift, poetry ascended to a vaguely floating position above fiction and drama"; the poetess particularly signified "elevation," or separation from the taint of the business world.[42]

While there seemed to be a powerful need to publish the intimate sentiments that the woman-as-poem evoked, that project was steeped in ambiguity and ambivalence. Hawthorne's Sophia is the perfect Poem that he is unable to write, but what would happen if his Poem were to write a poem? The offspring would prove both a distillation of purity and a treacherous impostor, for her poetic identity resides both in her status as Hawthorne's possession and in her own dispossession. Writing and publishing her own poem would damage this formulation, even while the formulation encourages and sanctions this act. While proffering a remedy for America's problems of the spirit, then, women's poetry also threatened betrayal. For how does one publish private sentiments without either violating them or proving them to be a sham in the first place? How does a woman sell her soul and still convincingly present herself as pure of commercial taint?

For while women's poetry promised to spiritualize the literary marketplace, it also successfully marketed the spirit. As much as women poets and their purveyors insisted that their motivation for sharing their spontaneous effusions with the public was altruistic, many profited financially. Despite Charvat's claim that no poet achieved professional status until after 1865, when Longfellow managed to earn a subsistence income from his publications, the first professional American poets were arguably women.[43] By 1830, Lydia Sigourney was selling her poetry to over twenty periodicals. She received as much as twenty-five dollars a poem, and *Godey's Lady's Book* paid her 500 dollars for the right to use her name as an editor in the early 1840s.[44] Twenty years Sigourney's junior, Frances Sargent Osgood's correspondence with editors and publishers shows her to be a shrewd bargainer fully aware that her poems might be sold at a premium rate.[45] Osgood seems to have largely supported herself and two daughters through her writing after her husband left for the west coast during the Gold Rush. Completely personal and radically public, constituted by and constitutive of lyric media, expressive because of rather than in spite of their conventionality, poetesses recognized, exploited, and critiqued – but did not transcend or subvert – the possibilities and limitations of their paradoxical lyric identities.

THE GENIUS OF MIMICRY: POETS, POETESSES, POETICS

Theodore Adorno insists that lyric's "relation to social matters" "must not lead us away from the works, it must lead us more deeply into them."[46] Exploring social networks of lyric performance affords a fresh vantage-point from which to revisit questions of genius and imitation that figure centrally in nineteenth-century theories of lyric form and their critical legacy.

"Genius" held conflicting meanings in the nineteenth century. According to Noah Webster's 1828 *American Dictionary*, genius could signify both a good or evil spirit that "presides over a man's destiny in life" and an uncommon or particular human intellectual power.[47] An inhabiting force or an innate quality, genius hinges on the question of possession. Although recent critics speak of literary "authority" rather than genius, romantic theories that both mystify and individualize intellectual production continue to underpin critical evaluations of nineteenth-century American lyric. This logic is apparent in Dickinson and Whitman studies, notwithstanding their recent cultural turn. According to Mark Maslan, for example, most of Walt Whitman's critics have either predicated his authority on exceptional self-possession, or they have claimed that he opposes individualism through experiments in identic disintegration, a radical strategy of dispossession. Combining and countering both strains, Maslan claims that Whitman authorizes himself by demonstrating the degree to which he is possessed by the cultural forces through which and for which he speaks. Maslan accounts for the ways that genius relies on inspiration for its effect; the poet is occupied by forces larger than himself which he nevertheless claims.[48] While arguments for the contingency of literary value have made genius a term that requires interrogation rather than a tool for critical evaluation, a study of Whitman's, Dickinson's, or even Poe's circle requires less strenuous justification and generates more immediate interest than a study of Osgood's or Oakes Smith's or Sarah Helen Whitman's circle because it can go without saying that the first three writers possess – and are possessed by – superior expressive powers. Indeed, this prevailing logic gives this book a title in which Poe's name anchors the orbit of unspecified others – his "circle" – even as I make a claim for the priority of the unnamed poetesses.

If genius signifies the presence of larger forces within the individual, mimicry fails to summon the object that it represents. Positing "a truthful relation between world and word, model and copy, nature and image, or, in semiotic terms, referent and sign, in which potential difference is subsumed by sameness," true mimesis would reproduce an object in the fullness of presence.[49] Mimesis implies its own impossibility, however, and imitations never live up to their originals. As a form of imitation that acknowledges and even celebrates this failure, mimicry has often borne the weight of contempt, even in dictionary definitions. According to Webster's dictionary, a mimic is "a buffoon who attempts to excite laughter or derision by acting or speaking in the manner of another"; "a mean or servile imitator." Mimicry produces an imperfect and inferior duplication that displays itself as such.

Long the sign of powerlessness, subjection, and subservience, mimicry has enjoyed renewed attention and respect in feminist and cultural studies as a means of subterfuge. If one assumes that individuals and signs cannot transcend the cultural terms that constitute them, then mimesis is a form of false consciousness, while mimicry holds the potential to subvert power structures from within. For Homi Bhabha, then, "the mimic man" "is the effect of a flawed colonial mimesis, in which to be Anglicized is emphatically not to be English."[50] A regulatory, disciplinary colonial power, mimicry is nevertheless always in danger of undermining itself by "disclosing the ambivalence of colonial discourse" (88). Judith Butler proposes that mimicry produces a similar effect on gender normativity. Drag's "parodic repetition" "reveals the imitative structure of gender itself – as well as its contingency."[51] Drag is paradoxically a more authentic form of representation, because gender poses as a stable identity, while drag's confessedly artificial reproduction exposes as false "the very notion of an original" (138).

Luce Irigaray – whose work informs Butler's – goes so far as to suggest that mimesis was always mimicry. In "Plato's Hystera," Irigaray suggests that the elaborate theater production in Plato's cave tricks its audience into believing in mimetic reproduction:[52]

This mimetic system is thus not referable to one model, one paradigm, to the presence of one reproduced thing. These "images," cut off from the genealogy of "own-ness" dominated by the Truth, are reinforced nonetheless, and moreover, by an echo, by voices – or a voice – which allow phantoms and fantasies to speak and thus authenticate their reality.[53]

Irigaray suggests here that "own-ness," the mimetic economy of possession which underpins and enables theories of genius, is actually an elaborate performance staged by talented mimics who convincingly project shadows and throw voices. Extending the logic, one could argue that genius is an effect of mimicry, a dishonest rendition that doesn't "tip its hand," but dupes the reader into believing in the possibility of a transcendent sign.[54]

Like Bhabha, Butler, and Irigaray, the writers in this study decline to enforce or accept a clear division between original and copy, genius and mimicry, poet and poetess. In a world besieged by mechanical reproduction, Poe, Osgood, Sarah Helen Whitman, and Oakes Smith share more recent skepticism about the possibility of true mimesis. Unlike contemporary theorists, however, the antebellum writers are hesitant to associate either side of the equation with subversion or acquiescence to cultural norms. This point of reticence offers a critical vantage-point from which to consider recent tendencies to associate particular political valences with certain formal traits. To begin doing so, I will look at two competing but interdependent genealogies of mimicry and genius in two distinct critical traditions, one rooted in the nineteenth-century figure of the poet, the other in the figure of the poetess.

While American poetesses were primarily restricted to lyric practice, poets like Poe and Emerson also produced theories of lyric reading, codifying models of reception that favored their own lyric practices. Emerson's legacy has been particularly influential in American traditions of literary criticism. In essays like "The Poet" and "Quotation and Originality," he offers a model of genius that contains mimicry within it; the containment structure contradicts what he acknowledges to be mimicry's power to overturn and exchange itself with genius. Harold Bloom has given theoretical authority to this model of lyric production and reception, in which the strong poets in each generation inherit and transmit the work of a culture in such a way that the collective imagination becomes the property of a representative individual, and the individual in turn becomes the property of the culture.[55] Maslan's reading of Whitman is a recent version of this argument that emphasizes synchronic rather than diachronic processes of absorption. Unlike his successors, however, Emerson is keenly aware that mimicry threatens to disable this model of transmission because it holds an insidious power to masquerade as genius so perfectly that inspiration and repetition become indistinguishable.

In "Quotation and Originality" mimicry and genius are difficult to separate from one another, and yet they are perpetually at odds. Emerson insists that, just as the "parasite" of Nature, "an aphis, teredo, or vampire bat," has "an excellent sucking pipe to tap another animal," so "admirable mimics" of the human variety "have nothing of their own," and "the self-supplying organs wither and dwindle."[56] Emerson is surely aware, however, that this gruesome scenario echoes the umbilical theory of cultural transmission that he advocates in the same essay, which converts women's reproductive processes to men's artistic prerogative via metaphor: "Swedenborg threw a formidable theory into the world, that every soul existed in a society of souls, from which all its thoughts passed into it, as the blood of the mother circulates in her unborn child" (436). Explicating Swedenborg's vision, Emerson imagines a democratic correspondence among "intelligences" as an extended version of the "coterie." The historically particular coterie serves as the negative counterpoint to Emerson's ideal communion, from which emerges genius:

does it not look as if we men were thinking and talking out of an enormous antiquity, as if we stood, not in a coterie of prompters that filled a sitting-room, but in a circle of intelligences that reached through all thinkers, poets, inventors, and wits, men and women, English, German, Celt, Aryan, Nenivite, Copt, – back to the first geometer, bard, mason, carpenter, planter, shepherd, – back to the first negro, who, with more health or better perception, gave a shriller sound or name for the thing he saw and dealt with? (*RWE* 436–437)

Unlike the prompters' gathering in a present moment – the moment of the salon – Emerson's circle reaches across time and space, establishing lineage back to the inaugural "negro" who "gave a shriller sound or name"; the superlative marks him as the best of his kind, and therefore the representative man. While "prompters" repeat in order to spur others to repeat a script, "men" retain presence of mind and force of character when "thinking and talking," so that even as they draw upon "an enormous antiquity," "there remains the indefeasible persistency of the individual to be himself" (437). Emerson therefore juxtaposes two kinds of mediumship, one that dissipates and one that fulfills.

He aligns himself with Swedenborg's fulfilled form by claiming intellectual lineage: the mystical thinker gave birth to a theory that now circulates like blood through Emerson's prose. Discriminating in his affiliations rather than his practices, Emerson acknowledges that he speaks in the name of Swedenborg but elides the influence of his contemporaries, who in the fifties and sixties were daily affirming the literal truth of Swedenborg's hypothesis. According to nineteenth-century proponents of Spiritualism, mediums received messages from "a society of souls" dwelling in the afterworld and transmitted them to people still living on earth. Emerson engages his audience in the terms of this national craze, even if he only acknowledges it obliquely. Typically contradicting himself, he encloses the notion of democratic (but still discriminating) circulation – personified in the poetess and practiced in the coterie and in ephemeral print media – within the distinguished figure of a "Representative Man": "Swedenborg; or, the Mystic."[57]

As Julie Ellison has noted, Emerson oscillates between a celebration of communal knowledge and unalloyed individualism. Ellison claims that for Emerson, "emulation results in crisis. . . . His integrity is threatened, not by a single influence, but by an incomprehensible multitude." Because he "desires freedom more than control," he seeks, via "transition," "always to break out of either a dominant or a subordinate stance" by both denying repetition and repeating.[58] But the crisis of emulation that registers as an internal dynamic of Emerson's writings is also a feature of antebellum literary culture. Harold Bloom and other influential critics have performed their own Emersonian relation to American literature by reinforcing historical lineages and downplaying lateral connections. In this way the creative, dynamic relations between and among individuals and across gender categories are recast as a process that occurs within a single exceptional mind, albeit one immersed in the culture of his time. In the chapters that follow I will emphasize instead the ways that literary creation occurs in transactions among writers, some of whom claim the exchange as a characteristic of their consciousnesses, and some of whose accomplishments are subsumed into the profiles of their more acquisitive, and therefore more memorable, peers. Such an emphasis reveals that fictions of lineage are shaped in competition with lateral models of creation that are less concerned with the preservation of names and the quest for literary authority. Rather than a description of literary process, Emerson's scenario has proved a highly influential fiction of cultural transmission whose instability later critics have neutralized by elevating Emersonian values of genius and downplaying the mimic traits he both performs and disowns. Whatever form they take, genius studies tend to bequeath collectively generated traits to superlative practitioners whose innovations depend on the work of their contemporaries as raw material. This lateral study of influence analyzes the dynamics by which that representation is achieved.

Even when stressing the opposite principles of collaboration and collectivity, feminist criticism of nineteenth-century American women's poetry has continued to work within an Emersonian framework. Both canonical and counter-canonical critical narratives depend upon an evolutionary model of artistic ingenuity that culminates in a more authentic modern sensibility. Canonical studies of American poetry have charted a development away from inherited and artificial British models towards a rebellious, more natural, distinctly American sphere of artistic genius; likewise, studies of nineteenth-century American women's poetry trace a growing rebellion against patriarchal oppression that results in an "emancipatory" twentieth-century feminist consciousness.

Particularly central to this strain of lyric criticism are nineteenth-century theories of reception that figure women's poems as "songs" that emerge straight from the heart. Nineteenth-century American women's poetry has consistently met with a double-edged response that centers on the question of lyric sincerity, the test of which is a believable expression of personal pain.[59] In the lyric tradition of Sappho, Charlotte Smith, and Felicia Hemans, these poems often attest to inconsolable sorrow. If readers find the suffering true, they say it is because the poem gives them direct access to the woman's personal experience. In her preface to *The American Female Poets*, Caroline May tells us that most of the poems emerge from "home, with its quiet joys, its deep pure sympathies, and its secret sorrows, with which a stranger must not intermeddle" (v). At the same time that the poetess is held up as the standard of confessional authenticity, however, she is reviled for the derivative qualities of her verse. For these women wrote of the most personal pain in the most conventional forms and the most common media. As May puts it with some alarm, American women, even more than their European counterparts, "have published volumes of poetry, and pieces of various merit have poured forth through our newspapers and other periodicals, with the utmost profusion" (v). If no stranger should intermeddle with a woman's secret sorrows, many have asked, then why does she publish them so profusely? And why do poems expressing personal sentiments bear such a strong stamp of generic similitude? Poetesses then stand accused of faking pain – mimicking the authentic expression of feeling – in order to cash in on a marketable fashion, the seemingly insatiable craving for an outpouring of female "song."

Recent recovery work reiterates these terms by imagining women's poems as utterances that enable the scholarly recuperation of lost female subjectivity. The strongest advocates for the study of women poets continue to oscillate between these two perspectives without reconciling them. Nineteenth- and twentieth-century critics alike have professed revulsion at "the Poetess as we know and despise her," condemning the derivative, soporific qualities of her verse.[60] In the introduction to her anthology of nineteenth-century women poets, Cheryl Walker declares: "Their lack of authority, finally, may make them imitative, on the one hand, or merely provocative on the other. One can readily see in women's poetry that freedom needs (some) power to express itself effectively" (*AWP* xxxix). Walker entitles her study of American women poets before 1900 *Nightingale's Burden* because the myth of Philomela "records the burden of woe the nightingale carries and the peculiarly autobiographical emphasis of her art."[61] If the nightingale represents the legitimate pathos of these suffering women, however, it does not legitimize the poems themselves, for here too Walker finds the women's poetic output fatally compromised: "These poems are manifestations of the fact that these women were so deeply trapped in their own powerlessness that they were afraid to disappoint the very critical expectations that kept them mired in mediocrity." In the introduction to her 1998 anthology of nineteenth-century American women poets, Paula Bennett admits that "when combined with the nineteenth century's fondness for regular meters and conventionally poetic diction, and its obsession with death and moral platitudes, the result can be a kind of narrow formulaic verse even sympathetic readers find indigestible."[62] On the other hand she singles out certain of these poems in order to lay claim to a prehistory of lesbian writing by arguing for the depth and sincerity of personal expression: "the love these poets inscribe is lesbian insofar as it projects a passionate and pervasively eroticized desire between women." These oscillations between apologies for the unconvincing quality of this body of work and celebrations of deeply authentic revelations of true feeling will be familiar to anyone following the recent efflorescence of critical literature on emotion, and particularly on sentimentalism, a word that, as Janet Todd explains, simultaneously evokes sincerity and duplicity: work by Elizabeth Barnes, Bruce Burgett, Julie Ellison, Glenn Hendler, Mary Louise Kete, Joycelyn Moody, Marianne Noble, Shirley Samuels, Julia Stern, and others.[63]

The tension has held renewed force ever since Ann Douglas condemned sentimentalism as morally and aesthetically bankrupt in the name of a Poetess, the Sweet Singer of Hartford Lydia Sigourney, and Jane Tompkins countered with her influential claim to sentimentalism's political power through her reading of a novel, Harriet Beecher Stowe's *Uncle Tom's Cabin*.[64] Tompkins' recourse to political and cultural work solved through circumvention the charges of aesthetic inadequacy and emotional inauthenticity. The lyric as practiced in the name of Sigourney was more difficult to salvage, apparently, and Tompkins and her followers left that task for later critics like Nina Baym and Sandra Zagarell, who made their case by minimizing Sigourney's substantial investments in elegy and foregrounding her poems that treat public themes like nation-building.[65] The substantial recovery efforts devoted to nineteenth-century women's poetry haven't met with the same success as the recovery of nineteenth-century women's prose, and it is worth asking why. The stakes of recovery are intense in the lyric, a form in which the expectations that someone will speak for and of herself are most extreme, and the failure subsequently more catastrophic and more inevitable, for what poem can speak the way a living person does, particularly a person who personifies an impossible ideal? Add to that the association of lyric with New Critical principles of hermetic enclosure, social disengagement, and temporal transcendence, and cultural criticism's resistance to considering poetry as a cultural form was all but ensured; only recently has this constellation been challenged by the provocative work of Paula Bennett, Joanne Dobson, Kirsten Silva Greusz, Virginia Jackson, Mary Louise Kete, Mary Loeffelholz, Elizabeth Petrino, and others.[66] Ridiculed or revived, the poetess leaves a legacy vital enough to continue affronting and engaging critical faculties. The connection between these polarized responses – visceral antipathy and intense attraction – is worth scrutinizing, for it helps to explain the dynamic relation among diverse critical investments in today's broadened cultural field.

I consider these questions in relation to the work of three poetesses and a poet who is invested in their work, literary figures whose divergent practices and productions complicate our received notions of what a poetess is supposed to produce. All the writers engage the mimic functions of lyric: echo, quotation, paraphrase, repetition. Using evaluative criteria that the poets actively reject, critics have consistently dismissed women's poetry of the period as overly derivative, echoic, and secondary. They have tended to valorize rebellious or subversive exceptions against the background of a poetic norm that is considered meaningless in comparison, except as an obstacle to overcome. In this model, poetry that cannot be identified as proto-modernist is more frequently condemned than interpreted. The search for another Emily Dickinson inadvertently reinscribes the terms that resulted in the initial dismissal of nineteenth-century women's poetry, for the elevation of the exception necessarily requires the rejection of all those figured as incapable of rising above formal or patriarchal constraint. By searching for "the emergence of a new and original kind" of women's poetry, we unwittingly reinforce the terms of valuation that render unreadable poetry that was highly influential in the nineteenth century.[67] Rather than circumvent or apologize for the derivative qualities of women's poetry, then, I will explore the ways in which lyric mimicry, a central function of much popular women's poetry of the nineteenth century, forges social networks and transmits cultural and formal understandings of value within and through time.

Each of the four chapters treats both an authorial figure and a related form of poetic communication. Chapter 1 demonstrates that Poe's transactions with his female contemporaries both enlivened and threatened the integrity of his work. Promoting the fantasy that his poems possessed mesmeric powers of attraction, Poe performed a "feminine" poetry for an audience of women poets in which he simultaneously mirrored and upstaged their own practices. Poe cast himself as a vampiric figure searching beyond the grave for lost, loved women. This image elicited the attention of women who wished both to provide solace and to recuperate their own displaced poetic practices. I go on to consider the legacy of Poe's experiments in female impersonation and exorcism in his critical history, which completes the eclipse of female influence. Ultimately, Poe receives credit for fathering mass culture, while the mass of women who helped make both Poe and mass culture are denied.

Chapter 2 attends to the question of the poetess' mass appeal, which Poe found so intriguing, through a reading of Frances Sargent Osgood's poetry in circulation. Here I argue that a symbiotic relation between two mediums, women poets and magazines, led the poetess to market an unlocalizable eroticism that conflated coquetry and print proliferation. Osgood cultivated a reputation as a living embodiment of poetic fancy while teasing her readers for their tendency to confuse poems with poetesses, particularly herself. Her poetic play resulted in a literary romance with Poe acted out in the pages of the *Broadway Journal* when he was editor. Poe responded to Osgood's emulation of her print environment by imitating it, making the *Journal*'s pages the active location of their love affair. Interjecting himself between the poetess and her popular audience, he claimed Osgood as his personal muse in an effort to curb her promiscuous circulation and enhance his own. By positioning himself as Osgood's patron, Poe retroactively designated himself as the source and destination of her public appeal, so that now she is remembered largely through her romantic association with Poe.

Whereas Osgood's modes of lyric transmission exploit the erotic potential of print circulation, Sarah Helen Whitman cultivates poetry's capacity to serve as a mode of spiritual communication and exchange. Comparing spiritualist and romantic theories of inspiration, chapter 3 claims that Poe and Whitman promoted a mystical understanding of their reciprocal mimicry during their public courtship, and that these collaborations helped prepare the ground for Poe's reception as an original genius. Whitman continued experiments with spirit channeling after Poe's death, forging an echoic form of poetry haunted by his ghost that reflects his own mirrored practices and ponders the immateriality of the poetic personality. Within the context of the spiritualist movement, she cultivated a telegraphic mode of poetic communication whereby she and other Poe fans could communicate with the dead poet, and with each other in his name. She presented her mystic version of Poe to Stéphane Mallarmé, John Ingram, and other poets, biographers, and critics who then claimed, revised, and transmitted Poe's portrait across the ages. The chapter concludes with an analysis of the ways that women's spiritualist practices inform the model of critical possession that underpins Poe's claims to literary authority.

While the second and third chapters explore the aesthetic consequences of accepting plastic forms of feminine generic identity, the final chapter investigates Elizabeth Oakes Smith's arguments against the terms she worked within. Intensely aware of the gendering of poetic traditions and practices, Oakes Smith didn't so much abnegate her poetess identity as try to convert it to genius by demonstrating the interdependence of masculine and feminine poetic traditions. She identified a conundrum based not on the difference, but on the similarity of gendered models of poetic achievement. After ventriloquizing received poetic forms – she imitated the work of Emerson, Coleridge, and others as well as Poe – she determined that contemporary terms of reception prevented her from claiming lyric subjectivity; ultimately, she paid tribute to an "unspeakable eloquence." Her concerns mirror Poe's from the perspective of the poetess, and for this reason this chapter serves as a bookend to chapter 1. Oakes Smith's preoccupation with future reception offers an opportunity to examine the persistent critical tendency to read nineteenth-century poetry in the light of modernism. Rather than arguing for Oakes Smith's status as an unjustly ignored proto-modernist, I explore the terms by which writers who were tremendously popular before the Civil War encountered their own obscurity by the end of the century. In a brief coda, I relate Oakes Smith's figuration of Poe as the sign of the forgotten poetess to the place of the nineteenth-century woman poet in recent literary studies. I suggest that attempts to recover women poets have obscured the terms by which they were forgotten, terms that, taking the lead from poetess-critics like Oakes Smith, we can productively explore.

CHAPTER I

"The Poetess" and Poe's Performance of the Feminine

Poe's "Israfel" tells the story of a poet who becomes a celebrity; the occurrence is so unlikely that it can only happen in Heaven. Looking on with envy, Israfel's human counterpart magnifies the heavenly poet's reputation by spreading the word on Earth:

> In Heaven a spirit doth dwell
> "Whose heart-strings are a lute;"
> None sing so wildly well
> As the angel Israfel
> And the giddy stars (so legends tell)
> Ceasing their hymns, attend the spell
> Of his voice, all mute.
>
> (*CWP* 175; 1–7)

Israfel's lyrical performance eclipses that of the other stars, who transform from celestial singers into his "mute" audience. The single word "giddy" feminizes the stars, but the gender of the audience is the subject of the second stanza, in which "Pleiads" "pause," while "Tottering above / In her highest noon, / The enamoured moon / Blushes with love." Israfel has a fan club of female singers who are awed into silence by his superior performance. Recounting the angel's triumph, the mortal poet impotently wishes that he "could dwell / Where Israfel / Hath dwelt, and he where I" (*CWP* 176; 45–47).

Poe's nameless poet's failure helped to ensure his own success. Bequeathing the poet's dilemma to Poe, admirers felt moved to give him Israfel's place. In a posthumous tribute shaped from the materials of Poe's poetry, "To Him 'Whose Heart-Strings Were a Lute,'" Sarah Helen Whitman equated Poe with his angel-poet, countering his speaker's insistence that he could never achieve the unearthly excellence of Israfel's music of the spheres (*LL*163). In her tributes "Echo Song" and "To One Who Swept the Sounding Lyre," Frances Osgood also conflated Poe with his celestial counterpart. By titling his biography *Israfel* Hervey Allen consolidated this trend, elevating Poe to immortal status within the American literary tradition.[1] Whitman, Osgood, and Allen all suggest that after death, Poe joined the ranks of the celestial poets; at the same time, they imply that even while living, Poe possessed other-worldly characteristics, or even connections, that made him a great poet. His poetic performance of failure mobilized fans to ensure his success.

Though "Israfel" helped to preserve Poe's name for posterity, it expressed an unlikely wish in the 1830s and 1840s, when the poem was printed and reprinted in the periodicals that he edited and in his collections of poems.[2] In a time when women poets were commanding the kind of attention that Israfel received, the story of his celestial success reads like a compensatory fantasy. Though they became Poe's adoring fans, many of his female contemporaries were objects of public admiration long before he achieved celebrity in 1845, with the publication of "The Raven." When *Graham's* began to list "Principal Contributors" on its cover in 1842, Poe was not among them. Several poetesses whom he knew and reviewed, however, were: Emma Embury, Elizabeth Oakes Smith, Frances Osgood, and Elizabeth Ellet appeared alongside male counterparts like Bryant and Longfellow. Poe was certainly aware that poetesses informed the social context through which his poetry circulated. In his 1836 review of poems by Lydia Sigourney, Hannah Gould, and Elizabeth Ellet, his interrogation of the legitimacy of female celebrity suggests that he had a personal stake in the matter. Singling out Sigourney, the most popular of the three, for censure, Poe juxtaposed two means by which writers can put their names "in the mouths of the people" (*ER* 874). While one may gain reputation by writing a single great work, another "with very moderate powers may build up for himself, little by little, a reputation equally great" through sheer quantity of production (874). Not only does Sigourney belong in the second category, but she also "stands palpably convicted of that sin which in poetry is not to be forgiven" (875). Sigourney's nickname, the "American Hemans," alone proves "that she has acquired this title *solely by imitation*" (875). The "almost identity" between the two poetesses' work lends a "ludicrous air of similitude to all articles of [Sigourney's] composition" (875, 876). Poe's forceful attempt to dismantle Sigourney's "*apparent popular reputation*" suggests that he would like to take her name out of the people's mouths and insert his own (874). His envy takes an even more curious turn, however, in "A Reviewer Reviewed," an unpublished piece that exposes his own acts of plagiarism as if he were someone else. Here Poe reveals that the credit for "one of Mr. Poe's most admired passages" – the concluding lines of "The

City in the Sea" – actually belongs to Lydia Sigourney, for "unfortunately" the lines originally appear in "a little poem called 'Musing Thoughts'" (*ER* 1052). Rather than convict Poe of the same poetic sin for which he convicts Sigourney, I want to suggest that his rhetorical gestures demonstrate the degree to which he was immersed in a mimic poetic economy saturated with the work of poetesses. At best, he could hope to carve out a space for his own mimic performances by shifting the terms of engagement to the male poet's advantage.

Because female reception was crucial to his poetic practices, Poe's solution to the dilemma of women's encroachment in the literary domain did not lie in a simple dismissal of their achievements. Instead he sought to reconcile their multiple roles of muse, literary competitor, and audience for his own poetry. Repeatedly in his poems and reviews, he literalized the generic figure of the poetess by identifying women so completely with their poems that they could not claim credit for their output; instead he claimed them as raw materials for his own work. While designating women as the natural site of poetic utterance, Poe also argued that poetic "truth" lies in a theatrical performance of the feminine. He consolidated his appeal for women poets by performing his rendition of their poetic practices. Identifying women poets with his poetic images of women, his poems enact dramas of evacuation in which speakers drain women of their poetic potency while claiming that the transfer of powers is in the spirit of feminine mimicry. Poetesses in turn were drawn by the recognition of their own practices in an alienated form, which they then sought to recuperate. For an audience of women poets, Poe performed a "feminine" poetry that both absorbed and negated their own poetic practices.

That he succeeded in shaping the terms of his reception – in collaboration with his female contemporaries – is suggested by the way in which the female corpse continues to stand in for women's corpus in Poe biography and criticism.[3] Studies consistently transpose gendered relations between texts into romantic relations between people, so that the body of women's work becomes the dead body of Poe's lost loves. Reiterating Poe's own absorption of the poetess, Poe studies depend upon women, even as they convert women into a figure of Woman that dwells within Poe's mind. Psychoanalytic interpretations that explicate his emotional difficulties through his poems and tales have a long, distinguished tradition in which women figure as phantoms that torment Poe.[4] The recurrent centrality of women in Poe's poetry, particularly dead women, is often considered a product and a sign of a psyche shattered by the repeated early loss of significant female figures: he has been diagnosed with a maternal complex, an oral fixation, a female-dependency syndrome. This critical inheritance obscures the relatively obvious point that some of the seemingly more peculiar traits of Poe's poetry are variations on conventional themes in nineteenth-century poetry, particularly in the poetry of women. Poe's inconsolable mourning served as a powerful draw for female sympathy: his primary audience consists of women who are moved at the plight of men who are unloved by women. Rather than evidence of social isolation, the themes of solitary suffering in Poe's poetry are signs of cultural engagement.

Parallel to the story of female loss runs a narrative of nationalist failure. Faulting the poetry's baroque sound patterns and derivative qualities, critics argue that Poe's poetry is obsessed with the past, capitulating to rather than conquering British literary tradition. Edwin Fussell argues that Poe unsuccessfully tried to break free from British constraint by further complicating meter, thus entrapping himself in ever more complex metrical patterns.[5] Mutlu Blasing claims that Poe both embraced and rejected British literary tradition, battling it by "us[ing] and abus[ing]" it.[6] Ultimately he failed to position himself in the American present: "the very thing [Poe] must acknowledge in order to begin to be a poet – temporality and the past, both personal and cultural – he proceeds to let annihilate him" (33). Displaced, maladjusted, emasculated in both psychological and historical narratives, Poe is figured as incapable of mastering inherited terms in order to craft a timely art. As the receptacle of everything unsalvageable, his poetry is readily excluded from recent studies that champion him as a savvy and masterful, if discontented and financially unsuccessful, analyzer and manipulator of mass cultural forms.

I would like to suggest instead that, rather than retreating into a fantasy world of British aristocracy, Poe produced and marketed the image of the wandering aristocrat lost in the new world, adapting the Byronic figure of the dark prince to the circumstances of an American literary marketplace and an international one that valued American images. Charles Baudelaire makes this connection: Poe was an "aristocrat by nature even more than by birth, this Virginian, this Southerner, this Byron astray in a wicked world."[7] In his new-world rendition of the Byronic hero, Poe conflated the European world with other worlds, most significantly with the land of the dead. He crafted himself into a vampiric figure with cloudy origins and mesmeric powers that encouraged readers to fantasize about his occult knowledge. A sympathetic icon of lost origins and other-worldly questing, his perpetual mourning fueled quests to the netherworld both to counter his female contemporaries' claims to superior spiritual access and to inspire them to provide the solace he so insistently seeks. These performances of visionary melancholy inspired readers to imagine themselves as a community of intimate insiders with shared insights into a supernatural realm. Through a species of niche marketing, Poe consolidated a small but passionate group of followers, "The Poe Cult," in the words of Eugene Didier, whose traditions descend to the present day.[8]

THE POE CULT

Capitalizing on contemporary fashions, Poe presented himself as a mesmeric poet at New York salons and in his writings. Initially associated with medical cures, mesmerism's meanings rapidly diversified once it spread to the US in the 1830s, gaining territory in the occult realms especially after it blended with the Spiritualist movement in the late forties, around the time of Poe's death.[9] Even before Spiritualism identified mediums or "spirit telegraphs" as a specific mode of communication between the living and the dead, many considered Poe to be such a conduit. During the final years of his life, his "mesmerizing" poetry readings, especially his recital of "The Raven," were a subject of gossip among New York literati: "People seem to think there is something uncanny about him, and the strangest stories are told, and, what is more, believed, about his mesmeric experiences, at the mention of which he always smiles. His smile is captivating!"[10] Oakes Smith recalled seeing "the childlike face of Fanny Osgood suffused with tears under [Poe's] wizard spell" at one of the literary gatherings.[11] Rufus Griswold evoked Poe's gripping salon presence in his infamous "Ludwig" obituary written for the *New York Tribune*:

His conversation was at times almost supramortal in its eloquence. His voice was modulated with astonishing skill, and his large and variably expressive eyes looked repose or shot fiery tumult into theirs who listened, while his own face glowed or was changeless in pallor, as his imagination quickened his blood, or drew it back frozen to his heart. His imagery was from the worlds which no mortal can see but with the vision of genius. . . . In a crystalline process of accretion, [he] built up his ocular demonstrations in forms of gloomiest and ghostliest grandeur, or in those of the most airy and delicious beauty, so minutely, and so distinctly, yet so rapidly, that the attention which was yielded to him was chained til it stood among his wonderful creations – til he himself dissolved the spell, and brought his hearers back to common and base existence, by vulgar fancies or by exhibitions of the ignoble passions.[12]

Griswold expands the mesmerist's "ocular" power to include poetic imagery, portraying Poe as a mesmeric poet who not only rivets people with his gaze, but also forces them to look upon and even dwell within his visionary landscape. Whereas mesmerists were often believed to seduce people without their knowledge or desire – Taylor Stoehr recounts a fictional experiment whereby a mesmerist throws a bouquet over a high wall, mesmerizing the girl who catches it – Poe captivates his audience not with an impersonal power, but with his personal magnetism.[13]

While Poe appears to be the dominant figure, feminizing the audience by riveting their attention with his spectacular demonstrations, he in turn is in thrall to his imagination, which has control over his body, quickening his blood or making him pale. The audience is not a separate and vulnerable entity that Poe controls, but an instrument like his own body that involuntarily registers and enhances the effects of his imagination. Griswold suggests that the readers understand this paradox – they "yield" their attention so that it may be "chained." The captivating aspect of the performance, then, is the dramatic interplay between domination and submission. Both mesmerizer and mesmerized, Poe displays himself as a medium who is under the spell of his own tyrannical imagination.

Griswold's depiction recalls the other-worldly figure of the poetess, whose supernaturalism is more complementary than opposed to Poe's. Whereas he transports his audience to ghoulish worlds where women are forbidden to wander, women's spiritual purity transports them to heavenly realms that are off limits to Poe's dark nature. Poe imports imagery "from the worlds which no mortal can see but with the vision of genius," while poetesses "repeat the songs to which they have listened, when wandering nearer than we may go to the world in which humanity shall be perfect again" (*LL*14). Griswold reserves origination as a male privilege: because men see and women hear, men convert worlds to words while women merely repeat. Purer mediums, women are lesser geniuses; more fully possessed, they cannot possess the words that move through them. Nevertheless, Poe's performance of self-subjection echoes and recalls the poetess' fuller form of mediumship.

Because it mirrored their own, Poe's performance of mediumship held special appeal for women poets. In the New York literary salons of the 1840s, his physical presence conveyed captivating signs. Elizabeth Oakes Smith recalls the attraction Poe held for women:

Perhaps no one received any more marked attention than Edgar A. Poe. His slender form, pale, intellectual face and weird expression of eye never failed to arrest the attention of even the least observant. He did not affect the society of men, rather that of highly intellectual women with whom he liked to fall into a sort of eloquent monologue, half dream, half poetry. Men were intolerant of all this, but women fell under his fascination, and listened in silence.[14]

According to Oakes Smith, Poe performs for women his inability to interact with them: his voice lacks "sympathetic vibration," and he is incapable of entering into a dialogue. Delivering his oracle to a spellbound audience, Poe again seems to be the dominant figure.

When Oakes Smith analyzes the substance of her own fascination, however, she finds that his status as victim inspires her pity. The basis for sympathy is Poe's inability to live in an adult world, his imprisonment within a childlike state of intolerably intense emotions:

> I noted his delicate organization – the white, fine skin of a face that had upon it an expression of questioning like that of a child, a shade of anxiety, a touch of awe, of sadness; a look out of the large, clear eyes of intense solitude. I felt a painful sympathy for him, just as one would feel for a bright, over-thoughtful child. I said at once: "Ah, Mr. Poe, this country affords no arena for those who live to dream."
>
> "Do you dream? I mean sleeping dream?" he asked quickly.
>
> "Oh, yes. I am a perfect Joseph in dreaming, except that my dreams are of the unknown, the spiritual."
>
> "I knew it," he said softly, "I knew it by your eyes; and I – the great shadowy realm of dreams, whose music, hidden from mortal ears, swells through all space, and dreams of more than mortal beauty ravish the eyes, comes to me – that is to dream!" and his eyes were far off in expression as if he saw them upon the instant. (116–117)

Oakes Smith identifies herself with Poe through their mutual capacity for dreaming. As soon as she notes his painful condition, he picks up on her cue, reversing the situation so that his state becomes emblematic of her emotional receptivity. Less an evocation than an empty marker, Poe's dream realm is at once syntactically incomprehensible and imagistically vague: he does not say what "dreams of more than mortal beauty ravish the eyes," but simply states that they do. Oakes Smith in turn does not see the dream world, but sees Poe seeing it, and becomes convinced that they have visited the same place. In this way, a clichéd expression, void of particularity, becomes the basis for a shared vision that provokes an intense sense of understanding. Poe and Oakes Smith are locked in a dual mirroring state in which each projects their own self-image upon the other. Their responses retroactively confirm each other's sense of identity.

Poe captivates his audience, then, by acting out his self-victimization. "I have often recalled this conversation as a key to his mental construction. He was entirely dominated by the imagination," Oakes Smith states at the end of the exchange, which is perhaps largely her own dreamwork, since the dialogue is more lengthy and detailed than most memories could encompass (about twice as long as what I have quoted). Poe is doubly dominated by the feminine, in his subjugation to his muse and to the needs of his female conversant. Oakes Smith and other female admirers embody the dual threat. Inseparable from his muse, they both inspire his vision and dictate its form. Poe serves in turn as both a conduit for feminine desire and its object.

Oakes Smith identified the mirror-like aspect of their interaction when she readily admitted that for her, there was no Poe there: "To me, Edgar was more spectral than human" (118). He possessed a "chameleon-like temperament, by which he assimilated to those with whom he associated, and thus each analyzer of Poe gives us a glimpse of his own idiosyncrasies rather than a revelation of this unique wonderful creation."[15] Poe's reactive surface offers his readers the pleasure of self-confirmation. Such a formulation suggests that Oakes Smith may be profiling herself when she portrays her mirror-like friend. How, then, are we to understand her sense of Poe's double-sided performance?

Men, such as Edgar Poe, will always have an ideal of themselves by which they represent the chivalry of a Bayard and the heroism of a Viking, when, in fact, they are utterly dependent and tormented with womanish sensibilities. I do not see that the sexes greatly differ, the strong of each and the harmonious of each being the exception and not the rule; if it were otherwise, novelists and poets would have nothing to do.[16]

In Oakes Smith's portrait, Poe suffers delusions of masculine strength while inadvertently exposing the psychic femininity he hides from himself. Striving to appear strong only increases the appeal of his weakness, since his audience notes the pathos in the discrepancy between his desired self-portrayal and the self he inadvertently reveals. Oakes Smith's speculations about the arbitrariness of gender in consciousness allows us to speculate that Poe's performance of feminine abjection allowed his female audience the chance to play the psychic part of men.

Though women actively recorded their experiences of captivation, they attributed their fascination with Poe to the ways that his lyric portrayals reflected their own. Frances Osgood wrote to Elizabeth Barrett that it would be "worth a trip to New York to see Poe's 'wild eyes flash through tears' when he read Barrett's poems": she wants to see Barrett hear Poe read Barrett (quoted in *EAP* 287). Recognizing and appreciating Poe's emulation, poetesses responded by making him over to look even more like themselves.

In "Echo Song," for example, Osgood quotes "Israfel" in order to hint that she inspires his celestial music:

> I know a noble heart that beats
> For one it loves how "wildly well!"
> I only know *for whom* it beats;
> But I must never tell.[17]

In making Poe into Israfel, Osgood aligns him with the figure of the poetess who writes "as if the singer's heart were a harp so delicate that even chasing sun and shadow swept it into music."[18] Her conversion suggests that she reads Poe's performances of writerly and emotional blockage as a plea for female assistance. Poe calls upon the loquacity of the poetess to give voice to his unspoken feelings, which, he implies, are also her own. Women felt moved to translate Israfel's "voice, all mute" for less ethereal beings who could not discern it. Their voluble assistance only reaffirmed Poe's need to render the ladies mute in turn. In a reciprocal dynamic, poetesses voiced Poe's mute suffering (which resembled their own), and Poe voiced the desires of the women he left speechless. The following sections will trace the textual play of this exchange in Poe's criticism, his poetry, and his critical reception.

THE POETESS' CRITIC

Poe's extensive interest in women's poetry suggests that he imagined women as the power generators of poetic discourse. Although his reviews of women poets outnumber those of male poets in his later criticism, they are rarely treated in studies of his poetics. When not ignored altogether, these frequently positive reviews are usually dismissed as either a display of vapid gallantry or an aberration in taste bearing little relation to his more serious considerations of male peers such as Hawthorne and Longfellow.[19] In his own time, however, Poe was a leading – and by far the most rigorous – critic of women writers, discriminating at one point between "poetesses (an absurd but necessary word)," and female poets worthy of admiration and serious critique.[20] To the second category belonged writers like Frances Sargent Osgood, Sarah Helen Whitman, Elizabeth Barrett, Amelia Welby, and Elizabeth Oakes Smith. In a review of Barrett's *Drama of Exile*, Poe lamented that "the inherent chivalry of the critical man" resulted in the "unhappy lot of the authoress to be subjected, time after time, to the downright degradation of mere puffery" (*CW* 12: 1). He promised, in contrast, to pay Barrett the respect of telling her "the truth" about her work (2). While proving his critical pronouncements "sincere" at any juncture would be a hopeless task, his treatment of women poets is comparable to that of their male counterparts.

Poe's analyses of women's poetry were torn between delimiting a separate character for female genius and rewarding poetesses by welcoming them into the male world of the "poet." He trounced anthologist Rufus Griswold, for example, for elevating "aristocrats" over "poets" in his *Poets and Poetry of America* and for relegating certain worthy writers, men and women alike, to the desultory category of "various authors." Poe lamented the disservice done to poets such as Sarah Josepha Hale, Horace Greeley, John Quincy Adams, and Frances Osgood ("one of our sweetest of poetesses") by "throwing openly the charge of their incompetency to sustain the name of Poets, and implying that they were only occasional scribblers[.] (This and of such men, is again from Rufus Wilmot Griswold!)" (*CW* 11: 241). More than once, Poe included women and "poetesses" under the rubric of "such men" and "Poets." He compared Barrett favorably to Tennyson; he also said that *The Sinless Child* demonstrated that its creator, Elizabeth Oakes Smith, had the potential, even if she lacked the discipline, to have written "one of the best, if not the very best of American poems" (*CW* 12: 16; 13: 85).

While Poe often measured all poets against a single standard, he also attributed superior artistic powers to the woman poet. He defended Maria Brooks against Charles Lamb's claim that her poem "Zóphiël" was so good that a woman could not have written it:

As for Lamb's pert query – "was there ever a woman capable of writing such a poem?" – it merely proves that Lamb had little understanding of the true Nature of Poets – which, appealing to our sense of Beauty, is, in its very essence, feminine. If the greatest poems have not been written by women, it is because the greatest poems have not been written at all.[21]

Because poems and women appeal interchangeably to the aesthetic sensibility, women make the best poets. By enforcing an equivalence between the "true Nature of Poets," Beauty, and women, Poe assigns to women an innate capacity for poetic expression. At the same time he suggests that the greatest poems have not been written because they literally *are* women; women embody an ideal of Beauty that cannot be reproduced in words. Though they can write poems, poetesses cannot write themselves within the terms that Poe provides them. As the mimetic embodiment of lyric, women can only imperfectly mimic themselves: saying more makes them less. Though Poe assigns them to failure, however, he doesn't ensure the male poet's success, because Israfel himself embodies the poetess ideal: "his voice, all mute" is powerful because it is melody freed from the constraints of human speech. While poets and poetesses are both doomed under the sign of Poe's poetic ideal, poetesses have a more compressed relationship to art that is at once more privileged and more impossible to fulfill.

While both Lamb and Poe were certainly familiar with the romantic commonplace that poetic accomplishment in men arose from their feminine aspect, Poe's formulation registers a dilemma: accepting a female claim to poetic authorship entails recognizing that women ostensibly contain more of the feminine element from which poetry emerges than men. That problem needed to be addressed if men were to compete.[22] Poe was not alone in this recognition. Rufus Griswold tried to work through the same problem in the introduction to *The Female Poets of America* (that this sequel to *Poets and Poetry of America* segregated women poets in a separate volume itself indicates male anxiety over female poetic achievement): "It does not follow, because the most essential genius in men is marked by qualities which we may call feminine, that such qualities when found in female writers have any certain or just relation to mental superiority. The conditions of aesthetic ability in the two sexes are probably distinct, or even opposite."[23] While Griswold's formulation reserves the creative power of the feminine for the male writer, elsewhere he insists that the poetess should emanate pure femininity, an accomplishment belonging pre-eminently to Frances Sargent Osgood: "All that was in her life was womanly, 'pure womanly,' and so is all in the undying words she left us. This is her distinction" (*LL* 16). In Griswold's aesthetic hierarchy, "'pure womanly'" poetry takes a diminutive second place to men's feminine accomplishments. By naturalizing the feminine to the domain of the woman's body – her womanliness – Griswold neutralizes its potential to fuel genius. The privileged vehicle for female poetic expression, lyric was also a natural extension of womanhood, so by definition it was not art. The complexity of such distinctions registers an unspoken anxiety that women's poetry might be superior to men's, since the feminine was indispensable to poetic production.

For Poe and his contemporaries, then, female verse inextricably linked the personal and the poetic, and the physical body and poetic form: Poe averred on more than one occasion that "a woman and her book are identical" (*CW* 12: 1). More than other purveyors of female verse, however, Poe stressed the convertibility between woman and medium.[24] Because he insisted on their identicality, her book could record the expressions of her heart, or her heart could record the expressions of a book. Reviewing Frances Osgood's "Elfrida, a Dramatic Poem, in Five Acts," Poe celebrated this transitive relation: "There is a fine feeling blending [sic] of the poetry of passion and the passion of poetry" (*CW* 13: 110). Emphasizing the equation of harp and heart in the conventional formulation of female poetic aptitude, Poe highlighted women's natural capacity to produce art. If women and poems were equally sources of beauty, then the woman poet displayed artlessly artful emotions. While much of the period's commentary stressed the naturalness of women's poetic utterance, Poe emphasized the poetess' natural capacity for the artistic.

Poe's theory of female artistry emphasizes women's dramatic abilities: if the body is drama's primary instrument, and women's bodies are naturally artistic, then women must make exceptional actors. For Poe – whose mother was a successful actress and his father a failure upon the stage – women possessed an uncanny ability to imbue their poems with an emotional presence that was often emphatically not their own (*EAP* 3–7). Poe's association of the dramatic with both the woman and the poet is clear in a review of a performance by actress Anna Cora Mowatt, whom he greatly admired: "her seemingly impulsive gestures spoke in loud terms of the woman of genius – of the poet deeply imbued with the truest sentiment of the beauty of motion" (*CW* 12: 187–188). Mowatt's art is bodily, her genius gestural. She is admirable not because she is naturally impulsive, but because she can feign spontaneity so convincingly. By equating acting with both the woman of genius and the poet, Poe implies that male poets must transform themselves into theatrical women if they wish to be geniuses.

The inevitable result of this intimate relation between women and art is the dramatic lyric, and Poe praised women's dramatic lyric performances as well. He voiced particular enthusiasm for "Lady Geraldine's Courtship" by Elizabeth Barrett, spoken in the voice of a male poet who has fallen in love with an aristocratic woman; an elegy by Amelia Welby, written from the point of view of a young man who mourns the death of his wife; and *The Sinless Child*, a story of a modern, blameless "Eva" told in the third person (*ER* 127, 907,1352). All the poems evoke an author figure obliquely, as the object of the narrative rather than the speaking subject. Any strictly autobiographical reading is impossible, even while autobiographical speculation is encouraged. For Poe, as for others of his time, the woman was the ultimate poet, or poem. The seamless performance, the very difficulty in distinguishing the artist from the production, or the woman from her role as artist, was the sign of the poetess.

Poe participated in public literary romances with two of the poetesses he admired, Sarah Helen Whitman and Frances Sargent Osgood, because he valued their status as embodiments of poetic sentiment. (This formulation counters the more familiar view that he admired their poetry because he was attracted to their personal charms.) Exchanging love poems with Whitman and Osgood in the pages of the literary journals and newspapers of the late 1840s, Poe participated in full-scale dramatic productions of personal life. Of Anna Blackwell, he inquired: "Do you know Mrs. Whitman? I feel deep interest in her poetry and character . . . Her poetry is, beyond question, poetry – instinct with genius" (quoted in *PH* 49). Enforcing an equation between woman and poem, Poe engaged Beauty in dialogue in hopes of absorbing some of its power, so that poetic romances might generate romantic poetry.

Of all the women poets, Frances Osgood symbolized poetry incarnate: "Mrs. Osgood was born a poetess only – it is not in her nature to be anything else. Her personal, not less than her literary character and existence are one perpetual poem" (*CW* 13: 105). Osgood was so poetic that she was incapable of writing any species of prose:

She begins with a desperate effort at being sedate – that is to say, sufficiently prosaic and matter-of-fact for the purpose of a legend or an essay; but in a few sentences we behold uprising the leaven of the unrighteousness of the muse; then, after some flourishes and futile attempts at repression, a scrap of verse renders itself manifest; then another and another; then comes a poem outright, and then another and another and another, with little odd batches of prose in between, until at length the mask is thrown fairly off, and far away, and the whole article – sings. (*CW* 15: 104)

In an ironic reversal, the "mask" of prose, associated with the real (the "prosaic"), is thrown off to expose the more artful genre, which is Osgood's true form of expression. Combining aspects of both genius and muse, Poe presents Osgood as a passive creator, the fecund site where wild poetry breeds and escapes into the world, against her will. However, "the warm abandonnement of her style," which makes her the visible manifestation of poetic process, prevents her from becoming a premier poet. Her amateurism reconfirms the poetry of her presence, which her output can never equal. With "more industry, more method, more definite purpose, more ambition," Mrs. Osgood "might have written better poems; but the chances are that she would have failed in conveying so vivid and so just an idea of her powers as a poet" (*CW* 13: 175). While Poe relegates Osgood to the realm of eternal amateur, her "astonishing facility" also renders her capable of emitting poetry in any vein, and of imitating the signature verse of another, which helps to explain why, when he felt incapable of producing a new poem to read before the Boston Lyceum, he asked her to write one that could pass as his own (*EAP* 286).

By emphasizing Osgood's incompleteness as a poet, Poe created a space for himself to finish what she so energetically started. Her work only "affords us glimpses . . . of a capacity for accomplishing what she has not accomplished and in all probability never will" (*CW* 13: 176). The ambiguous phrasing suggests that Osgood affords Poe glimpses of his own capacity to realize the latent potential of her own work. Poe's interactions with poetesses suggests that he imagined them as sites of poetic ore that he might mine, a theme that is familiar from his poems and tales, which often center on the death of a beautiful young woman. J. Gerald Kennedy has said that "in calling poetry the 'rhythmical creation of beauty,' and then designating the death of a beautiful woman as the most poetical of topics, Poe established an implicit metaphorical relationship between the death of beauty and poetic texts" that "dramatize[s] the writer's problematic relationship" to his work.[25] The metaphorical relationship is more properly between the death of a beautiful woman and Poe's generation of a poetic text. This equivalence implies a convertibility between the terms: if women are Beauty incarnate, and poetesses are poems, then figuring women within his textual practice can make their poems his own.

For Poe, the natural, somewhat banal terrain of the poetess becomes exotic territory when traversed by a male poet. Though a woman and her book cannot help but be identical, men are incapable of achieving identification:

> If any ambitious man have a fancy to revolutionize, at one effort, the universal world of human thought, human opinion, and human sentiment, the opportunity is his own – the road to immortal renown lies straight, open, and unencumbered before him. All that he has to do is to write and publish a very little book. Its title should be simple – a few plain words – "My Heart Laid Bare." But – this little book must be true to its title.[26]

The artfulness of Osgood's artless heart mirrors the poet's drive to accomplish a seemingly natural art that would bring him fame, fortune, and originality. The apparently simple task of writing from the heart is impossible for a man, however: "no man *could* write it, even if he dared. The paper would shrivel and blaze at every touch of the pen" (150). While success is impossible, the quote suggests Poe's strategy for outstriding his female contemporaries, even while increasing their adoration.

POETIC MESMERISM

If the popular success of women poets depended upon their capacity for mimicry, then male poets could not help but contemplate the potential of mimicry uncoupled from originality. Hoping to transfix poetesses with his version of their mimic performances, Poe staged a takeover of their powers. His poems dramatized the transfer of energy from a female poetic wellspring to a male lover's texts.[27] Draining women of substance, encouraging them to stand as markers for other things, Poe transformed his all-too-present female poetic rivals into marmoreal emblems, momentarily quieted so that his own work might take center-stage. His masculine rendition of the feminine draws attention to its "crime" by encasing the evidence, the female corpse, within the poem that has absorbed the female spirit. These poems take as their primary audience the poetesses whose materials they borrow. Poe's figure of the mesmeric poet mirrors the mediumistic figure of the poetess: the difference lies in the extent to which the poet possesses the vision, rather than the reverse.

Comparing odes by Poe and Sarah Helen Whitman clarifies this duplicative, evacuative process. Regardless of whether the poets were aware of the affinities, Whitman's "Moonrise in May" and Poe's "The Sleeper" are in close dialogue. In addition to iambic tetrameter rhymed couplets, the poems share a similar setting: the speakers stand in the moonlight near a graveyard and contemplate, in Whitman's words, "the dead Past – the shrouded woes / That sleep in sculptural repose" (*SHWP* 11). Whereas Whitman's poem stresses the fullness of communion between the female speaker and landscape, however, Poe's male speaker disrupts that positive relation. "Moonrise in May" celebrates the healing power of natural beauty:

> Outspread beneath me, breathing balm
> Into the evening's golden calm,
> Lie trellised gardens, thickly sown
> With nodding lilacs, newly blown;
> Borders with hyacinthus plumed,
> And beds with purple pansies gloomed;
> Cold snow-drops, jonquils, pale and prim,
> And flamy tulips, burning dim
> In the cool twilight, till they fold
> In sleep their oriflammes of gold.
>
> (*SHWP* 9)

In the tradition of romantic promontory poems, the speaker stands above the landscape, displaying visual control of the scene she surveys. The garden is cultivated, rather than wild, however, and the speaker demonstrates more interest in mastering floral names than in imaginatively colonizing unknown territories. Through persistent personification, she turns the flower bed into a catalogue of female sexual possibilities: the lilacs' awakening, the hyacinths' narcissistic self-admiration, the jonquils' and snowdrops' virginal frigidity, the tulips' burning lust. Nowhere is the connection between woman and flower made explicit: it relies on conventional associations of women, and particularly female sexuality, with flowers.[28] The speaker extends this vision of feminine unity in her address to the moon – "Enchantress of the stormy seas, / Priestess of Night's high mysteries!" – that "doth interfuse / The magic world wherein I muse" (*SHWP* 11). The speaker's identification with the landscape soothes her sorrow and allows "a heavenly odor" to "bloom" by the end of the poem: "And lilies of eternal peace / Glow through the moonlight's golden fleece." Both evoking and expressing the speaker's tranquillity, the lilies' glow establishes a perfectly reciprocal relation between poetess and landscape.

"The Sleeper" methodically eliminates the inspirational unity that Whitman's poem reinforces. In an earlier version of the poem entitled "Irenë," a singing moon akin to Whitman's drips "an influence dewy, drowsy, dim," on to the landscape and "hums" into a woman's ear. By the time "The Sleeper" was published fourteen years later in 1841, the moon's song belongs to the male speaker.[29] While Whitman's moon animated the landscape with feminine sexual possibilities, Poe's speaker channels the moon's energy to sedate the landscape and its feminine inhabitants:

> At midnight, in the month of June,
> I stand beneath the mystic moon.
> An opiate vapour, dewy, dim,
> Exhales from out her golden rim,
> And, softly dripping, drop by drop,
> Upon the quiet mountain top,
> Steals drowsily and musically
> Into the universal valley.
> The rosemary nods upon the grave;
> The lily lolls upon the wave,
> Wrapping the fog about its breast,
> The ruin moulders into rest;
> Looking like Lethe, see! the lake
> A conscious slumber seems to take,
> And would not, for the world, awake.
> All Beauty sleeps! – and lo! where lies
> Irenë, with her Destinies!
>
> (*CWP* 186–187; 1–17)

Poe's speaker mesmerizes the landscape through a series of alliterative redundancies that heighten the iambic tetrameter's insistence ("And softly dripping, drop by drop"). He withstands the "opiate vapour" that puts Beauty to sleep. He is immune because he is an interloper in the scene, manipulating rather than blending with the landscape, as Whitman's speaker does. While Whitman's lady is the voluble source of poetic insight, "the lady sleeps" in Poe's poem, encased within a room so that she has only a mediated relation to the natural environment.

Like Whitman, Poe evokes a conventional landscape: the "rosemary nods," the "lily lolls," and the "ruin moulders." While Whitman's flowers signify modes of feminine sexuality, however, Poe's images redundantly signify death. Conventional images gain particularity in "Moonlight in May," but in "The Sleeper" only the words remain, in their singular and personified state. Fetishized, they summon the "universal valley," a primeval land of pure convention. Since historical usage establishes convention, convention's source can only gain priority retroactively. This process is figured in the forgetful lake, a mirror that suppresses the source of its reflection in order to assert the primacy of its secondariness. A lake of Lethe rather than a river evokes the deliberate stagnation and stasis that is prerequisite for the poem's duplicating process. By asserting itself as the form of form, the replica of a replica, the landscape becomes curiously "original" and originary.

That process extends to the speaker's relation with the "lady," a figure he also doubles in order to authorize. He casts himself as a vampire who takes her voice and uses her body to construct his poem. Standing in the moonlight, the speaker has no apparent need to move in order to survey the still and speechless figure within the chamber. His disembodied voice enjoys a superior freedom of movement:

> Oh, lady bright! can it be right –
> This window open to the night?
> The wanton airs, from the tree-top
> Laughingly through the lattice drop –
> The bodiless airs, a wizard rout,
> Flit through thy chamber in and out,
> And wave the curtain canopy
> So fitfully – so fearfully –
> Above the closed and fringed lid
> 'Neath which thy slumb'ring soul lies hid,
> That, o'er the floor and down the wall,
> Like ghosts the shadows rise and fall!
>
> (187; 18–29)

Synonymous with the "bodiless airs," the speaker's voice infiltrates the lady's unguarded window and then obsessively hovers around her coffin or bed: "fringed lid" could describe either a closed coffin, or a shut eye, replete with lashes. Assuming a threatening stance, the speaker all but begs the lady to be afraid of his ominous presence.

As the poem progresses, however, the speaker makes himself increasingly anxious about the status of the sleeping woman, generating confusion about whether he wants her to die and cannot kill her, or wants to revive her and cannot wake her up. When she does not respond with fear, presumably because he has deadened her to sensation, her impervious disregard threatens him. He compulsively questions her as if she could answer:

> Oh lady dear, hast thou no fear?
> Why and what art thou dreaming here?
> Sure thou art come o'er far-off seas,
> A wonder to these garden trees!
> Strange is thy pallor! strange thy dress!
> Strange, above all, thy length of tress,
> And this all solemn silentness!
>
> (187; 30–36)

Sedating the woman increases rather than decreases the speaker's fascination, because death or unconsciousness intensifies rather than destroys her personal integrity. While at the outset of the poem he suggests that he has captivated her, by the middle, she has mastered his attention.

Though the speaker claims verbal omnipotence, moreover, it is difficult to see what kind of threat a disembodied voice could pose to a dead female convention, for even pure body in this poem does not imply physicality. Irenë alludes only to other literary figures: Sleeping Beauty, for example, or Tennyson's dead women. The speaker, who ominously begins the poem by drugging the world in preparation for an act of violence, only commits his crime in a self-consciously literary landscape; he violates not a woman's privacy or her corpse, but the convention of the sleeping or dead woman. If he wished the reader to take him seriously, he would not foreground the "posing" of the threat and the theatricality of the scene: the bodiless airs are "a wizard rout" that try to animate an empty stage by "wav[ing] the curtain canopy" and making "shadows," not bodies, "rise and fall." While he evokes his magical power to animate or deaden, he also drains his assertion of its potency, confessing that he cannot raise the dead, or kill the living. Instead, he observes the scenario he has evoked, waiting for the woman to take on a life of her own that would simultaneously annihilate and animate his creation.

Killing the lady would remove the source of the speaker's inspiration; reviving her would remove the purpose of the poem and reintroduce the competition that he evades. He therefore seeks to maintain a state of suspended animation, a "conscious slumber." To this end, the overly regular iambic tetrameter breaks down at precisely the wrong moments: on the descent "into the universal valley," for example, the final unstressed syllable undermines the finality of the arrival. Perfect rhymes occur at the cost of proper syntax, as in the anticlimactic couplet "Looking like Lethe, see! the lake / a conscious slumber seems to take." Sedation and stimulation also vie in the sporadic disruption of perfect end rhymes with perverse off-rhymes: June-moon, dim-rim, drop-top, musically-valley is a typical sequence. The over-use of exclamation points indicates monotonous utterance, which might be sleep-inducing, if the speaker were not yelling the phrases: "The lady sleeps! Oh, may her sleep, / Which is enduring, so be deep!" (187; 37–38). We might expect a sinister visitor in a sleeping lady's chamber to whisper: this speaker repeats his self-evident assertion so often and loudly that we begin to think that he is trying to wake her. The incompatibilities between form and sense both shock and anesthetize the reader along with the lady, who is the figure for the poem's reception.

While the speaker addresses a feminine figure that he simultaneously animates and sedates, masters and submits to, in the final lines he suggests that *he* is the living dead who has escaped from the tomb in order to avenge himself on her crimes of appropriation:

> Far in the forest, dim and old,
> For her may some tall vault unfold –
> Some vault that oft hath flung its black
> and winged panels fluttering back,
> Triumphant, o'er the crested palls,
> Of her grand family funerals –
> Some sepulchre, remote, alone,
> Against whose portal she hath thrown,
> In childhood, many an idle stone –
> Some tomb from out whose sounding door
> She ne'er shall force an echo more,
> Thrilling to think, poor child of sin!
> It was the dead who groaned within.
>
> (187; 48–60)

The speaker suggests that "she" should be condemned for a seemingly trivial crime: she has thrown stones against the door of a family tomb while fantasizing that the echoes were the voices of the dead. Her echo-forcing duplicates the speaker's own apostrophes to the entombed source of his poetic reverie. The doubling of the speaker and the lady is so strong at this point that he addresses her for the first time as "My Love!" and proclaims the source of his fascination. By calling Irenë "child of sin," he inverts the title of Elizabeth Oakes Smith's *The Sinless Child*, reversing Eva's purity and summoning the specter of American female literary competition. The tomb's "crested palls" link it to British aristocratic tradition. The scenario suggests that all American writers, male and female, are secondary in relation to British literary tradition. Poe's speaker sedates Irenë for committing an identical crime – generating echoes – and reminding him of his own secondariness.

The redundancies that structure "The Sleeper" also forge continuities within Poe's corpus, reinforcing the reader's impression that the same speaker moves across poems, and that he revisits rather than invents that "wild weird clime" he repeatedly describes. In "Dreamland," for example, the speaker again champions his position as expert on sentiment by touring the source of sentimental convention "that lieth, sublime, / Out of SPACE – out of TIME," and coming "home" to tell about it (*CWP* 344; 7–8). If the poem evokes a sense of déjà-vu, we are correct in feeling that we have visited this place previously: a stagnant lake ("Their lone waters, lone and dead") and a "lolling lily" also appear in "The Sleeper." Unlike "The Sleeper," however, "Dreamland" is devoid of women; instead the landscape itself is primordially feminine. The poem portrays a liquid place with "bottomless vales and boundless floods" and "forms that no man can discover / For the tears that drip all over." Intensifying the elements of sentimental poetry, Poe's poem evokes a sentimental sublime. A place of no measure, drowned in tears and melancholy, Dreamland is absolutely and luxuriously tragic. The realm is so effusive, weeping endlessly over infinite loss, that its contours are undetectable. At least, "no man" can discern its geography, and poetesses rarely visit Heaven's dark inversions in their lyrics. Poe's speaker takes advantage of this restriction to assert his proprietorship over this primordial realm of elegiac tears, the origin of all mournful sentiment. The "home" that the wanderer returns to is the form of the formless infinite, and he serves as the medium that connects domesticated literary conventions to mystical and profound possibilities.

If "The Sleeper" and "Dreamland" dismantle the continuity between woman and landscape that poetesses like Sarah Helen Whitman maintained, Poe more directly staged the poetess' disappearance for the poetess herself when he sent Whitman the second "To Helen," along with a request for her autograph in June 1848 (he then published the poem in the *Union*

Magazine). The poem offers a funereal portrait of the poetess "clad all in white, upon a violet bank" that celebrates the "poetry of [her] presence" while highlighting its conversion to the presence of his poem (*CWP* 445; 16). In the initial image of Whitman among the flowery creations for which she was known – "roses that grew in an enchanted garden" – poetess and poems share one landscape and are illuminated by yet another feminine figure, "dear Dian": "I saw thee half reclining; while the moon / Fell on the upturn'd faces of the roses, / And on thine own, upturn'd – alas, in sorrow!" (18–20). Almost immediately, however, the roses die of an excess of sameness: even their odors "died in the arms of the adoring airs" (446; 35). The speaker dismantles both the landscape ("in an instant, all things disappeared") and Whitman ("thou, a ghost amid the entombing trees / Didst glide away") until "only thine eyes remained" (29, 50–51). Her eyes – "two sweetly scintillant Venuses, unextinguished by the sun" – linger in order to illuminate the post-apocalyptic landscape (447; 65–66). The bizarre juxtaposition of the lingering eye-stars and the departed Helen underscores the need for the integrity of even a ghostlike body and returns the reader to the recalcitrance of Poe's poetic dilemma: he needs her to stay in order to provide the materials for his poem, and he needs her to go in order to make his poem anew.

Poe's poems seek to become the source of feminine convention by asserting themselves as prior originators of previously established cultural codes. Poe cannot dismantle, reject, or deny the source since he must refer to it in order to stake his claim; instead he embeds it within his poems. Through imitating the imitative, Poe asserts a curious brand of primacy that temporarily inverts the status of shadow and form. The titles of his poems alone suggest the reflective nature of his poetics: "A Dream Within a Dream," "Eulalie," "Ulalume," "A Dream," "Fairyland," "The Lake," "The Sleeper," "Dreamland," "Lenore," "Annabel Lee," "The Bells," etc. The words echo each other and even themselves: "Ulalume," for example, mirrors itself, recalls "Eulalie," and begins to spell "emulate" backwards. These strategies of exaggerated repetition foreground convention while emptying it of meaning. Poe documents rather than hides his evacuations of conventional form, which he specifically identifies as feminine in the tableau of the dead or sleeping woman. His male poet-speakers persistently toy with the idea of supplanting the feminine realm entirely, yet just as persistently draw back, unable to imagine a world without the constitutive force of the feminine.

Poe's evacuative aesthetic is most clearly propounded and performed in "The Raven" and its critical companion piece "The Philosophy of Composition." While "The Philosophy of Composition" works as an extension of the poem it interprets (and I will discuss this effect presently), "The Raven" serves as a study of composition, particularly as it relates to the interplay of gender and genre. His poem works from an identifiable female rhythmic prototype, "Lady Geraldine's Courtship" by Elizabeth Barrett. Highlighting her influence, Poe dedicated *The Raven and Other Poems* (1845) to Barrett. In a review of her *Drama of Exile* that appeared shortly before the first publication of the "The Raven," he paid special attention to her own poem's secondary status:[30]

With the exception of Tennyson's "Locksley Hall," we have never perused a poem combining so much of the fiercest passion with so much of the most ethereal fancy, as the "Lady Geraldine's Courtship," of Miss Barrett. We are forced to admit, however, that the latter work is a very palpable imitation of the former, which it surpasses in plot or rather in thesis, as much as it falls below it in artistical management, and a certain calm energy – lustrous and indomitable – such as we might imagine in a broad river of molten gold. (*ER* 127)

Dueling referential "it"s generate uncertainty about the status of "the palpable imitation," and about the attribution of qualities to the original and to the copy. By highlighting Barrett's derivativeness shortly before he presents his own heavily allusive poem, Poe affiliates himself with a second-comer and consolidates his identification with the poetess seeking to establish legitimacy within a masculine tradition.

Together, "Lady Geraldine's Courtship" and "The Raven" encourage a contemplation of the differences between models of female and male poetic achievement. A comparison of just two lines highlights this process:

BARRETT: With a murmurous stir uncertain, in the air, the purple curtain
     Swelleth in and swelleth out around her motionless pale brows.[31]
POE: And the silken, sad, uncertain rustling of each purple curtain Thrilled me –
     filled me with fantastic terrors never felt before. (*CWP* 364; 13–14)

In both poems, a male poet speaks of his unattainable love. Barrett's poet closely observes Lady Geraldine's queenly presence, framed and enhanced by the swelling curtains, which register her unspoken passion. Poe's poet, on the other hand, records his own sensations about the curtains which only obliquely recall the lost Lenore: the curtains are "sad," but their sadness "thrilled" the speaker, who expresses the vicarious pleasure of observing his pain at a remove. Whereas thrushes and songbirds, emblems of poetic musicality, populate Barrett's poem, Poe centers his poem on a single "croaking" bird that repeats a human word it does not understand. Even this scant comparison suggests that "The Raven" parodies its reliance upon the imitation of a feminine precursor and asserts its originality by highlighting its secondariness.[32]

The poem takes as its subject a symbiotic – or, with the presence of the scavenger bird, an explicitly parasitic – process of poetic composition. Aligned with the raven, the lyric speaker replaces female inspiration by drawing from it. Whereas the beautiful woman inspires the poem, her evacuation is prerequisite to its existence. Contemplating the memory of his departed lover, the speaker sits in the velvet chair that was her habitual resting place in order to compose his poem:

> This and more I sat divining, with my head at ease reclining
> On the cushion's velvet lining that the lamp-light gloated o'er,
> But whose velvet violet lining with the lamp-light gloating o'er,
> She shall press, ah, nevermore!   (*CWP* 368; 75–78)

Not only does Lenore's absence inspire the poet to link "fancy unto fancy," but he literally occupies her vacated space while composing his poetic tribute. The gloating lamplight partially illuminates a crime of dispossession, expressing the speaker's displaced pleasure over his occupation. The speaker thus underscores the suggestion that Lenore's death has provided him with an opportunity for poetic generation even as he professes sorrow over her loss. The speaker simultaneously proclaims his desire to forget and stimulates his desire in remembering by repeating the tantalizing word Lenore, an ambivalent marker for a banished presence, or a presence of banishment.[33]

> "Respite – respite and nepenthe from thy memories of Lenore;
> Quaff, oh quaff this kind nepenthe and forget this lost Lenore."
> Quoth the Raven "Nevermore"   (368; 82–84)

Caught in an insoluble dilemma, the speaker cannot completely erase Lenore and still retain the poem's reason for being: the elegiac occasion of "Mournful and Never-ending Remembrance" (*ER* 25). He professes his need to remember Lenore, the source of his inspiration, even while asserting his need to forget her in order to assert his poetic primacy.

Dramatizing his appropriation of the feminine, the speaker encourages readers to ponder the implications of an aesthetic that foregrounds its exploitative tendencies. Although in "The Philosophy of Composition" Poe states that the tone of "The Raven" is characterized by sadness, this contemplation of "the death of a beautiful woman" results in titillation, "the most delicious because the most intolerable of sorrow" (*ER* 19). The speaker promotes himself to the reader as an expert on suffering who has achieved heightened sensibility through Lenore's death, which provides him with an occasion to give guided tours through "fantastic terrors never felt before." He stresses the ways that his poem provides an occasion for novel entertainment:

> For we cannot help agreeing that no living human being
> Ever yet was blessed with seeing bird above his chamber door –
> Bird or beast upon the sculptured bust above his chamber door,
> With such name as "Nevermore."   (367; 51–54)

The collective pronoun aligns the speaker with the reader in admiration of his brand-new, never-before-seen amalgamation. The poet thus makes himself into an observer of his own performance who celebrates its vicarious qualities as the basis of readerly identification. At a dramatic remove from the incident of even a fictional lover's death, the narrative is concerned with the thrill that the theatrical portrayal of a loss would evoke in an audience to which the speaker himself belongs. Voyeur to the speaker's preoccupation with his own sensation, the reader never gains insight into the memory of a dead lover, unless she understands the speaker's narcissistic aestheticization of grief as an attempt to block the memory of the beloved. Against the backdrop of a feminine poetics predicated upon the ability to simulate heartfelt emotion, Poe's speaker openly disowns his grief, transforming it into a show for the viewer's pleasure.

The vicarious quality of Poe's poetry was not lost upon his contemporaries. One reader even literalized this impression, accusing Poe of killing his wife in order to have a mournful subject for "The Raven." With "passions controlled by the presence of art until they resembled sculptured flame," according to one published accusation, Poe "deliberately sought [Virginia's] death that he might embalm her memory in immortal dirges" (quoted in *EPC* 42–43). This peculiar type of character assault, which hovered around Poe, found its starting point in his own poems, which encouraged scandalous readerly fantasies. Such accusations collapse the distinction between material and poetic worlds that underpins Poe's appropriative play. In "The Raven," as in other poems by Poe, a dead woman stands in for a publicized robbery of feminine forms. Not surprisingly, a poetess, Sarah Helen Whitman, recognized this distinction and defended Poe against the charge of wife-killing in the name of art: "A serious objection to this ingenious theory may perhaps be found in the 'refractory fact' that the poem was published more than a year before the event [Virginia's death] which these persons assume it was intended to commemorate." Whitman's eloquent and influential defense testifies to the paradoxical power of Poe's poetic crime scenes to mobilize female sympathy.[34]

Underscoring its recycled qualities and proudly confessing its secondariness, "The Raven" echoes "Lady Geraldine's Courtship" as well as any number of other precursors. While I have focused on this single pairing, Poe frequently embeds identifiable fragments or aspects of poems written by women within his own forms. T. O. Mabbott frequently identifies women's popular poems as possible sources for Poe's work. He suggests, for example, that in "Ulalume," the speaker replicates the plot of Elizabeth Oakes Smith's "The Summons Answered," in which a reveler arrives unwittingly at his wife's tomb (*CWP* 411). Burton Pollins claims that Poe's "Lenore" is indebted to Frances Osgood's "Leonor." Buford Jones and Kent Ljungquist have argued that Osgood's "The Life Voyage" is a model for Poe's "Annabel Lee."[35] Contemporaries would have been able to identify many of these "plagiarisms," particularly if they were part of a group of writers who followed each other's work in the literary journals. Displaying rather than hiding his female influence, Poe generates a masculine poetics of appropriative flattery that particularly appealed to female poets.

CRITICAL VOICE

If within his poetry Poe establishes a cross-gendered identification with women poets even as he attempts to upstage them, in his critical essays he negates that relation in order to establish an affective tie with the "race of critics" who "are masculine – men" (*CW* 12: 1). Poe further masculinizes the traditionally masculine genre of the critical essay, advertising its analytical stronghold over the poetic realm of feminine feeling. His titles alone drive home this point: "The Rationale of Verse," "The Poetic Principle," and "The Philosophy of Composition" all celebrate the critic's ability to arrive at distilled truths which are invisible to readers and common authors alike. This gesture towards dominating the terrain of poetry with an alien rhetorical force, however, becomes Poe's attempt to extend his poetic claims by expanding his performance of emotional distance via the poetic feature of voice. Linked to his lyric speakers by authorial signature, Poe's critical voice is detached from the poet's agony not from lack of feeling, but from excess.[36] In this scenario, a tortured soul finds relief in the realm of thought, but blankly recalls, like one in shock, the source of pain: the poem. Overlaying critical and lyric voices creates a model of emotional suppression, an enduring constellation signifying masculine literary sentiment that Poe helped to organize. Rather than a separate genre, Poe's essays are more accurately demonstrations of poetic mastery, which relocate the ground of affective authenticity from the heart of the poetess to the page of the critical essay.[37]

As the companion piece to "The Raven," "The Philosophy of Composition" offers the clearest example of this process. Published in *Graham's Magazine* in April 1846, the essay rode the wave of the poem's success. Poe reminds his readers that he wrote the poem that many had found haunting, even as he adopts an incongruous critical voice that offers to "render it manifest that no one point in the poem's composition is referable to either accident or intuition" (*ER* 14–15). People who had heard Poe's readings of the poem had testified to the uncanny quality of the event; by revealing that impression to be a product of the reader's imagination, Poe hoped to create a second sensation. The dramatic difference between his critical and poetic voices enhances his authorial mystique; in trying to reconcile the disparity between the essay and the poem, readers must posit an author who stands behind both texts, but remains elusive.

Poe's critic displays and disowns the emotions of his lyric speaker. While the essay purports to tell the tale of the poem's purely rational construction – "which proceeded, step by step, to its completion with the rigid consequence of a mathematical problem" – more accurately, the critic decomposes the poem into its elements in order to expose the fiction of lyric voice (*ER* 15). "Commencing with a consideration of an effect," he relocates the source of melancholy regret from the lyric speaker to a universal reader who would agree that "the death ... of a beautiful woman is unquestionably, the most poetical topic in the world – and equally is it beyond doubt that the lips best suited for such a topic are those of a bereaved lover" (13, 19). Because his conclusions seem to result from an individual obsession rather than a scientific survey of the reading population, however, this disavowal of sentiment closes the distance between Poe, the living poet, and the poem's "Mournful and Never-ending Remembrance" (25). For once the speaker is gone, who but Poe might own "the lips ... of a bereaved lover"?

Poe contrasts this emotionally detached state favorably against that of other poets who make claims to an artless art. Like a showman, he opens the curtains on the theatricality of lyric: "Most writers – poets in especial – prefer having it understood that they compose by a species of fine frenzy – an ecstatic intuition – and would positively shudder at letting the public take a peep behind the scenes" (14). Reversing the feminine terms of evaluation, Poe exposes the theatricality of the poet's performance of the natural and naturalizes theatricality as the poet's authentic environment. His gesture of sincerity is to expose others' fraudulent version of it. He lets the public stare "at the wheels and pinions – the tackle for scene-shifting – the step-ladders and demon-traps – the cock's feathers, the red paint and the black patches, which, in ninety-nine cases out of the hundred, constitute the properties of the literary *histrio*" (14).

Removing authenticity from the body of the poetess to the masculine realm of rational inquiry, Poe engineered a critical lens that validated absence and distance rather than presence and proximity. His disjunctive poetics both rival and recall his portrait of the poetess. Whereas he claims that "the poetess speaks because she feels, and what she feels – but what she feels is felt only by the truly poetical" – he starts as far away from lyric speech as possible in "The Philosophy of Composition," working backwards from the poem's imagined "effect" on its readers (*CW* 13: 115; *ER* 13). While "poetical" emotion dictates the form of women's utterance, Poe selects through analytical process the most *"universally* appreciable" focus at every stage of composition (*ER* 16). If the poetess spontaneously erupts into lyric speech, Poe valorizes conscious selection and choice. If she emits pure poeticality, he insists that his compositional process consists of "originality of combination," rearranging received forms into new constellations (21). An "obvious" and "easily attainable . . . source of interest," originality in verse is crafted, banal, and mechanically deducible (13). Anti-inspirational, Poe's poetic method is original in its extreme lack of any claim to originality. The precise inversion of the practices he ascribes to poetesses, his pronouncements must have instilled an odd sense of familiarity, as if he encouraged readers to recognize the image and the influence of the feminine in the labor he invested in reversing it.

This reversal further suggests that Poe's aesthetic system is designed to convert the poetess from the ideal producer of poetry into an ideal consumer of his own. Poe imagines readers in the image of the poetess, the ultimate home of Beauty, when he ascertains that the most poetical topic in the world is the death of a beautiful woman, and that the male lover's lips best express this idea (*ER* 19). This formulation makes a captive audience of one sector of Poe's literary competition. For it was undoubtedly seductive for women to imagine themselves into the position of Poe's lost love and object of his poetic tributes. The multiple bids for the role of the inspiration of "Annabel Lee" are well known: at least three women believed the poem was written for her alone.[38] If the most poetical topic in the world is a man's longing for his female lover, then women would have difficulty imagining themselves into the role of poet with the same level of authenticity that a male poet could claim. While Poe was particularly drawn to poems by women told from the perspective of a bereaved male lover, he naturalized the link between himself and that figure in his criticism.

Positioning women as readers and himself as the poet with superior claims to emotional authenticity, Poe's critical essays attempt to stabilize the fluid, imitative play of cross-gendered poetic exchange. Instead of a systematic attempt to disenfranchise poetesses, however, his critical negotiations seek to carve out a masculine poetic space. By annexing the critical essay to the "province of poetry," Poe creates a hybridized model of masculine literary sentiment. Rather than a separate sphere of discourse, his essays overlay his poetry in order to create a composite portrait of an authentic male artist. Confirming and extending this aesthetic fusion of critic and poet, critic (and poet) Daniel Hoffman locates the key to Poe's artistic sensibility at the point of generic comparison. "A remarkable achievement in candor," "The Philosophy of Composition" offers the second half of a confession that begins in Poe's poems:[39]

What is the relation between his claim that imagination is a rational and orderly premeditated process and his need to drape it in crepe at the bier of a beautiful woman? What is the connection but that the straitjacket method enables the poet to deal with his obsessive and inescapable subject by compelling him to think about something else, something other than the woe vibrating within him which to think of would overcome him. So the method of his art enables the madness of his matter to be spoken. (92)

"The woe vibrating within" Poe is made visible through generic juxta-position. His critical assertions of aesthetic rigor authenticate the poems' obsessive crepe-draping. If the rigidity of the "straitjacket method" betrays the power of the contained emotion, then criticism is a more radical form of artistic self-containment than poetry-writing and is therefore, paradox-ically, the location of authorial self-revelation.

Present in Poe but missing from his descendants is an acknowledgment of his aesthetic exchange with his female contemporaries. Following cues from Poe's essays while ignoring the evidence from his poems, critics have consolidated a tradition of scholarship in which the figure of the poet-ess has suffered an ever more radical absorption into the figure of the male poet. Baudelaire's mid-century interpretations have played a key role in this process. In appropriating Poe for his own poetico-critical project, Baudelaire suppresses Poe's expressions of female identification and indebt-edness, while exaggerating his literary misogyny. Looking to Poe in order to ask how to write an elite poetry within a market economy, Baudelaire finds an answer in the exorcism of female influence.

In his 1856 introduction to his translations of Poe's works, Baudelaire portrays a monstrous America, founded at a point of civilizational decline that is articulated in its democratic organization, whose unchecked impulses and enormous energy find their outlet in indiscriminate productivity. In the American literary marketplace, excessively prolix writers proliferate: "America babbles and rambles with an astonishing volubility. Who could count its poets? They are innumerable. Its bluestockings? They clutter the magazines."[40] Deprived of the protective milieu surrounding his aristocratic European forebears, the great American poet confronts a throng of profit-oriented writers whose dubious poetry stands on equal footing with great literary works. The productivity of "the money-making author" mimics the mindless generativity of mass production and threatens to drown the true artist – Poe – adrift in the modern world.

Baudelaire finds Poe's theatrical strategies successful in combating the encroachment of literary materialists in this "maelstrom of mediocrity": Poe distinguishes himself "as a caricature" (122, 123). The prototype for his "charlatanry" is also its audience: the writers whom he conquers through his duplicative and dismissive play. Baudelaire contrasts the masculine arti-ficiality of Poe's work with the natural femininity of those writers aligned with market forces. Taking his cue from Poe, Baudelaire links Poe's mas-culine literary style to an artificial performance of the feminine. He says of *Marginalia*'s advocacy of an analytical approach to writing:

The lovers of a fine frenzy will perhaps be revolted by these cynical maxims; but everyone may take what he wishes from them. . . . After all, a little charlatanism is always permitted to genius, and is even proper to it. It is, like rouge on the cheeks of a naturally beautiful woman, an additional stimulus to the mind. (156)

Whereas Karen Halttunen argues that antebellum theatricality opposes sincerity and embodies the threat of hypocrisy, Baudelaire suggests that theatricality is a form of transparency that sets off natural beauty.[41] He maps this set of associations on to literary styles, associating the inferior "fine frenzy" with the rougeless female and Poe's "deliberate," premeditated style with both theatricality and the made-up woman.

The logical conclusion of Baudelaire's argument would be that Poe is a literary transvestite whose charms are superior to the "naturally beautiful" women he imitates.[42] And indeed, he advances precisely this claim, reveal-ing in the process that the ultimate threat to the male writer's autonomy is the female writer, the spirit not of the home, but of the marketplace. Poe's rendition of the feminine beats the literary women on the very terms that they should excel: intensity and emotional sincerity. Baudelaire's logic is associative:

As for [Poe's] intense preoccupation with the horrible, I have noticed among a number of men that it was often the result of an immense unused vital energy, or sometimes of a stubborn chastity, or of a deeply repressed sensibility. The unnatural pleasure that a man may feel on seeing his own blood flow, brusque and useless movements, loud cries uttered almost involuntarily are analogous phenomena. Pain relieves pain, action rests one from repose. Another characteristic of his writing is that it is completely anti-feminine. . . . Women write and write, with an exuberant rapidity; their hearts speak and chatter in reams. Usually they know nothing of art, or measure, or logic; their style trails and flows like their garments. . . . In the books of Edgar Poe the style is concatenated; the prejudice or the inertia of the reader cannot penetrate the meshes of this network woven by logic. (78–79)

Baudelaire suggests that Poe's preoccupation with self-inflicted pain is a sign of a heightened capacity for strong feeling that he represses into such perversions in order to protect himself from his less sensitive contemporaries. Baudelaire links Poe's unnaturally heightened sensibility to his "anti-feminine," highly crafted writing style, which counters women's "natural" "reams." After likening Poe's preoccupation with the horrible to men who enjoy "seeing their own blood flow," Baudelaire repeats this image in transmuted form when describing feminine style, which "trails and flows like their garments." The parallel articulates the difference between feminine and masculine styles in terms of control. Advertised in their flowing clothing, women's lack of control is superficial. Internalizing their fashion accessories, women write thoughtlessly and without depth. The male writer, on the other hand, is a detached observer of his own uncontrol, which registers not superficially, in his clothes, but crucially, on his body.

While Baudelaire draws a stark contrast between men and women, ultimately he casts masculinity as a theatricalized extension of femininity. Poe's emotional distress is repressed into a physical symptom that expresses a desire for suicide, a pleasure in seeing blood come to the surface. The analogy – that blood is to man as clothing is to woman – implies that bleeding, as an externalized expression of agony, is men's way of becoming feminine. A man's bleeding cut is the hysterical equivalent of a woman menstruating. A perverse form of mimicry, men's bleeding is an unregenerative, even deadly version of women's fertility. To Baudelaire, Poe's lack of emotional receptivity is the sign of a "deeply repressed sensibility," and his mechanistic tendencies (his "concatenated" style) are a sign of "unused vital energy": the stylistic traits substitute for what cannot reveal itself. As I have argued in relation to "The Philosophy of Composition," Baudelaire believes that Poe's theatricality contributes to the reader's impression of his sincerity rather than undercutting it. Canonical values lie in a reaction to a female-identified aesthetic of proximity to the marketplace; however, the masculine performance of distance as a sign of heightened emotional sensitivity contains all the traits of the poetess in inverted form.

Baudelaire's hyper-masculine version of Poe's aesthetic has influenced not only the American reception of Poe, but also the development of an aesthetic that has almost entirely erased the contributions of nineteenth-century women poets. Critics continue to read Poe as Baudelaire read him: the embattled, heroic artist awash in a sea of female poetry that was indistinguishable from marketplace motions, and that therefore appealed to the degraded popular readership that could not appreciate his genius. In investing Poe with the feminine, Baudelaire and other later critics have divested literary history of the significance of women poets, whose presence was a mixed blessing for Poe, a pure evil for Baudelaire, and an incomprehensibility for later scholars. Daniel Hoffman, for example, calls Poe "the first critic in this country to insist that literary work be measured by literary standards alone," but he simultaneously expresses bafflement about Poe's interest in poetesses:

True, [Poe's] own standards were not only high but a little odd: he couldn't keep himself from overpraising poetesses who wrote elegies to dead lovers, finding in the effusions of such nobodies as Mrs. Amelia Welby and Elizabeth Oakes Smith the nearly articulated intimations of the theme which became the sole burden of his own verse, and its undoing. But when I read Poe's notes on poetry – not on contemporary poems . . . Poe on poetic principles makes a lot of good sense.[43]

Hoffman denies the feminine influence that Poe himself identifies in the poetess' "nearly articulated intimations" of his work. Echoing Poe's critical gesture of female exorcism, Hoffman dismisses the poetesses on the basis of Poe's "poetic principles" only by disregarding Poe's reviews.

In forgetting the women, Hoffman and others have stripped Poe of his ties to a market-based dynamics of literary exchange in order to render him an impermeable critic of those forces. That external vantage-point, as Poe more than his followers might readily acknowledge, is a fiction constructed by antebellum writers themselves. In order to elevate Poe, critics have needed to forget that Emerson called him "the jingle man," aligning him with "the female poetasters," those "anti-poetic influences of Massachusetts" that the great writer must struggle against.[44] Often, critics have needed to forget Poe's poetry entirely in order to make of him "a brilliant analyst of a market he was never able fully to exploit";

generally speaking, the canonical (and masculine) Poe is the Poe of fiction and criticism.[45]

Although some scholars have located the systematic dismissal of female literary achievement in the antebellum period, Poe's case suggests that antebellum writers were more open to considerations of the value (not simply the saleability) of women's poetry than later critics. While writing was obsessively categorized according to supposedly gendered qualities, cross-gendered literary interactions were pervasive among writers who considered themselves peers. Poe's struggles, and those of his critics, demonstrate that women poets played a formative role in the creation of literary tastes in the antebellum period, and not simply as a repulsive force that impelled great male writers to create works of art in resistance to mass mediocrity.[46] Later critics have tended to accept as accurate the dismissive characterizations of antebellum poetesses that their competitors promulgated in the period. When looking for the reasons why nineteenth-century women poets have been forgotten, we should consider the lyric voice of the critical essay as much as its aesthetic pronouncements and recognize the influence of the poetess in reactive rhetoric. Rather than peripheral, trivial, or obviously frivolous, antebellum women poets posed central aesthetic challenges. Any historical understanding of American poetry requires a thorough re-evaluation of the significance and influence of the nineteenth-century poetess.

CHAPTER 2

Frances Sargent Osgood, Salon Poetry, and the Erotic Voice of Print

The title page of Frances Sargent Osgood's final collection of poetry, published in 1850, the year of her death by tuberculosis at the age of forty, features a portrait of a precocious child (fig. 4). Wearing an off-the-shoulder gown, a butterfly on her finger, the little girl looks directly into the reader's eyes. Beneath the image are lines from Osgood's poem, "On Parting With An Infant's Portrait," that send the "fair image of my fairer child" out into the world to win acclaim for her painter-husband, Samuel Osgood, who crafted and signed their daughter's picture. Poem and picture refer to their places in a duplicative series: the couple produced the child and then reproduced her likeness in word and image; the volume's publication then multiplied those replicas. Underscoring the relation of genetic and artistic progeny, the butterfly signals metamorphosis, from girl to woman, and life to art. Poem and picture so stress the living properties of the "fairy child" that the reader wonders how the mother-poet can bid her to journey alone into the world and "gaze smiling into stranger hearts" without worrying that she might come to harm at the hands of predatory adults (*FSOP* 201).

Why does this figure greet us at the outset of Osgood's volume? Should we imagine her as a portrait of Osgood's poems, the sisters of this fair image, sent off into the world to earn money and reputation for their author through readerly seduction? Should we associate the precocious child with the authorial persona of Osgood, under whose name the image floats the way a portrait of the artist might? Or should we experience difficulty distinguishing the artist from the artwork, the mother from the daughter, the husband-painter's vision from the outlook of his living Muse?

The hallmark of Osgood's work is precisely the unlocalizable eroticism that derives from these conflations. Hailed as "our American Sappho" and the "Cleopatra of song," Osgood stole the hearts of men and women in the 1830s and 1840s with a wayward, coquettish poetic performance that placed her "first in the rank of literary women of this country" over the old favorite,

Fig. 4: Title page, *Poems by Frances Sargent Osgood.* Painting by Samuel Stillman Osgood; engraved by J. I. Pease. Verse from Frances Osgood's "On Parting With an Infant's Portrait."

Lydia Sigourney. Offering pieces that were "informed and 'o'er informed' with passion and imagination," Osgood marketed the poetry of romance as successfully as Sigourney capitalized on the elegy.[1] Like Sigourney, she personified the poetess; her portrait serves as the frontispiece for Caroline May's 1848 anthology, *American Female Poets* (fig. 5). But while Sigourney was a national icon of mourning, Osgood was a figure of Fancy, an ethereal feminine sprite with enchanting gifts of mobility, spontaneous invention, and seduction. Her amatory model of author–reader relations appealed to a rapidly expanding readership across gender divisions. Contrary to claims that antebellum women wrote "by, for, and about women," Osgood won not only the praises but the hearts of men, including many of the most important critics, editors, and publishers of her day: John Neal, Hiram Fuller, R. H. Stoddard, Rufus Griswold, and – most famously – Edgar Allan Poe.[2] Presenting herself as a renegade muse that had managed to escape the bounds of the male imagination, Osgood captivated men with fantasies that they might recapture their lost inspiration and regain their footing among the literary women; she captivated women with fantasies that they might harness the seductive powers of print through lyric expression.

A number of mid-century reviews make clear that Osgood's popularity was a force to be reckoned with:

We may still differ in opinion upon the old lyceum question about the equality of mind in the sexes, but stern facts and ugly, tell-tale figures leave no one in doubt as to which sex bears away the palm of popular meed at the present day. The most successful works of Irving and Cooper have been distanced in the race of popularity by those of Mrs. Stowe and Miss Wetherell. Mr. Bryant stands to-day the noblest of all our American poets; but Mrs. Osgood has a hold upon the heart and sympathy of the American public never accorded to Bryant. This is a wonderful revelation in literature – a reversing of the state of things in all former ages.[3]

Greater literary merit ("nobility") lies with Bryant, but Osgood has never-theless performed the intriguing feat – one Bryant could not manage – of winning the public's love. Fearsome and wondrous, the rise of the woman writer inverts the natural order.

The secret to Osgood's success, as well as to her subsequent failure to remain within the scope of literary admiration much beyond the time of her death, lies in a literary practice that obliquely related the embodied figure of the poetess with a disembodied figure of female "voice" in order to explore the erotic potential of the print media through which poems circulated.[4] Working within both a coterie tradition of lyric performance and a newer logic of mass publishing, Osgood presented a hybrid, paper self that combined the traits of a salon socialite with the properties of

Fig. 5: "Frances S. Osgood," Frontispiece, *American Female Poets*, ed. Caroline May (Philadelphia: Lindsay and Blakiston, 1848). Painting by Samuel Stillman Osgood; engraving by J. Sartain.

a widely circulating magazine. Sharing her cover girl's innocent promiscuity, Osgood's capricious poems reached out indiscriminately to an ever-increasing number of readers. They stirred desires to pick them up and hold them, to buy them and bring them home, to incorporate them through reading, recitation, and song.[5] Osgood explored the blurred line between the erotic pleasures of producing text and the textual pleasures of producing erotic relations. We can never be sure if we are hearing the voice of female desire or the voice of print as it rapidly proliferated in the magazine age.

Reading Osgood's poetry in circulation requires an adjustment of recent critical delineations of antebellum women writers' place in the production of privacy and publicity. While challenging the idea that the public sphere is purely masculine, recent studies nevertheless attribute a subordinate place to women's "voices." Caroline Levander, for example, argues that "men's attention to women's voices both marginalizes women from public life and consolidates the masculinity of an emerging public arena."[6] Levander shows that nineteenth-century linguists celebrated the morally elevating capacities of women's tonal utterance while denying their intelligibility. When women tried to "develop a more openly content-oriented speech," associations of verbal expression with sexual promiscuity enforced their exclusion from political debate (21). Reformers like Melville and E. D. E. N. Southworth then challenged this political exclusion by physically dislocating women's voices from their bodies, enabling their "heroines to circumvent the strategies that contain their speech and thereby to recover command over the sexually specific subject matter that women have surrendered in their attempt to raise the nation's vocal standard" (38). Though these fictional representations of voice are disembodied, Levander nevertheless locates the voice's origin within the woman's body; she then links the expressive fiction to the status of real women's political expression. In this formulation, women's ability to talk about sex in public is a subversive, liberatory force.

While Levander's analysis of nineteenth-century linguistic theories and their implications for women's political speech is persuasive, it does not extend to the function of sexual expression in antebellum women's lyric. This chapter suggests that lyric figurations of female desire constitute the print public sphere in such a way that they cannot be expunged, suppressed, or marginalized, nor can they serve as a disruptive or liberatory force. Poetesses like Osgood write about sexual relations in generic terms that constitute a standard medium of exchange. The poetess' lyric carries a range of impersonally personal erotic messages that bear no clear relation to anyone in particular. Osgood foregrounds the ways that women do not speak for themselves when they speak about sex. She teases her readers' tendency to mistake printed lyric "voice" for embodied utterance and the figure of the poetess for an actual person. Male readers most frequently mistake Osgood's poetic "speech" for the embodied utterances of an actual woman. The final section of this chapter will explore Poe's enforcement of this equation as an attempt to curb Osgood's poetic dissemination and assume her intimate relations with print under his own signature.

POETESSES IN PRINT, 1830–1850

Osgood's practices marked a shift in the possibilities for female poetic expression in a rapidly changing American literary scene. Because the capacity to inculcate morally uplifting sentiments was attributed to both women and poems, women's poetry promised to provide the public world of print with a soul. The understanding that women wrote from the heart, however, also threatened to undermine the poetess' moral purity, for it marked her poetry as a product of body as well as soul. The published poetess evoked both angelic purity and sexual promiscuity, spiritual amateurism and capitalist professionalism. Arguably the first American professional poet, Sigourney pioneered in negotiating this ground, and Osgood closely followed her. One of the earliest American purveyors of poetry to a mass audience, Sigourney negated associations of female sexuality with print proliferation in order to establish the literary sphere as an ethereal realm, distinct from the material world, with its own properties and modes of relation and exchange. Osgood and other poetesses of a later generation worked to populate and animate the lyric public sphere with disembodied figures of female sexuality. Detached from the person of the author, but affiliated with the personification of the Poetess, these figures relied upon Sigourney's previous work distinguishing the literal from the literary.

Perhaps the two most popular and highly paid women poets of their time, Sigourney and Osgood forged radically different poem- and print-based fantasies of intimacy. In order to make sense of Osgood's poetics of promiscuity, then, we must first take a look at its more proper predecessor. While the signed lyric poem was not precisely the woman's publicly displayed body, it held enough resemblance to inspire comparisons. In 1827 Lydia Sigourney's husband complained of her "lust of praise, which like the appetite of the cormorant is not to be satisfied" and her "apparently unconquerable passion of displaying herself." Equating female publication with prostitution, Mr. Sigourney asked Mrs. Sigourney, "Who wants or would value a wife who is to be the public property of the whole community?"[7] Mr. Sigourney's link between sexual indiscretion and female publication was a familiar one, but while his chastisements may have helped to inspire Mrs. Sigourney's maintenance of a relentlessly impersonal poetic self-presentation, they did not keep her from reaching an agreement with editors who offered to pay more for signed contributions.[8] While increasing the money value of the poem, the addition of the signature also intensified the poem's identification with the woman's sexualized body. This formulation then stood in heightened contrast with the expectation that a woman's poem express spiritual purity.

Lydia Sigourney responded to the association of female public expression with prostitution by specializing in the elegy. Her posthumous tributes consistently drain the life force from the body, anticipating and negating any possible perception of sexual exuberance emanating from the poetess. Recurrently at the center of Sigourney's poetry is an iconic image of a dying infant, a figure doubly purged of the sexual by dissipation and immaturity. In "Death of an Infant," for example, the infant, already marmoreal, becomes increasingly statue-like throughout the poem:

> Death found strange beauty on that polish'd brow,
> And dash'd it out. There was a tint of rose
> On cheek and lip. He touch'd the veins with ice,
> And the rose faded.[9]

The poem compares the emotions aroused by the poetic image of the dying child and those aroused by looking upon a corpse. Though Death expunges the infant's "strange beauty," it is nonetheless recorded within the poem. Indeed, the description of Death's erasure engraves the infant's image, demonstrating the transformation of the dying infant into the living poem. Sigourney's memorials promise to convert grief over the lost soul into an aesthetic contemplation of the poetic memento.[10] Consistent with the goal of establishing a realm of public sentiment discrete from individual bodily function, Sigourney's seemingly obsessive re-enactment of the drama of the spirit leaving the body distinguishes the properties of a poetic from those of a material world.

While neutralizing the specter of the female body in the poem, Sigourney encouraged readers to develop metaphysical forms of identity. If death is the great leveler, then a writer cultivating an American mass readership of unprecedented proportions would rightly focus upon elegiac emotion as the key to touching the broadest range of readers. Sigourney's own dying words, "I love everybody," borrowed from one of her novels' heroines, neatly contain the paradoxes of a poetry that simultaneously assures each reader of an intimate bond with the poet, and of membership in a community of readers who share a single emotional register.[11] Sigourney worked to express and evoke universally appropriate elegiac feelings in poems custom-designed to speak to readers' individual plights. Countless readers shared her fantasy. The bereaved Eliza Banks, for example, begged Sigourney to "pour Balm and Oil in a deeply wounded heart – and be entitled to its everlasting gratitude."[12] An elixir of solace, Sigourney's poetry offered a liquid form of sympathy that readers could imbibe from the print.[13] This elegiac poetic realm offered an opportunity for interpersonal identification when sentiment overcame the physical boundaries that separated individuals and texts. The resulting homogenization of taste offered a ritual cure for the loneliness of individual suffering in an increasingly anonymous, urban world.

Critics have repeatedly condemned Sigourney for the generic sentimentality that is arguably a great accomplishment. Even those seeking to recuperate her reputation have done so by downplaying the centrality of elegiac sentiment in her work. According to Nina Baym, for example, critics "invented" the death-obsessed Sigourney as a caricature to dismiss: "a mildly comical figure who embodies the worst aspects of domestic sentimentalism"[14] Baym herself notes, however, that Sigourney characterized herself as an elegist. According to Baym's own estimate, moreover, no small percentage of Sigourney's work was elegiac (32 percent, in an informal review). And several works not included in the tally increase that percentage. *The Weeping Willow* presents a range of mourning scenarios, as a sampling of titles indicates: "The Son of the Widow," "Orphan's Second Birthday," "The Mother's Parting Gift." Sigourney wrote *The Faded Hope*, a prose memoir, on the occasion of her son's death. More than one-third of *Letters to My Pupils* memorializes "my dead," former students who had passed away.[15] Turning away from elegy, Baym argues for "the construction of a very different Sigourney" that she calls the "republican public mother" (58). She distinguishes between Sigourney's private poetry of sentiment and her historical writings that have "a public resonance" and are "much more political and much less emotional" (58). Baym concludes that "all history writing, in Sigourney's literary approach to it, is a memorial to the past.... (And this point allows us to think of her elegiac verse as another, individualized, form of history writing)" (68). This formulation leaves unresolved the relationship between terms that Baym formerly opposed: private elegy and public historical memorial.

In fact, the two projects are one, in which elegiac sentiment is the building block of Sigourney's republican project.[16] In the preface to *The Weeping*

Willow, she identifies a social need for lyric solace: "An increasing desire among those who endure the sundering of affection's ties for some simple lyric, fashioned to their own peculiar wound, marks our state of society, and perhaps, the age in which we live" (v). Arguing that condolences from friends may prove too painful to bear ("The voice of even the dearest, may inadvertently touch some chord, whose vibration is anguish"), Sigourney advocates the use of generic poetic sentiment as a superior balm: "the sigh of sacred poetry steals without startling." Poetry binds individuals together with ties as strong as the pain it converts to solace: "The friendships that take root in affliction have peculiar vitality and fervor. Their office and ministry of consolation supply all deficiencies in date, giving them the force of an attachment that time had tested." Offering her services to the cause, Sigourney claimed that poetry converted private suffering into communal bonds.[17]

Sigourney's poems registered ambivalence about the value of an immaterial, aesthetic realm even as they were highly effective in securing that imaginary space and encouraging readers to visit it. In "A Shred of Linen," for example, when the speaker contemplates the contrast between the physical labors of the housewives of olden times and the literary labor of making poems, she cannot fully define or justify what literature can accomplish that has the indisputable present of a well-knit sweater or a wheel of cheese. She addresses a scrap of cloth she encounters in her housecleaning in order to confront charges that her domestic labors suffer because she writes poetry.[18] Thankful that "no neat lady, train'd in ancient times / Of pudding making" sees the scrap, the speaker imagines the accusations she would incur: "'This comes of reading books,'" and "'This comes of writing poetry.'" Tracing the shred's origins, the speaker imagines the farmer and his wife laboring to transform the flax to linen and reminisces about the times when "there was less of gadding, and far more / Of home-born, heart-felt comfort, rooted strong / In industry, and bearing such rare fruit / As wealth might never purchase." Her tone is equivocal, however, for while chiding the insubstantiality of "gadding" and "wealth," or poems and money, the speaker has opted for the paper economy in writing her poem. The shift allows her to work for herself rather than stocking a husband's larder like the wife of an earlier generation, whose "many a keg / And pot of butter, to the market borne, / May, transmigrated, on his back appear, / In new thanksgiving coats."

Uncertainty about the difference between the immaterial, affective work of writing poetry and modes of material production generates a corollary confusion about the differences between paper and what is written on it. Like the poem that will eventually be inked onto its remade surface, the shred of linen, a "defunct pillow-case" has, sponge-like, absorbed the experiences of the people who have laid their heads on it: the dreams of babes, lovers' sighs, the "sick one's moan." Unlike the poem, however, the shred "wilt tell no secrets." Conflating the shred with a poem, the speaker considers its muteness mutiny and sends it to the "jaws" of the "paper-mill" (itself transmogrified into a hungry human), where it may undergo "renovation" and emerge as a more perfect surface to register human experience. But if the speaker cannot see the linen as anything but a mute poem and imperfect writing paper, her own poem cannot break its nagging relation to the shred. The speaker perceives her output as scrap-like and herself as incapable of "tracing" the "hallow'd lineaments" of "wisdom and truth" "for posterity" upon the paper, leaving that task for "a worthier bard." For Sigourney, who situates herself on the threshold of an ethereal economy where paper goods are exchanged for paper money, printed poems seem flimsy and two-dimensional beside the manufacture of pots of butter and the "groaning" "weight of golden cheese": things, Sigourney fears, speak louder and more persuasively than words or the money they bring.

For this reason, perhaps, Sigourney was oddly materialistic about matters of aesthetic output, often valuing quantity of poetic production over any distinguishable quality. She darned socks while she wrote poems and recorded the number of sweaters knit and poems written in a single notebook. Her meticulous attention to literary quantity resulted in a lifetime publishing total, tallied by herself, of 56 books and 2000 articles.[19] Preoccupied with the question of artistic bulk upon a visit to the Louvre, Sigourney was impressed by "that astonishing collection of 1500 arranged pictures, and probably as many more for which the halls of its sumptuous gallery have no space."[20] Civilizing America for Sigourney meant populating it with a similarly substantial number of artworks. Writing to Elizabeth Oakes Smith, a poetess of the next generation, Sigourney praised her contributions to a national literature in terms of her prolixity:

Indeed, I marvel at the energy and rapidity with which you complete your intellectual performances, as much as rejoice in the high popular acclaim which they gain, and deserve. It is pleasant to know and feel that your efforts to elevate our national literature are appreciated. . . . Please let me know as a curiosity, on how many literary labors you are at present engaged; and how you find time for them, and for maternal and social intercourse.[21]

Hardly mentioning the qualities of the work she admires, Sigourney wonders at the efficient method by which Oakes Smith generates her "literary performances." While Sigourney considered quantity essential to "efforts to elevate our national literature," Oakes Smith relentlessly questioned and criticized her own work's merit and regretted the financial constraints that required her to write quickly and voluminously. Indicative of a later generation of women writers, such concerns quickly overshadowed Sigourney's fascination with mass production.

Frances Osgood also published a poem about the relation of cloth scraps to writing paper that clarifies this shift in perspective. In *The Cries of New York* (1846), a collection of poems about urban occupations, a maternal figure explains to a child the relation between the book she narrates and a rag collector's activities:

> Scorn not the rag-man's poor employ!
> This very page, his form revealing,
> Where now thy young eyes rest in joy,
> Was formed from bits like those he's wheeling.
>
> Those "airy nothings" yet may turn,
> To some rare page of song or sermon,
> Where "thoughts that breathe and words that burn,"
> May charm you, when you're grown a woman.[22]

While Sigourney is ambivalent about whether the cloth or the poem should prevail, Osgood clearly subordinates rags to the world of print they fuel. Initiating the child into that world, the speaker identifies continuities and correspondences between physical and literary occupations where Sigourney's speaker found only discontinuities and contrasts. While the book's abstractions give meaning to physical materials, those materials are "'airy nothings'" until they are poetry. The rag-man's labor results in a book that imprints his image and justifies his occupation on its pages. Quoting Thomas Gray, the maternal speaker promises the little girl adult reading pleasures – "'thoughts that breathe and words that burn'" when she's "grown a woman" – as a way to indoctrinate her into a paper economy.[23] Osgood playfully suggests that charming women is the ultimate goal of industrial processes, and that books, not men, instill and inspire women's passion.

By 1848, the publication date of two major anthologies of women's poetry, the aesthetic represented in Osgood's work had overtaken that in Sigourney's. Griswold, for example, included Sigourney in his anthology but dismissed her significance on the grounds that her poems lacked interiority. He complained that "we know too little of her secret experiences to form an opinion" as to the reasons for "the absence of any deep emotion or creative power" in her work.[24] Osgood, on the other hand, was the ultimate poetess, because there was "a very intimate relation between Mrs. Osgood's personal and her literary characteristics" (*LL* 21). For Griswold, Sigourney's poetry provided only a faulty window to the soul, while Osgood's work blended the "literary" and the "personal." Griswold neglected to note or had already forgotten that Sigourney's aesthetic was impersonal by design, even while it operated under the sign of transparency. Sigourney presided over an emotional transmission between readers and poems which proffered immediate and complete understanding. Osgood, however, who was supposedly more directly accessible in her poems, flaunted a poetics of opacity, of masks and costumes, characters with an oblique relation to herself, urbane coquetry and dissemblance. In her marriage of "personal" and "literary" characteristics, in other words, the literary not only became a vehicle for personal expression, but the personality became an increasingly literary creation. Griswold's praise of Osgood contains this ambiguity: the "intimate relation" is not between Osgood and her readers, but between Osgood and her poems. Readers like Griswold were voyeurs to Fanny's love affair with poetic self-creation.

If Sigourney imagined mass publication as an activity that addressed the needs of embodied individuals, Osgood celebrated a textual landscape of aesthetic and erotic experience distinct from physical bodies. Sigourney's utilitarian poems offered her readers solace through codified rituals of mourning; Osgood celebrated ornamental pleasures. Sigourney cultivated the principles of duty, dedication, and loyalty; Osgood promoted the delights of self-indulgence. While readers valued Sigourney for writing about others' suffering, they loved Osgood for talking about herself. In short, while Sigourney marketed emotional products, Osgood became one: an object of endless and often contradictory readerly fantasies.[25] Mary Loeffelholz charts the ways that women's poetic practices shift over the course of the nineteenth century from didactic to aesthetic contexts – "from school to salon"; the contrast between Sigourney and Osgood underscores and confirms this trajectory.

The shift from elegiac to amatory verse indicates a rapid and dramatic reconfiguration of the expectations and possibilities surrounding the professional female poet. While Sigourney confronted the association of women's writing with sexual indiscretion by specializing in the elegy and draining bodies of animation, a decade later Osgood embraced the association of female promiscuity with publication to forge an image of a literary coquette who could proclaim that "love-lays are my vocation."[26] While dying infants populate Sigourney's poetry, there is hardly a death or an infant in all of Osgood's poetry. Instead, the central character in Osgood's poetic drama is the erotic child: little girls who have the sentiments of adult women, or women who possess a childlike innocence that enhances and excuses their sexual charm. Because Osgood's speakers ground their being in words rather than bodies, they have far greater sexual license. Contrary to Walt Whitman's later experiments with inscribing physical presence in his poems in order to generate a homosexual politics of union, Osgood's erotic play depends upon a negation of bodily presence.[27] Her lyric speakers present themselves as flirtatious fairies, drained of physicality but saturated with erotic force. Her poems offer an outpouring of words inflected with human desires unmoored from physical origins. Rather than bodily presence, they project the sensual mobility and modulations of voice.

LYRIC COQUETRY

Studies of nineteenth-century American women writers have tended to concur that the print public sphere severely restricted expressions of female sexuality, while private arenas offered greater expressive freedom – Emily Dickinson's milieu, for example, or diaries, letters, and unpublished works. Joanne Dobson has made such a claim with respect to Osgood's lyric eroticism: "the forum of the salon, with its urbane constituency, allowed Osgood to go further than she would – or could – in her published work."[28] According to Dobson, the salon's restricted circulation enabled the sexually explicit play that the literary marketplace prohibited. The argument that local, elitist social gatherings cultivated expressive freedom in reaction to constricting market demands has a precedent in critical narratives that pit the writers of the American Renaissance against the popular writers of the period.[29] But such formulations overlook the reciprocal relation between coterie culture and the publishing industry, a relation that converts personal exchanges into forms of public display. Lyric eroticism played a key role in this process, a role that Osgood's poems both exploit and critique.

Though some of Osgood's manuscript poems treat the subject of sexual transgression, so do many of her published poems.[30] In one of her more provocative unpublished poems, for example, a speaker encourages a potential lover to commit suicide so that their sexual liaison would be socially acceptable:

> Won't you
> die and be a spirit
> Darling, say
> What's the use of keeping on
> That robe of clay
> If you only were a spirit
> You could stay.[31]

Urging her lover to divest of his body so that he can "stay" with her, the speaker dramatizes the intensity of her desire in the extremity of her proposed solution – suicide – even as she mocks the social prohibitions that would spur such a drastic act. Alluding less concisely to a scene of physical seduction, the published poem "Would I Were Only a Spirit of Song" confronts readers with the identical irony that only within the bodiless realm of poetry may the speaker explore bodily feelings:

> Oh! Would I were only a spirit of song,
> I'd float forever around – above you!
> If I were a spirit it wouldn't be wrong,
> It *couldn't* be wrong to love you!
> (*FSOP* 423)

The poem plays with the notion of an "I" at once identified with the authorial body of Osgood, who laments the taboo against physical intimacy with the poem's recipient, and the poem's "I," who can indeed "float . . . around – above" her lover without censure. Taunting the reader, the lyric speaker enacts a poetic "touch" that mimics physical bodies touching, yet leaves the author blameless.

While Dobson posits an oppositional relation between a private, sexually sophisticated salon world and a more restrictive public world of print, a study of the literary magazines of the period suggests that, far from hiding her salon performances of "sex, wit, and sentiment," Osgood, along with many of her peers, publicized them. Osgood attended fashionable New York salons, among them Ann Lynch's at Waverly Place. There she trumped those who recited their poetry by performing spontaneous lyric generation. Oakes Smith attests: "I have seen little Fannie Osgood write with a pencil upon slips of paper in her lap surrounded by a room full of company; indeed, she rarely wrote in solitude – she needed the inspiration of human companionship to give form and force to her pen" (*HL* 283). Against the background of celebrity reports in the literary magazines of the 1840s, Osgood cultivated a reputation as a coquette whose poetry was an outgrowth of salon flirtations. She published numerous sketches in which female characters, who both identified themselves with their author and flaunted their fictional status, riveted the attention of male onlookers with lyric performances. These scenarios served as models of reception that trained readers to think of themselves as spectators for Osgood's disembodied poetic performance on the printed page.

In her sketches for *Graham's Magazine* and other periodicals, Osgood combined an insider's story of the salon scene with patent fictions, encouraging readers to sort or blend fact and fable as they wished. Bestowing her own pseudonyms – Kate Carol, Violet Vane – upon the flirtatious poetesses in her sketches, Osgood commodified her authorship as a form of promiscuous exchange, stressing that her signature qualities add up to no one in particular. In "Life in New York: A Sketch of a Literary Soirée," she "daguerrotypes" herself in precisely these terms.[32] Evoking Lynch's salon, Osgood depicts a number of New York literati, including Elizabeth Oakes Smith, N. P. Willis, Bayard Taylor, Rufus Griswold, and Poe. She places herself among these figures as the one without character, and even that characterization is a quote from Poe, who had said in a review that her work possessed exceptional "grace – that Will-o'-the-Wisp which in its supreme development may be said to involve nearly all that is pure and ethereal in poetry."[33] Osgood borrows his phrase to cast herself as a personification of poetry:

> There . . . was that little "will-o'-the-wisp," V—, whom nobody knows what to make of – wild, wayward, capricious as an April day – changeable as the light spring cloud, and restless as the wave – the spoiled child of Fancy. (178)

The character's name, V—, hints at Osgood's pseudonym Violet Vane. Her chameleon-like versatility renders her everyone and no one, potentiality incarnate. Poe is her counterpart, "an antithesis personified" combining "the wildest conceits – the sharpest satire – the bitterest, maddest vituperation – the most exquisite taste – the most subtil appreciation of the delicate and beautiful in his subject – the most radiant wit – the most dainty and Ariel-like fancy – with a manner and mean the most quaint, abrupt, and uncouth imaginable – it is like nothing in nature, or rather it is so exceedingly natural that it seems almost supernatural." Sitting side by side at the salon, the two reflect each other's status as personified literary potentiality.

Foregrounding the poetess' shape-shifting capabilities, Osgood puts her poems in the mouths of the different salon characters (these poems later appeared in her collected works), who take turns reading from a book of poems, "the only copy in the country." Written by "Anon," each poem

suits the sentiments of the reciter. This psychic versatility stimulates the
reader's efforts to glean the elusive Osgood's sentiments from her characters' recitations. The Rufus Griswold figure recites a poem that seems to
charge Elizabeth Ellet with vicious hypocrisy and scandal-mongering over
Osgood's relationship with Poe, for example:

> I've heard that voice – 'tis very sweet, I own,
> Almost too much of softness in its tone;
> I've heard its tender modulations tried,
> On one you'd just been slandering – aside.
>
> (178)

The poem both hints at and obscures the relation between public utterance
and personal exchanges among insiders. The expressed sentiments hold a
definite but disavowed and irretrievable relation to Osgood the author.

V— gives the last recitation, which comments on the sketch's haphazard
structure and its relation to Osgood's authorial persona:

> They call me a careless coquette;
> That often, too often, I *change*; they chide
> Because every being on earth I've met,
> Of the glorious mark in my hope falls wide.
>
> (179)

V—'s celebration of capriciousness summons Osgood's performance of
poetic versatility within the sketch, affiliating her authorship with the figure of the coquette. Speaking for all the salon attendants as if they composed a single, multi-faceted individual, Osgood composes the figure of
the celebrity author, which is also the figure of New York salon culture.
The promiscuous gathering of voices under a single signature expresses the
erotic capacities of print circulation that belong at once to everyone and
no one.

In an epistolary sketch in the *Columbian Magazine*, Osgood creates a
character for her other pseudonym, Kate Carol, who contrasts her poetry
of passion with the moral verse of her peers: "If I have the gift of song . . .
I can't always be singing psalm tunes; I must sing only when my heart asks
me to and what it asks; I must interpret its throbs in love-lays or glees or
dirges or paeans." Kate's mission is, like the bee, "to gather honey every
day, / from every opening flower."[34] Like Violet Vane, she locates these traits
within the literary salons that she and her correspondent habitually attend:
"Valentine's evening, Mary! How I wish I were with you at the gay party
in Waverly Place" (203). Kate quotes from numerous valentines, which she
attributes variously, but which display the characteristics of Osgood's own

verse (and appear later in her collected poems). Taking self-promotion to
the point of absurdity, she even confesses to posing as her own admirer:
"you offered me the pen to *finish myself* with, and . . . *for the sake of a rhyme*,
Mary, I was obliged to flatter myself in the most unheard of manner, and
with what a demure countenance I heard it read aloud in the evening"
(203). More than one of the valentines written in Kate Carol's signature
style are addressed to herself, whom she encourages readers to identify:
"The one which follows was addressed to one of the liveliest of beings –
lovely in mind, heart, and person. The verses convey some impression of
coquetry on her part; but that must be a mistake" (203).

The coquetry that "must be a mistake" is the centerpiece of both the
letter and the embedded poems, which both perform and justify Kate
Carol's poetic promiscuity:

> Reprove me not that still I change
> With every changing hour,
> For glorious Nature gives me leave
> In wave, and cloud, and flower.
> . . . .
> So yield I to the deepening light
> That dawns around my way:
> Because *you* linger with the *night*,
> Shall *I my noon delay?*[35]

Foregrounding her poetic eroticism as well as her fictional status, Kate
Carol defends her right to find her noon wherever it may lie. Her insistence on sexual license is qualified, however, by the possibility that she
is addressing herself. The self-confrontation offers a distilled equation of
the public circulation of emotion in which unleashed desire defines itself
against moral control. At the point of maximum circulation, the celebrity
author figure can only see herself, whom she does not possess and cannot
recognize. Osgood underscores this poetics of dissociation by attaching a
real and a fictive name to her work. Kate Carol signs the letter, but Frances
Osgood undersigns it; her name appears beneath the title, simultaneously
authorizing the work and foregrounding the fictive qualities of authorship. Osgood's auto-mimicry foregrounds the irretrievability of authorial
identity.

Osgood diagnoses and analyzes the poetess' role in the commodification
of literary celebrity most extensively in her satire of New York literary culture, *A Letter About the Lions, A Letter to Mabel in the Country* (1849).[36]
Advertised as an insider's report to an intimate friend, this twenty-four-
page booklet comes in an envelope postmarked January 1 in New York
City and addressed alliteratively in a facsimile of Osgood's handwriting to

"Miss Mabel Montagu, Montpelier, Montgomery County, Massachu-setts."[37] The letter-book teases the reader with the possibility of intercept-ing secrets intended for a friend, even as its mass format and the publisher's return address – the envelope is stamped "Forwarded by G. P. Putnam, 155 Broadway, New York" – belie this fiction. This fantasy of epistolary intimacy with a New York celebrity cultivates a fascination with urban lit-erary culture that disseminates from the city center via expanding circuits of print.

Ostensibly responding to her country friend's request to tell "all I hear and see / In this bewildering Babel" (3), Osgood charts the linguistic chaos of the New York literary scene that arises from a self-promotional mania fostered by urban anonymity. A "belle" curls her hair "with love notes by the dozen"; a "blue" "buys boquets / And sends them to *herself*"; a man "writes some stuff / In praise of all his books," and a critic "read[s] no book he praises" (3–5). In an arena characterized by both personal and professional competition, the figures promote their reputations at the expense of their authenticity. Identifying the superficial source of her admirers' attraction, the belle applies love notes where they were originally inspired in order to multiply desire; puffing himself, the writer disregards what readers think of his work; and the critic refuses to dilute his opinions by reading what he reviews. Self-promotion has evacuated people's emotional investments and reduced the communicative capabilities of language to marketing "stuff" and unread words.

While the "babble" bewilders, however, it also exhilarates, and Osgood is less concerned with critiquing the marketplace than with exploring the ways it shifts meaning from insides to surfaces via the figure of the poetess. Placing poetesses at the center of New York literary culture, Osgood challenges the slant of James Russell Lowell's better-known *Fable for Critics* (1848), which screens out almost all of the women writers, except for a nasty portrait of Margaret Fuller. Osgood suggests instead that the newer, most vigorous poets are women, whose prolixity and ubiquity have seemingly drained the male poets of their energy. Bayard Taylor, Lowell, and Whittier are still productive, "and Longfellow still nobly writes," but "the Raven" has disappeared; Hoffman has "furled" his "starry flag"; "Willis sleeps, with silken curls / Upon his lyre and laurels"; "Halleck sings no 'Fanny' now / And Bryant mute reposes" (18–19). Silenced by an unnamed force, the male poets are sleepy, dysfunctional, dejected, and blocked. Osgood even suggests that fashionable salon society renders men impotent: "Our beaux, who should our spirits raise, / Can only raise moustaches" (24).

A more flexible form of currency, poetesses meet and respond to the reading public's desires. Referring to a group portrait of women writers (all

Fig. 6: "Contributors to Graham's Magazine," Frontispiece, *Graham's Magazine*, vol. 22 (January 1843). Engraving by R. W. Dodson.

of whom are poets, with the exception of Catherine Sedgwick) published in
Graham's (fig. 6), Osgood compares the pleasures of surfaces and interiors
for consumers of women's literature:

> I know a Magazine, that shows
> A constellation cover,
> Of every "star" whom Genius knows
> In his *blue* Heaven a rover:
>
> But look *within* and you shall catch
> No ray of all that glory;
> The love-tale there can never match
> The wondrous outside *story*.   (6)

The "blue" writer's fusion with the magazine is complete; the cover girls
beckon readers to look within, and their "love-tales" imprint the pages.
The marriage of woman and magazine, however, inverts its promise to
reveal interiority. Readers' fascination with the poetesses' self-promotion
surpasses the intrigue of the love-tales they write. The "wondrous outside *story*" sustains not in spite of, but because of its obvious artificiality.
Rather than critiquing the hypocrisy of this constellation, Osgood avers
that the pleasures of the sham outweigh the pleasures of the real. Instead of
complaining that middle-class readers experience life vicariously, Osgood
encourages readers to participate in the public making of fantasy selves.[38]

Osgood evaluates idealized forms of female authorship by comparing
the ways that three anthologies package women poets. She is least favorable
to Thomas Buchanan Read, who "has been a book inditing," rather than
editing. Casting him as a "minstrel-painter" (and suggesting an analogy with
black-face), Osgood complains that Read covers up the women's literary
ambitions: "The first has portraits of the blues / Not blue since he has
crowned them; / A halo all "coleur de rose" / He kindly flings around them"
(9). Osgood portrays this unbidden makeover as a form of vampirism: he
"drew out his share" of women's "souls" by "draw[ing]" them the way he
wanted.[39] His engraver completes the process: "His graver's a divining-
rod, / That finds where Beauty should be, / And makes us all – however
odd – / Not as we were but *would* be" (10). Read drains the poetesses of
their particularity in order to convert them into his own artistic project.

Rufus Griswold gets top billing because he differentiates among the
women rather than fusing them into one ideal body: "Like Tennyson, he
gives the world / His 'vision of blue women,' / And paints them with
impartial pen, / And critical acumen" (10). Each poetess represents an individualized feminine stereotype. Lydia Sigourney, is the "kindly pilot" "upon

the sea of verse"; Osgood's protégée, Grace Greenwood, is an impetuous, "glorious girl of girls" who should not be chastised for her "lays of 'Love and daring!'"; Amelia Welby casts mystic spells; Emma Embury "like a zephyr, plays / The 'Eolian harp' – how sadly!"; Fanny Forester "her bird-song warbles gladly"; Elizabeth Oakes Smith "sweeps her Sapphic lyre, / As if a seraph fanned her"; and so on (11–16). Poetesses animate and sexualize poetic styles – the Sapphic ode, the Keatsian ode – by personifying them. In this way they transmit strains of literary sentiment in pleasurable, consumable forms. As literary professionals, according to *Letter About the Lions*, poetesses were not confessional even and especially when they were most sexually expressive; rather, their eroticism functioned as a medium for the public circulation of lyric. Mediated through purveyors of sentiment like Griswold and Read who intuited and responded to public demand, poetesses were both products and producers of the literary marketplace.

IMPRINTING PERSONALITY

Recognizing her status as literary commodity, Osgood cultivated a lyric personality that anticipated, promoted, and responded to the desires of magazine readers. Because antebellum readers were accustomed to associating female publication with promiscuity, Osgood could reverse that equation so that female sexuality functioned as an expression of print promiscuity. Her poems corresponded to Poe's 1846 call in *Graham's* for a new form of writing adapted to the magazine age. Quarterly journals didn't meet the challenge:

Not only are they too stilted, (by way of keeping up a due dignity), but they make a point . . . of discussing only topics which are *caviare* to the many, and which . . . have only a conventional interest even with the few. Their issues, also, are at too long intervals; their subjects get cold before being served up. In a word, their ponderosity is quite out of keeping with the rush of the age. We now demand the light artillery of the intellect; we need the curt, the condensed, the pointed, the readily diffused – in place of the verbose, the detailed, the voluminous, the inaccessible. (*ER* 1415)

Osgood's poetry filled Poe's order, personifying his new style in an enticing feminine form. Weightless, airborne sprites repudiated "ponderosity"; their short attention span and craving for novelty prevented subjects from "get[ting] cold before being served up"; and their fleeting, ethereal mobility and hunger for readerly attention composed a sensibility that kept pace with the "rush of the age."

Osgood crafted this exotic figure in the name of Fancy rather than Imagination. Before the nineteenth century, Fancy held a prominent role as the feminine personification of poetic inspiration that "scatters from her pictured urn / Thoughts that breathe and words that burn."[40] By the end of the eighteenth century, however, according to Julie Ellison, Fancy had become an "inferior but therapeutic faculty," subordinated to the imagination because it "treats experience, including feelings, as matter that can be managed but not transformed."[41] Fancy's "operations" include "associating, collecting, combining, embellishing, mixing" ideas and images; and "fancy enjoys mimicry, the exotic, nomadism, displacement, strangeness, and hybridity."[42] Osgood anachronistically embraces this characterization while denying Fancy's subordinate status. She casts the sprite as a feminine figure who has escaped from imprisonment by male writers who had harnessed her for their creative ends.

The male poet in Keats' "Fancy" (a prototype for Osgood's poem "The Fan") urges the sprite's liberation, insisting that in order to find poetic inspiration one must "let the Fancy roam," "let winged Fancy wander," "let her loose."[43] His descriptions of the luscious scenes that Fancy encounters in her unfettered wandering demonstrate the effectiveness of his prescription. Taking more extreme liberties, Osgood's Fancy has entirely escaped from the poet's control – she no longer needs him to "let" her wander – in order to wreak rebellious havoc and to find her own enjoyment, often at the expense of men's fulfillment. Directing her attention away from male poets, Osgood's Fancy takes advantage of her supposedly inferior qualities to gain the upper hand with male readers. "A Flight of Fancy," for example, puts her brand of poetry on trial for sexual scandal and wins the case even while it is proven guilty. Before "Judge Conscience," Reason stands charged of allowing himself to be swept off his feet by Fancy's manipulations:

> "They say that young Fancy, that airy coquette,
> Has dared to fling round you her luminous net;
> That she ran away with you, in spite of yourself,
> For pure love of frolic – the mischievous elf."

> "The scandal is whispr'd by friends and by foes,
> And darkly they hint, too, that when they propose
> Any whisper to your ear, so lightly you're led,
> At once to gay Fancy you turn your wild head:
> And she leads you off to some dangerous dance,
> As wild as the Polka that gallop'd from France."
> . . . .
> "Then she talks such a language! melodious enough,
> To be sure, but a strange sort of outlandish stuff!

> I'm told that it licenses many a whopper,
> And when once she commences, no frowning can stop her;
> Since it's new, I've no doubt it is very improper!
> They say that she cares not for order or law;
> That of you, you great dunce, she but makes a cat's paw.
> I've no sort of objection to fun in its season,
> But it's plain that this fancy is *fooling* you, Reason!"
>
> Just then into court flew a strange little sprite,
> With wings of all colours and ringlets of light!
> She frolik'd 'round Reason, till Reason grew wild,
> Defying the court and caressing the child.[44]
>
> > (*AWP* 108–110)

The scandal arises from Reason's tapping his feet to a beat more akin to an exotic French polka than an American hymn. His head has been turned from important matters by a frivolous, new-fangled, feminine melody. While Fancy inspires Reason's desire, however, she has no intention of fulfilling it; instead she is interested in the powers of seduction. She ultimately forces Reason to lose his case even before he defends himself because he cannot help but publicly "caress the child," admitting Fancy's power. Although the testimonies of "maidens of uncertain age . . . a critic, a publisher, lawyer and sage" send her to jail with Reason as her gatekeeper, she ultimately escapes through the "hole / In the lock in the door which she could not undo," because her ethereal nature is not subject to the laws of the material universe. The crime resonates with sexual transgression only as it is emptied of it, since the man and the child are clearly allegorical figures. The fable playfully taunts its audience, encouraging them to pin a crime on to a fictional entity and then exposing the fallacy. Even as she urges readers to conflate the poetess and her spritely creation, Osgood foregrounds the difference between the two.

Rather than staging a drama of heterosexual attraction between poet and muse, a longstanding tradition, Osgood twins Fancy with the figure of the poetess and then exploits this identification to attract male readers.[45] Inherited terms of romantic desire stipulate that the male lyric subject finds the muse alluring because she is more elusive than a real woman, "a dancing Shape, an Image gay / To haunt, to startle, and waylay."[46] Writing as the female "Shape" (Wordsworth's lines serve as the epigraph to a tribute to Osgood published in *Graham's* in 1847), Osgood explores the range of an erotic voice unmoored from a woman's body, projected from the printed page, understanding that this disjunction promotes the reader's desire by leaving it unsatisfied.

"The Coquette's Vow," for example, compares the plight of a physical woman consigned to monogamy with a female voice that, inhabiting the realm of Fancy, delivers herself into the hands of any number of readers and emerges unscathed. The poem projects a distinctly female and seductive voice that lacks a corresponding body. In an airy realm where the laws of gravity and the gravity of laws are irrelevant, the speaker obeys Fancy's rules, vowing fidelity to change by a shape-shifting cloud rather than swearing to principle on an immutable book. Her insubstantiality renders her incapable of monogamy and immune to criticism or consequence:

> I promise *while* I love you,
> To love you true and well;
> But, by that cloud above you,
> How long – I dare not tell.
>
> I promise to be tender,
> And docile to your sway;
> I promise to surrender
> My soul – at least – *a day*.
>
> But if – but if – to-morrow
> I chance to grow more wise –
> If Love should dream you borrow
> Your light from Fancy's eyes;
>
> If I should weary, playing
> On one eternal lyre,
> And touch, with fingers straying,
> Some other chords of fire;
>
> If they should answer willing,
> In sweeter tones than you,
> Forgive my heart for thrilling,
> And own *my ear is true*.
> . . . .
> Yet though unlike most lovers,
> I vow at once to change
> If fancy e'er discovers
> A nobler field to range.
>
> Of this at least be sure,
> That even when I go
> I'll probably be truer
> Than some who swear they're so.
>
> And though less true than truant,
> I shall not *fall* in love;

> But of some star pursuant,
> Still rise to light above.
>
> Then, since around your Real
> My Fancy deigns to fly,
> Keep up to my Ideal,
> Or you are false as I.[47]

Reception is so crucial to poetic production that the speaker's lyre is the reader, whom she "plays" while warning that any hint of chordal monotony will cause her to stray. Underscoring the ways in which textual mediation seduces the reader into wishing that poems were women, the speaker recognizes that her appeal increases in inverse proportion to her availability. "My Fancy" hovers around the reader's "Real," stimulating a desire that relies on the knowledge that the womanly figment cannot materialize.

Osgood frequently positions her readers in a voyeuristic relation to an eroticized process of self-composition. In "The Fan: A Lover's Fantasy," for example, poetess and poem engage in a symbiotic mimicry whereby each becomes a version of the other before the reader's eyes. The speaker is a verbal magician who, with the help of Fancy's animating powers, conjures womanhood while drawing attention to her sleight of hand:

> Dainty spirit that dost lie
> Couch'd within the zephyr's sigh,
> Murmur in mine earnest ear
> Music of the starry sphere!
> Softest melody divine
> Lend unto each lyric line
> Till the lay of love shall seem
> Light and airy as its theme.
> Ah! Not unto mortal wight
> Wilt thou whisper, frolic sprite!
> Fancy! wave thy fairy wing
> While the magic Fan I sing![48]

Summoning Fancy to animate her Fantasy of the Fan, the speaker imagines that homomorphism enables the transmission of energy from one word/idea to the next; if her poem imitates a waving fan, which in turn imitates Fancy's "wing," it will absorb Fancy's spirit. "Fanny" is an additional, unmentioned member of the "Fan" word family; just as the fan provokes curiosity about the face that it obscures, the poem draws attention to the signature of the poetess by "hiding" it.

The poem centers on the conceit of a young woman holding a fan before her face; even as vocal and visual metaphors obscure the written nature of the poem, the figure of the hand underscores it.[49] The speaker's address to her fan thinly veils the poetess' address to her poem. In both cases, a woman's need to maintain protective silence in matters of the heart heightens her identification with mediums that uncannily resemble herself in their mute impressionability:

> All have made thee plaything fit
> For a maiden's grace and wit.
> She can teach thee witchery's spell
> Make thy lightest motion *tell*,
> Bid thee speak, though mute thou art,
> All the language of the heart.
>
> . . . .
>
> Queen of fans! the downy pressure
> Of her snow-white, dimpled hand,
> As it clasps the costly treasure,
> Wrought in India's glowing land,
> Has it not a soul impress'd
> On the toy by her caress'd?   (98–99)

Fan is to face as poem is to voice: an aesthetic substitute for the human aspect it obscures. The operator manipulates these prosthetic extensions to create the illusion of human animation. Just as the "dimpled hand" impresses the holder's "soul" upon the fan, the writing hand imprints the author's speech upon the page. Using "tell" as a metaphor for gesture underscores the poem's literal muteness and foregrounds the figurative nature of poetic "voice."

Rather than naturalizing the familiar equation of female body and poem, Osgood's sleight of hand shows how metaphors of face and voice personify the poetess through lyric writing. She stages a process of poetic composition that animates the feminine figure while exposing corporeal presence as a verbal illusion. Casting "witchery's spell," the speaker invests the fan with feminine qualities so that it becomes increasingly indistinguishable from the "maiden" who holds it:

> Showing, like her temples fair,
> Through her curls of lustrous hair,
> Tints of richest glow and light,
> From a master's palette bright,
> On the parchment rarely wrought,
> Till the painting *life* has caught –
>   (98)

Taking on an animal glow, the fan's painted surface grows to resemble a made-up woman. Its parchment, also writing paper and skin, mediates insides and outsides while ensuring that the specific boundary is indiscernible; because we cannot tell where the woman ends, she is everywhere. As the fan becomes human-like, the human gains the sheen of the fan's artificial beauty:

> Softly wave each careless curl
> O'er her brow – the radiant girl;
> Fan each pure and precious tint
> Feeling on her cheek doth print;
> Wake it from its pure repose,
> Till the dear blush comes and goes.
>
> (100)

Whereas earlier the girl's hand gave life to the fan, now the fan animates the "radiant girl." It both "print[s]" its color on her cheek and "wake[s]" her feeling "from its pure repose." A paper lover, the fan-poem's rhythmic seduction makes the girl blush in waves.

Instructing readers to respond with desire for the lyric figure of the poetess, the speaker embeds a portrait of reception within the poem. Blinded by amorousness, admirers see the imitation woman as the real thing even as it is exposed as an illusion:

> Airy minister of fate,
> On whose meaning motions wait
> Half a hundred butterflies,
> Idle beaux – more fond than wise –
> Basking in the fatal smile
> That but wins them to beguile.
>
> (97)

A swarm of male butterflies mistake a lady's fan for an attractive female butterfly: the paper decoy draws the real thing. Its coy verisimilitude seduces the live fans – here Osgood seems to play on the modern meaning of the word – only to enjoy the pleasure of deception.[50] Osgood encourages readers to find the author in the poem even while she exposes the illusion; she has the last laugh when their fingers close around air.

Osgood more directly explores mass circulation's influence on printed voice in "To My Pen," in which a bemused magazine poet observes that publication pressures exaggerate writing's automatic elements, resulting in indiscriminate self-disclosure. Baffled about how to adapt diary or letter-writing modes to address a vast audience of magazine readers, the writer addresses her own pen as "thou." Even as they compose each other, lyric voice and writing hand are at odds: the pen betrays the voice that chastises the pen. Disavowing personal volition, the speaker insists that the pen writes her poems, while the pen transcribes her vain attempts to discipline its motions:

> Dost know, my little vagrant pen,
> That wanderest lightly down the paper,
> Without a thought how critic men
> May carp at every careless caper, –
>
> Dost know, twice twenty thousand eyes,
> If publishers report them truly,
> Each month may mark the sportive lies,
> That track, oh shame! Thy steps unruly?
>
> Now list to me, my fairy pen,
> And con the lessons gravely over;
> Be never wild or false again,
> But "mind your Ps and Qs," you rover!
>
> While tripping gaily to and fro,
> Let not a thought escape you lightly,
> But challenge all before you go,
> And see them fairly robed and rightly.[51]

Having attributed the powers of authorship to the pen, the speaker's task of discipline is impossible, for the pen can only write, not think. Its muteness confirms that the speaker dictates her poem to a mechanical device, but her sense of release from responsibility encourages her to take expressive liberties. Under pressure to satisfy her mass readership, she has no time or inclination to clothe her thoughts and sends them out naked. Precisely the circumstances that would warrant discretion – forty thousand "eyes" all watching for improper behavior – encourage "unruly" "steps" and "sportive lies."[52]

Under these conditions the speaker feels impelled to say whatever comes to mind, which is less an individual's thoughts than unprocessed text, recycled maxims. Unconcerned about composing a coherent lyric consciousness, the speaker is the mouthpiece for both personal and impersonal forces without distinguishing between them. She fluctuates between celebrating the mindless flow of ink and playing the moralist who vainly attempts to educate and enlighten that flow. The didactic genre of the Sigourneyesque poem or "letter to a mother" spars with a rebellious, wayward child-poem, spawned of amoral print itself.[53] She admonishes the pen to subordinate desire to duty and let "truth constrain each truant caper"; but she also encourages it to "roam as thou wert wont to do / In author-land, by rock and river" (171). She chides the pen for loving the voluptuous qualities of language unmoored from meaning: "You know that words but dress the frame / And thought's the *soul* of verse, my fairy! / So drape not spirits dull and tame / In gorgeous robes or garments airy." Yet she also encourages it to indulge the propensities she just condemned: "Be like the wand in Cinderella; / And if you touch a common thing / Ah, change to *gold the pumpkin yellow!*" The speaker advocates both more and less discipline, profundity, and clarity of purpose. The effect is not simply incoherence. The odd tone cannot be called ironic, satiric, or parodic, for neither perspective gains the upper hand. Instead the speaker juxtaposes discursive modes while suspending resolution, mimicking and transmitting cultural perspectives that are not her own.

Possessed by the automatic elements of her craft, the speaker portrays herself as an involuntary register of received wisdom and the pen's thoughtless velocity. As the pen gains momentum, writing blends into printing:

> But what is this? you've tripp'd about,
> While I the mentor grave was playing;
> And here you've written boldly out
> The very words that I was saying!
>
> And here as usual on you've flown
> From right to left – flown fast and faster,
> Till even while you wrote it down,
> You've *missed* the task you ought to *master*.

The "right to left" motion reverses the usual direction of English writing, suggesting that the speaker is not thinking about what she is saying, and that she is describing a mechanical rather than a manual process. The anticipation of publication converts writing to printing and privacy to publicity even before the poem goes to press: publishing is an afterthought. Though the process she describes is automatic, however, the poem is nevertheless confessional; Osgood's lyric speaker exposes to her readers her intimate relation to impersonal media. Displaying her unrevised composition process, she showcases her rhetorical incoherence and her mechanized mode of lyric production as an alluring mark of textual vulnerability. Writing for a mass audience engenders an indiscriminate, seductive, and impersonal form of confession. The author's intimacy with her readers is largely an effect of mass publication, one that Osgood successfully mocked and exploited.

AUTHORIZING FANTASIES

Offering proof of Osgood's success, Rufus Griswold attested that the "com-plimental verses" composed in her honor "would fill a volume."[54] Numerous fan letters profess love, propose marriage, and offer suggestions for future poems. Readers spoke as if Osgood herself inhabited the magazine pages, as if her poems were seductive visits from the poetess. Men imagined Osgood as their renegade muse who, recaptured, would restore to them the creative powers that had fled to the poetesses. Women writers mimicked Osgood's figures of liberated Fancy because of their demonstrated ability to maximize the poetess' circulation.

Fantasies of the author reiterated the tensions between adult seductress and innocent child that Osgood cultivated in her poetry and sketches. Struck by the force of her erotic wizardry, Bayard Taylor called Osgood "the *potentest* of Circes," while Rufus Griswold identified "an almost infantile gaiety and vivacity . . . possessed only by her and the creatures of our imagination that we call angels."[55] The mother of two girls brought out maternal urges in Elizabeth Oakes Smith, who saw in her "a weird, tender child whom one wanted to shelter . . . so fragile, so dependent that maternity looked distorted upon her."[56] Oakes Smith averred that the angelic poetess' wayward innocence was often mistaken for passion. Alluding to the sexual scandal involving Osgood and Poe, she said: "I never think of her without a pang, for she was unjustly traduced by those who could not understand the purity of her heart."[57] In a memorial tribute Rufus Griswold told readers that he needed literally to spell out Osgood's death for her because she was too childlike to understand it on her own:

> I wrote the terrible truth to her, in studiously gentle words, reminding her that in heaven there is richer and more delicious beauty, that there is no discord in sounds there. . . . She read the brief note . . . and then turned upon her pillow like a child, and wept the last tears that were in a fountain which had flowed for every grief but hers she ever knew. (*LL* 16)

Griswold was clearly mistaken in his estimation of her childlike oblivion, for on March 28, 1848 Osgood wrote to Sarah Helen Whitman with chilling nonchalance, "Do write to me and tell me what you are doing in the literary way. As for me I have a terrible racking cough which is killing me by inches and there are not many inches left now" (quoted in *PH* 48). Since Osgood was obviously capable of acknowledging her decline, we may conclude that she played the part of ingénue for Griswold even as she observed the slow, painful progress of her own death. That Griswold felt moved to compose

Osgood's final epiphany testifies to her ability to inspire men to create in her name.

Such fantasies suggest that Osgood's fans – particularly men powerful in the New York literary establishment – experienced a sense of proprietorship over the author. Hiram Fuller asked Osgood if he could have the pleasure of sketching her: "Will you ask Graham, when he publishes your portrait, to let me illustrate the plate?"[58] Osgood's admirers liked to custom-design the figure of the poetess, and men frequently cast her as the product of a male artist's imagination. Reverend Dr. Davidson, for example, compared her to Fonqué's water sprite:

There is nothing mechanical about her. . . . In her almost childlike playfulness, she reminds us of that exquisite creation of Fonqué, Undine, who knew no law but that of her own waywardness.[59]

Davidson portrays Osgood as a magic toy that the male imagination brings to life. She is less an artist herself than an inspiring figure that naturalizes male creativity by proving its fecundity. Calling her "the first live poet who ever lived up to my ideal," Hiram Fuller imagined that he could make Osgood by naming her. He wrote in amorous effusion of the new names she acquired, first from her literary creations and then from him:

I am at loss how to address you with all your new names . . . Undine – Florence – I wish I had a catalogue of the Angels at hand . . . or even a list of the Fairies, – but I'll look through Heaven and earth for a [word unclear] that shall go beyond them all. Have I not already called you "Sunbeam of Summer" – "Rose of the Desert" – "Lily of the Valley" – . . . Have I not already crowned you "Queen of American Song"?[60]

Osgood's tendency to generate characters (Florence and Undine) that allude in obvious but oblique ways to the author encourages Fuller to do the same. Once begun, the logic of multiplication takes on a life of its own. Her "new names" inspire his hyperbolic attempts to outdo previous appellations. Their collective force exponentially increases the author's singularity and makes her into a celebrity. For Fuller, naming has a talismanic power that authorizes Osgood while making him her author and thus the co-author of her work.

In a letter dated May 14, 1845, William Mitchell Gillespie told Osgood which of her characters composed her and to what degree. Though he usually ignored his *Graham's* when it arrived at his house,

this number I have just been pouncing upon like a tiger – for I saw it advertised, that it contained an article by a certain (or more properly a very *uncertain*)

Mrs. Osgood. I found that it was not that wicked New Orleans story, which so shocked me when I read it in your little parlor after good and great Mr. Channing's sermon. . . . but it was darling "Lulu," a stranger to me – and yet not a stranger, for I well know her eyes "with their shy startled look," and I have often seen how "Her soul trembles in them / Like light on brook."[61]

Osgood's personification of the magazine enables Gillespie to express his passion: while he would have to control his desire for the married woman, he is free to pounce on the magazine and even tell her about it. Gillespie loves and lovingly repeats "Lulu," a poem about a sprite-like woman who seduces everyone with her child-like innocence (*FSOP* 37). At the same time he is so deliciously scandalized by Osgood's "wicked New Orleans story" that he prefers to read the sketch in her parlor rather than speaking to the poetess, who was also presumably present at the time.

Men's investment in their Muse led them to instruct Osgood on her literary output as if she were writing their pieces. Gillespie told her about poems he wished her to write, including one on "Venetian glass": "Do it carefully – do not leave even those pretty blemishes, which you are sometimes careless of . . . When you have written [it], please to send me a copy – I am *so lonely*." As if verbally mimicking glittering surfaces could capture and transmit the poet's seductive charm, poems about reflective objects serve as surrogate companions who administer to Gillespie's intimate emotional needs. He requests another poem on "Queen Mary's Mirror – which I saw in her chamber at Holyrood Palace. Pray its adamantine surface to reflect back to our eyes some portion of that loveliness which has so often emparadised its heart."[62] Imagining Osgood as a specialist in mimesis, he thinks she can capture in a poem about a mirror the woman whose image the mirror had held. (To my knowledge Osgood never fulfilled Gillespie's wishes; it would go against her capricious image to submit to his will.)

To some current readers, Osgood might appear to play within the circumscribed bounds of the "female complaint" deemed allowable in the public sphere because it posed no threat to patriarchy. A number of her contemporaries, however, claimed that Osgood's complex negotiations changed the rules of the literary game, turning the tables on powerful men with their consent. Grace Greenwood, a slightly younger poet who went on to become popular in her own right, wrote in the *Home Journal* in 1846:

And how are the critical Caesars, one after another, "giving in" to the graces, and fascinations, and soft enchantments of this Cleopatra of song. She charms *lions* to sleep, with her silver lute, and then throws around them the delicate network of her exquisite fancy, and lo! when they wake, they are well-content in their silken prison. (*LL* 18)

The promise of poetic power rooted in seduction contributes to Osgood's appeal for Greenwood, who expresses her own identification with her role model in the language of romantic love:

long, long before we met, I loved you, with a strange, almost passionate love. You were my literary idol. I repeated some of your poems so often, that their echo never had time to die away. (18)

Greenwood describes a mimic process of self-composition in which her lyric voice emerges from repeating Osgood's poems; her tribute advertises her indebtedness by adopting Osgood's vocabulary of erotic fancy. The romantic spell that Osgood casts upon Greenwood is synonymous with literary aspiration, "an 'intense and burning,' almost unwomanly ambition." Osgood, along with other poetesses of the 1830s and 1840s, opened to a younger generation of women the possibility of being read and desired by men as well as women. She cultivated a consumptive passion, or a passion for poetic consumption, that revised codes of genteel conduct discouraging public displays of female sexuality.

Desiring Osgood meant desiring her seemingly effortless capacity to be desired, an important talent in a market economy. She allowed others to possess her without seeming to be diminished in any way; on the contrary, their possessiveness added to her worth. The key to this alchemy was the poem's reproducibility: everyone could own a copy, while Osgood was the unattainable original. The relation between individual and copy perfectly stimulated a romantic love predicated on lack. Only with Poe did Osgood meet her match, when his desires to possess female poetic accomplishment overwhelmed her insistence on remaining ethereal in order to elude male entrapment.

SIGNATURE EMBODIMENT: THE OSGOOD–POE AFFAIR

Though her work appeared in major anthologies throughout the nineteenth century, Osgood's reputation had waned by the beginning of the twentieth century. In Poe studies, her erotic allure has migrated from her poems to her embodied self, which has increased in appeal while appreciation of her work has diminished. Playing a tiny role in Poe biography, Osgood appears as the attractive, flirtatious, married poetess "with a talent for facile literary composition" with whom Poe carried on some kind of affair while his wife was dying (*EAP* 280). Their mutual compliments at the New York City literary salons, as well as their ongoing exchange of romantic poems in the pages of the *Broadway Journal,* elicited gossip. The relationship ended in a scandal when another poetess, Elizabeth Ellet, supposedly caught a glimpse of a compromising letter from Osgood on a visit to Poe's house. The ensuing controversy alienated him from many of the New York literati.[63] Poe scholars continue to speculate about the affair; John Evangelist Walsh has even argued that Osgood had Poe's baby. Some critics have attributed Rufus Griswold's vindictive demonization of Poe to jealousy over Osgood.[64] According to Poe lore, it was a case of fatal attraction: Osgood's physical charms generated rivalries that damaged Poe's reputation. Her talent for flirtation also purportedly explains why powerful literary men admired her poetry: dazzled by her allure, they came to believe that she was a talented poet.[65]

Osgood has traditionally been portrayed as a supplicant trading on flattery to gain Poe's literary compliments. Alternatively, Mary De Jong has cast her as Poe's "protegée" in an unequal "literary alliance," in which Poe stood to gain from promoting her work even though he was the more powerful figure.[66] Both readings minimize Osgood's poetic power, which generated as much rivalry as condescending patronage on the part of male writers, including Poe. During her lifetime, Osgood shared the stage with Poe as a successful poet and outstripped him in popularity. Then too her trademark was erotic charm, but that eroticism was firmly associated with her poetry. In redistributing her appeal from her poems to her body, commentators have minimized the fact that Poe published Osgood's work before he met her, when he was the editor of *Graham's*, and that he came to her attention only after she learned that he had identified her as one of the best female poets of the age in a public lecture and "recited a long poem of mine exquisitely, they said" (quoted in *EAP* 282).

In order to imagine that Poe and Osgood had a physical love affair, critics have extrapolated from elusive textual evidence: the poetic exchange in the *Broadway Journal*, Osgood's suggestive sketches in *Graham's* that alluded to an affair, and the letters between the poets that may or may not have ever existed.[67] In her landmark defense of Poe, Sarah Helen Whitman locates Osgood's seductive powers in her verse. Referring to the rivalry between Griswold and Poe, Whitman meditates upon a painting of Osgood:

Looking at the beautiful portrait of this lady – the face so full of enthusiasm, and dreamy, tropical sunshine – remembering the eloquent words of praise, as expressed in the prodigal and passionate exaggerations of her verse, one ceases to wonder at the rivalries and enmities enkindled within the hearts of those who admired her genius and her grace – rivalries and enmities which the grave itself could not appease.[68]

Following the painter's lead, Whitman personifies Osgood as a figure of poetic fancy in terms consistent with her contemporary reception. Osgood's face gains its appeal from the legible presence of poetic reverie. It is a visible sign of the lyric coquetry that generated her reputation.

Rather than presume that Poe's romantic interest in Osgood explains his interest in her work, I want to suggest that he staged a public literary romance because he valued her capacity to captivate readers by personifying a poetic muse. Poe recognized and sought to appropriate Osgood's insights about the ways authors could promote their circulation within mass print media. In an 1845 review, he states that "we have no poetess among us who has been so universally *popular* as Mrs. Osgood" and attributes her appeal to poetic "*grace*. . . . It is this rod of the enchanter which throws open to her the road to all hearts."[69] Reckoning with her popularity, Poe dramatized a takeover of Osgood's poetic powers within the course of the literary affair. Through a series of gestures that embodied the elusive, ethereal poetess, he publicly made her his personal muse, promoting the idea that his poetic powers could arrest her attention, and therefore her circulation. Osgood validated the impact of Poe's mesmeric efforts in her tributes, which she directed for the first time towards a particular love object; in doing so, she cultivated his reputation at the expense of her own. Their exchange, then, tells us little about their private lives, but much about the public role of the celebrity poet at mid-century, a role crucially informed by gender.

While both poets had cultivated the art of provoking readerly desire for their lyric subjects, the *Broadway Journal* exchange encouraged readers to identify the poets as the objects of each other's desire. The more restricted address had the effect of animating the printed page itself. Poe's arrangement of their writings and signatures in close proximity suggested an analogy with lovers conversing intimately in a salon setting. Occupying dual roles of editor and suitor, he encouraged readers to speculate about the logic informing the selection and placement of material, and to wonder whether they were uncovering clues to an inside story, or projecting fantasies upon a neutral arrangement.[70]

In the April 12, 1845 issue, near the start of the print flirtation, a lewd illustration offers a visual template for the coterie flirtation that Poe stages on the magazine page (fig. 7).[71] "A Presentation at a Literary Soirée" depicts two men leaning exaggeratedly over a petite woman in order to view her prominently displayed cleavage under the guise of attending to her recitation. The cartoon is too abstract to assign particular identities to the figures (though they resemble Poe, Griswold, and Osgood), but at any rate the woman's sexualized body distracts the men from hearing her words: their

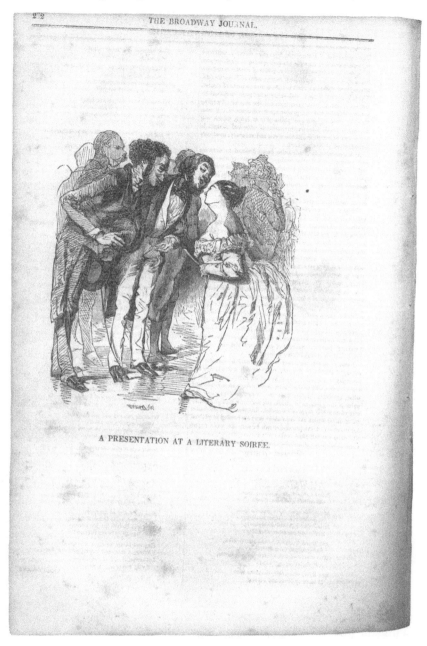

A PRESENTATION AT A LITERARY SOIRÉE.

Fig. 7: "A Presentation at a Literary Soirée," *Broadway Journal* (April 12, 1845).

interest in her physical "presentation" eclipses their attention to her verbal one. The image indicates the extent to which fantasies of the embodied woman informed readings of the poetess' work. In the same issue, on the reverse side of the same page, Poe identified Osgood as an object of attraction by publishing two of her poems – one signed by herself, the other by "Violet Vane"(fig. 8).[72] The juxtaposition of two different signatures draws attention to her characteristic poetic diffusion while enclosing it within a smaller-than-customary frame (this happens in the April 5 issue as well, which contains poems by Kate Carol and Violet Vane).[73] Putting himself in dialogue with the poetess in this restricted scenario, Poe addressed tributes both to Osgood ("To F__") and to one of her pseudonyms ("Impromptu: To Kate Carol") in the April 26 issue.[74]

As Poe gained editorial control over the *Journal*, he encouraged readers to imagine the page as a place and the literary pieces as inhabitants, events, or obstacles to overcome.[75] Within this terrain, he placed his own and Osgood's work to suggest that the paper's surface was the active location of their love affair.[76] On August 30, for example, when the pair had already become town talk, Poe published Osgood's poem "Slander" on the front page (fig. 9).[77] Representing the scandal-mongering it condemns, the body of the poem divides Poe's name as editor from Osgood's signature; the names themselves are aligned. Poe's arrangement thus identifies the couple as the object of gossip (something Osgood had refrained from doing) and conveys the message that their emotional bond endures under stress. His signed story "William Wilson" appears directly underneath Osgood's poem and occupies the entire column beside it. By surrounding her poem on three sides of the page, Poe enacts all-encompassing desire. In this visual context, the opening words of his story allude to the erotically charged space that it inhabits: "Let me call myself, for the present, William Wilson. The fair page now lying before me need not be sullied with my real appellation."[78] William Wilson's address draws attention to the printed voice's location on the page, and his fears of sullying the medium position the magazine as an arena for sexual exchange and transgression in a way that echoes, albeit in a sinister way, Osgood's own erotics of print. In this particular case, however, the text of Osgood's poem works against Poe's visual and verbal implications. Her speaker stresses the disjunction between words and facts. A "little meaning" voice "wanders round, / From ear to lip – from lip to ear," until it finally breaks a heart with the lethal power of a baseless "report." While the poem laments the false impression of an adulterous affair that irresponsible verbal circulation generates, Poe's editorial play implies that the words on the page are themselves conducting an erotic exchange.

The cultivation of accuracy in MS., thus enforced, will tend with an irresistible impetus to every species of improvement in *style*—more especially in the points of concision and distinctness—and this again, in a degree even more noticeable, to precision of thought, and luminous arrangement of matter. There is a very peculiar and easily intelligible reciprocal influence between the thing written and the manner of writing —but the latter has the predominant influence of the two. The more remote effect on philosophy at large, which will inevitably result from improvement of style and thought in the points of concision, distinctness, and accuracy, need only be suggested to be conceived.

As a consequence of attention being directed to neatness and beauty of MS. the antique profession of the scribe will be revived, affording abundant employment to women— their delicacy of organization fitting them peculiarly for such tasks. The female amanuensis, indeed, will occupy very nearly the position of the present male type-setter, whose industry will be diverted perforce into other channels.

These considerations are of vital importance—but there is yet one beyond them all. The value of every book is a compound of its literary value and its physical or mechanical value as the product of physical labor applied to the physical material. But at present the latter value immensely predominates, even in the works of the most esteemed authors. It will be seen, however, that the new condition of things will at once give the ascendancy to the literary value, and thus *by* their literary values will books come to be estimated among men. The wealthy gentleman of elegant leisure will lose the vantage ground now afforded him, and will be forced to tilt on terms of equality with the poor devil author. At present the literary world is a species of anomalous Congress, in which the majority of the members are constrained to listen in silence while all the eloquence proceeds from a privileged few. In the new *régime*, the humblest will speak as often and as freely as the most exalted, and will be sure of receiving just that amount of attention which the intrinsic merit of their speeches may deserve.

From what we have said it will be evident that the discovery of Anastatic Printing will not only not obviate the necessity of copy-right laws, and of an International Law in especial, but will render this necessity more imperative and more apparent. It has been shown that in depressing the value of the *physique* of a book, the invention will proportionally elevate the value of its *morale*, and since it is the latter value alone which the copy-right laws are needed to protect, the necessity of the protection will be only the more urgent and more obvious than ever.

Original Poetry.

LOVE'S REPLY.

I 'll tell you something chanced to me,
　(A quaint and simple story,)
Before I crossed, with beating heart,
　Old ocean's gloom and glory.

Around me came three graceful girls,
　Their farewell whisper breathing,—
Julie,—with light and lovely curls,
　Her snowy shoulders wreathing;

And proud Georgine,— with stately mien,
　And glance of calm hauteur,
Who moves—a Grace,—and looks—a queen,
　All passionless and pure;

And Kate, whose low, melodious tone
　Is tuned by Truth and Feeling;

Whose shy yet wistful eyes talk on,
　When Fear her *lips* is sealing.

" From what far country, shall I write ?"
　I asked, with pride elated,
" From what rare monument of art
　Shall be my letters dated ?"

Julie tossed back her locks of light,
　With girlish grace and glee,—
" To me from glorious Venice write,
　Queen-city of the Sea ?"

" And thou, Georgine ?" Her dark eyes flashed,—
　" Ah ! date to me your lines
From some proud palace, where the pomp
　Of olden Honor shines !"

But Kate,—the darling of my soul,
　My bright, yet bashful flower,
In whose dear heart some new, pure leaf,
　Seems to unfold each hour,—

Kate turned her shy, sweet looks from mine,
　Lest I her blush should see,
And said—so only Love could hear—
　Write from your *heart* to *me !*"

　　　　FRANCES S. OSGOOD.

SPRING.

She has come and brought her flowers,
　Loving, child-like, happy Spring !
Smiling out through sudden showers,
　Lo ! the Peri plumes her wing !

She has come — the wood-bird, listening,
　Knows her step and warbles low ;
Every cloud and wave is glistening,
　Where her light feet go.

Every leaf with love she blesses ;
　Even the little violet's heart
Throbs beneath her dear caresses,
　While its purple petals part.

In the skies, a changeful glory,—
　In the woodlands, bloom and glee,—
All things tell a joyous story :—
　What has Spring brought *me ?*

Hope—her promise-buds revealing !
　Joy, with light and dazzling wing !
Fresh and ardent founts of Feeling !
　These should come with sportive Spring.

When she came of old, she found me
　Gay as any bird she knew ;
Hope her wild-flowers showered around me,
　Friends were fond and true.

Do not look so glad and bright,
　Loving, laughing, joyous Spring !
Weep awhile amid thy light,
　Frolic Ariel, fold thy wing !

Weep for me ! my heart is breaking,
　'Neath thy blue eyes' careless smile !
Mine, with hidden tears are aching,—
　Weep with me awhile !

No ! the winter of the spirit
　Melts not in the breath of Spring ;
Birds and flowers her joy inherit ;
　Let *them* gaily bloom and sing !

Sing and bloom for those who never
　Wronged their own hearts, pure and free ;
Let her smile on field and river—
　Spring comes not to *me !*

　　　　VIOLET VANE.

Fig. 8: "Love's Reply," by Frances S. Osgood; "Spring," by Violet Vane (née Frances Osgood). *Broadway Journal* (April 12, 1845).

THE BROADWAY JOURNAL.

VOL. 2.   NEW YORK, SATURDAY, AUGUST 30, 1845.   NO. 8.

Three Dollars per Annum.
Single Copies, 6 1-4 Cents.

EDITED BY
EDGAR A. POE AND HENRY C. WATSON.

Published at 135 Nassau St.
by JOHN BISCO.

Slander.

A whisper woke the air—
A soft light tone and low,
Yet barbed with shame and woe;—
Now, might it only perish there!
Nor farther go.

Ah me! a quick and eager ear
Caught up the little meaning sound!
Another voice has breathed it clear,
And so it wanders round,
From ear to lip—from lip to ear—
Until it reached a gentle heart,
And *that—it broke.*

It was the *only* heart it found,
The only heart 't was meant to find,
When first its accents woke;—
It reached that tender heart at last,
And that—it broke.

Low as it seemed to *other ears,*
It came—a thunder-crash to *hers,*—
That fragile girl so fair and gay,—
That guileless girl so pure and true!

'Tis said a lovely humming bird
That in a fragrant lily lay,
And dreamed the summer morn away,
Was killed by but the gun's *report,*
Some idle boy had fired in sport!
The very *sound*—a death-blow came!

And thus her happy heart, that beat,
With love and hope, so fast and sweet,
(Shrined in *its Lily* too
For who the maid that knew
But owned the delicate flower-like grace
Of her young form and face!)
When first that word
Her light heart heard,
It fluttered like the frightened bird,
Then shut its wings and sighed,
And, with a silent shudder,—died!

FRANCES S. OSGOOD.

William Wilson.

What say of it? what say CONSCIENCE grim,
That spectre in my path?
CHAMBERLAIN's PHARRONIDA.

LET me call myself, for the present, William Wilson. The fair page now lying before me need not be sullied with my real appellation. This has been already too much an object for the scorn—for the horror—for the detestation of my race. To the uttermost regions of the globe have not the indignant winds bruited its unparalleled infamy? Oh, outcast of all outcasts most abandoned!—to the earth art thou not forever dead? to its honors, to its flowers, to its golden aspirations?—and a cloud, dense, dismal, and limitless, does it not hang eternally between thy hopes and heaven?

I would not, if I could, here or to-day, embody a record of my later years of unspeakable misery, and unpardonable crime. This epoch—these later years—took unto themselves a sudden elevation in turpitude, whose origin alone it is my present purpose to assign. Men usually grow base by degrees. From me, in an instant, all virtue dropped bodily as a mantle. From comparatively trivial wickedness I passed, with the stride of a giant, into more than the enormities of an Elah-Gabalus. What chance—what one event brought this evil thing to pass, bear with me while I relate. Death approaches; and the shadow which foreruns him has thrown a softening influence over my spirit. I long, in passing through the dim valley, for the sympathy—I had nearly said the pity—of my fellow men. I would fain have them believe that I have been, in some measure, the slave of circumstances beyond human control. I would wish them to seek out for me, in the details I am about to give, some little oasis of *fatality* amid a wilderness of error. I would have them allow—what they cannot refrain from allowing—that, although temptation may have erewhile existed as great, man was never *thus,* at least, tempted before—certainly, never *thus* fell. And is it therefore that he has never thus suffered? Have I not indeed been living in a dream? And am I not now dying a victim to the horror and the mystery of the wildest of all sublunary visions?

I am the descendant of a race whose imaginative and easily excitable temperament has at all times rendered them remarkable: and, in my earliest infancy, I gave evidence of having fully inherited the family character. As I advanced in years it was more strongly developed; becoming, for many reasons, a cause of serious disquietude to my friends, and of positive injury to myself. I grew self-willed, addicted to the wildest caprices, and a prey to the most ungovernable passions. Weak-minded, and beset with constitutional infirmities akin to my own, my parents could do but little to check the evil propensities which distinguished me. Some feeble and ill-directed efforts resulted in complete failure on their part, and, of course, in total triumph on mine. Thenceforward my voice was a household law; and at an age when few children have abandoned their leading-strings, I was left to the guidance of my own will, and became, in all but name, the master of my own actions.

My earliest recollections of a school-life, are connected with a large, rambling, Elizabethan house, in a misty-looking village of England, where were a vast number of gigantic and gnarled trees, and where all the houses were excessively ancient. In truth, it was a dream-like and spirit-soothing place, that venerable old town. At this moment, in fancy, I feel the refreshing chilliness of its deeply-shadowed avenues, inhale the fragrance of its thousand shrubberies, and thrill anew with undefinable delight, at the deep hollow note of the church-bell, breaking, each hour, with

Fig. 9: "Slander," by Frances S. Osgood; "William Wilson," by E. A. Poe. Front page of the *Broadway Journal* (August 30, 1845).

Osgood responded to Poe's editorial advances by limiting the circulation of her name in order to publicize his. She first alluded directly to Poe in "Echo-Song," published on the *Journal's* front page on September 6 (fig. 10). Quoting "Israfel," the speaker professes to know but refuses to tell a secret lover's identity:

> I know a noble heart that beats
> For one it loves how "wildly well!"
> I only know for whom it beats;
> But I must never tell!
> Never tell!
> Hush! Hark! How Echo soft repeats, –
> Ah! Never tell! . . .[79]

While the speaker encourages the reader to identify the "noble heart" with Poe and the unnameable lover with Osgood, her refusal to "tell" leaves both positions empty and unspecified, stimulating speculation while refusing to satisfy it.[80] Even if the reader equates the lovers in the poem with the poets themselves, however, "Echo-Song" suggests that Poe loves Osgood for quoting Poe, or, in other words, that Poe loves himself. The fact that Poe publishes the song on the front page of the *Journal* – directly under his name and surrounded by the text of his story "Why the Little Frenchman Wears his Hand in a Sling" – shows that he understands and appreciates the poem's gift of publicity. Whereas Poe has often been portrayed as someone who gallantly "puffs" undeserving poetesses, here Osgood puffs Poe and legitimates his poetic allure. The famously elusive poetess stages her own captivation by Israfel's irresistible song.

A more conflicted interaction is evident in the November 22 issue, when Osgood meditates on the dynamics of poetic captivation in "To __," while Poe takes credit for her thoughts (fig. 11).[81] Defending a "star" from accusations of flirting with a lake, the speaker is one of many waves that involuntarily register its image on their reflective surfaces. Although literary convention may encourage the reader to assume that the star is male and the waves are female, Osgood refrains from assigning gender to either position:

> . . . Smile on then undimmed in your beauty and grace!
> Too well e'er to doubt, love, we know you; –
> And shed, from your heaven, the light of your face,
> Where the waves chase each other below you;
> For none can e'er deem it your shame or your sin,
> That each wave holds your star-image smiling within.

THE BROADWAY JOURNAL.

VOL. 2.   NEW YORK, SATURDAY, SEPTEMBER 6, 1845.   NO. 9.

Three Dollars per Annum.
Single Copies, 6 1-4 Cents.
EDITED BY
EDGAR A. POE AND HENRY C. WATSON.
Published at 135 Nassau St.
By JOHN BISCO.

Echo-Song.

I know a noble heart that beats
For one it loves how "wildly well!"
I only know for *whom* it beats;
But I must never tell!
Never tell!
Hush! hark! how Echo soft repeats,—
Ah! *never* tell!

I know a voice that falters low,
Whene'er one little name 't would say;
Full well that little name I know,
But that I 'll ne'er betray!
Ne'er betray!
Hush! hark! how Echo murmurs low,—
Ah! ne'er betray!

I know a smile that beaming flies
From soul to lip, with rapturous glow,
And I can guess who bids it rise;
But none—but none shall know!
None shall know!
Hush! hark! how Echo faintly sighs—
But *none* shall know!

FRANCES S. OSGOOD.

Why The Little Frenchman

WEARS HIS HAND IN A SLING.

It's on my wisiting cards sure enough (and it's them that's all o' pink satin paper) that inny gintleman that plases may behould the inthertisthin words, "Sir Pathrick O'Grandison, Barronitt, 39 Southampton Row, Russell Square, Parrish o' Bloomsbury." And shud ye be wantin to diskiver who is the pink of purliteness quite, and the laider of the hot tun in the houl city o' Lonon—why it's jist mesilf. And fait that same is no wonder at all at all, (so be plased to stop curlin your nose,) for every inch o' the six wakes that I've been a gintleman, and left aff wid the bog-throthing to take up wid the Barronissy, i'ts Pathrick that's been living like a houly imperor, and gitting the iddication and the graces. Och! and would'nt it be a blessed thing for your sperrits if ye cud lay your two peepers jist, upon Sir Pathrick O'Grandison, Barronitt, when he is all riddy drissed for the hopperer, or stipping into the Brisky for the drive into the Hyde Park.— But it's the iligant big figgur that I ave, for the rason o' which all the ladies lov'd me. Isn't it my own swate silf now that'll misure the six fut, and the three inches more nor that, in me stockings, and that am exceedingly will proportioned all over to match? And is it ralelly more than the three fut and a bit that there is, inny how, of the little ould furrener Frinchman that lives jist over the way, and that's a oggling and a goggling the houl day, (and bad luck to him,) at the purty widdy Misthress Tracle that's my own nixt door neighbor, (God bliss her) and a most particuller frind and acquaintance? You perceave the little spal-

peen is summat down in the mouth, and wears his lift hand in a sling; and it's for that same thing, by yur lave, that I'm going to give you the good rason.

The truth of the houl matter is jist simple enough; for the very first day that I com'd from Connaught, and showd my swate little silf in the strait to the widdy, who was looking through the windy, it was a gone case althegither wid the heart o' the purty Misthress Tracle. I percaved it, ye see, all at once, and no mistake, and that's God's thruth. First of all it was up wid the windy in a jiffy, and thin she threw open her two peepers to the itmost, and thin it was a little gould spy-glass that she clapped tight to one o' them, and divil may burn me if it did'nt spake to me as plain as a peeper cud spake, and says it, through the spy-glass, "Och! the tip o' the mornin to ye, Sir Pathrick O'Grandison, Barronitt, mavourneen; and it's a nate gintleman that ye are, sure enough, and it's mesilf and me forfin jist that'll be at yur sarvice, dear, inny time o' day at all at all for the asking." And it's not mesilf ye wud have to be bate in the purliteness; so I made her a bow that wud ha broken yur heart althegither to behould, and thin I pulled aff me hat with a flourish, and thin I winked at her hard wid both eyes, as much as to say, "Thrue for you, yer a swate little craythure, Mrs. Tracle, me darlint, and I wish I may be drowndhed dead in a bog, if its not mesilf, Sir Pathrick O'Grandison, Barronitt, that'll make a houl bushel o' love to yur leddy-ship, in the twinkling o' the eye of a Londonderry purraty."

And it was the nixt mornin, sure, jist as I was making up me maind whither it wouldn't be the purlite thing to sind a bit o' writin to the widdy by way of a love-litter, when up cum'd the delivery sarvant wid an illigant card, and he tould me that the name on it (for I niver cud rade the copper-plate printin on account of being lift handed) was all about Mounseer, the Count, A Goose, Look-aisy, Maiter-di-dauns, and that the houl of the divilish lingo was the spalpeeny long name of the little ould furrener Frinchman as lived over the way.

And jist wid that in cum'd the little willian himsilf, and thin he made me a broth of a bow, and thin he said he had ounly taken the liberty of doing me the honor of the giving me a call, and thin he went on to palaver at a great rate, and divil the bit did I comprehind what he wud be aither the tilling me at all at all, excipting and saving that he said "polly wou, woolly wou," and tould me, among a bushel o' lies, bad luck to him, that he was mad for the love o' my widdy Misthress Tracle, and that my widdy Mrs. Tracle had a puncheon for *him*.

At the hearin of this, ye may swear, though, I was as mad as a grasshopper, but I remimbered that I was Sir Pathrick O'Grandison, Barronitt, and that it wasn't althegither gentaal to lit the anger git the upper hand o' the purliteness, so I made light o' the matter and kipt dark, and got quite sociable wid the little chap, and afther a while what did he do

Fig. 10: "Echo Song," by Frances S. Osgood; "Why the Little Frenchman Wears His Hand in a Sling," by E. A. Poe. Front page of the *Broadway Journal* (September 6, 1845).

THE BROADWAY JOURNAL.   367

that the glasses of the instrument, as worn by the old lady, had been exchanged by her for a pair better adapted to my years. They suited me, in fact to a T.

The clergyman, who merely pretended to tie the fatal knot, was a boon companion of Talbot's, and no priest.— He was an excellent "whip," however; and having doffed his cassock to put on a great coat, he drove the hack which conveyed the "happy couple" out of town. Talbot took a seat at his side. The two scoundrels were thus "in at the death," and, through a half open window of the back parlor of the inn, amused themselves in grinning at the *dénouement* of the drama. I believe I shall be forced to call them both out.

Nevertheless, I am *not* the husband of my great, great, grandmother; and this is a reflection which affords me infinite relief;—but I *am* the husband of Madame Lalande—of Madame Stephanie Lalande—with whom my good old relative, besides making me her sole heir when she dies—if she ever does—has been at the trouble of concocting me a match. In conclusion: I am done forever with *billets doux*, and am never to be met without SPECTACLES.

                                        EDGAR A. POE.

To ——

Oh! they never can know that heart of thine,
    Who dare accuse thee of flirtation!
They might as well say that the stars, which shine
    In the light of their joy o'er Creation,—
Are flirting with every wild wave in which lies
One beam of the glory that kindles the skies.

Smile on then unblamed in your beauty and grace!
    Too well e'er to doubt, love, we know you;—
And shed, from your heaven, the light of your face,
    Where the waves chase each other below you;
For none can e'er deem it your shame or your sin,
That each wave holds your star-image smiling within.

                                    FRANCES S. OSGOOD.

Critical Notices.

We have again to apologise to our publishing friends for the brevity of our Critical Notices. In our next number we shall devote more than usual attention to this Department. There are several important works now lying before us, of which it is our intention to speak in detail:—Mrs. Kirkland's new book, for example—Von Raumer's America—and the Life of Schiller—one of the Appleton series. We wish to say much, also, of the Annuals and Gift-Books—very especially of "The Missionary Memorial," "The Dialena," "The Rose," and "The Mayflower"—the best of th ese works, as far as we have yet had an opportunity of judging. For the present (owing to the haste consequent upon removing our office) we must content ourselves with a mere announcement of the books on hand for notice.

Wiley & Putnam's Library of American Books. No. 7. Western Clearings. By Mrs. C. M. Kirkland, Author of "A New Home," etc.

Wiley & Putnam's Library of American Books. No. 8. The Raven and Other Poems. By Edgar A. Poe.

Appleton's Literary Miscellany—a New Series of Choice Books. No.5. The Life of Frederick Schiller: Comprehending an Examination of his Works by Thomas Carlyle, Author of "French Revolution," "Sartor Resartus," "Past and Present," etc. A new Edition revised by the Author. New-York: D. Appleton & Co. 200 Broadway.

Trifles in Verse: A Collection of Fugitive Poems. By Lewis J. Cist. Cincinnati: Robinson & Jones.

The Oath, a Divine Ordinance and an Element of The Social Constitution: its Origin, Nature, Ends, Efficacy, Lawfulness, Obligations, Interpretation, Form and Abuses. By D. X. Junkin, A. M. Pastor of the Presbyterian Church, Greenwich, N. J. New-York: Wiley & Putnam.

The Mass and Rubrics of the Roman Catholic Church, Translated into English, With Notes and Remarks. By the Rev. John Rogerson Cotter, A. M., Rector of Inishannon, etc. New-York: D. Appleton & Co.

The Diadem for 1846. A Present for all Seasons. With Ten Engravings, after Pictures by Inman, Leutze, etc. Philadelphia: Carey & Hart.

The Missionary Memorial: a Literary and Religious Souvenir. New-York: E Walker, 114 Fulton St.

The Rose: or Affection's Gift for 1846. Edited by Emily Marshall, Illustrated with Ten highly finished steel engravings. New-York: D. Appleton & Co.

The May-Flower, for 1846. Edited by Robert Hamilton. Boston: Saxton & Kelt.

Harper's Library of Select Novels: No: 62. Amaury. Translated from the French of Alexandre Dumas. By E. P. New-York: Harper & Brothers.

The O'Donoghue. A Tale of Ireland Fifty years ago. By Charles Lever, Author of "Harry Lorrequer," "Charles O'Malley," etc. With Illustrations by Phiz. To which is added St. Patrick's Eve, or Three Eras in the Life of an Irish Peasant. Philadelphia: Carey & Hart.

Cosmos: a Survey of the General Physical History of The Universe. By Alexander Von Humboldt. Part 2. New-York: Harper & Brothers.

Harper's Library of Select Novels. No. 61. Only a Fiddler! and O. T. By the Author of "The Improvisatore, or Life in Italy" etc. Translated by Mary Howitt.

Lucy of Lammermoor: Grand Serious Opera in Three Acts; Founded on Sir Walter Scott's Celebrated Novel. The Music by Donizetti. Words by Messrs. G. Bowes and Rophino Lacy. New-York: George Trehern.

Morse's Geographic Maps. No. 4. Contents—Texas, Kentucky—Tennessee—Indiana—and South Carolina. New-York: Harper & Brothers.

The Devotional Family Bible. By the Rev. Alexander Fletcher, A. M. Containing The Old and New Testaments, with Explanatory Notes, Marginal References, etc. Every Part embellished with a Highly Finished Engraving on Steel; Including Views of the Principal Places mentioned in Scripture, from Drawings taken on the Spot. Part 12. New-York: R. Martin & Co., 26 John St.

The Edinburgh Review, for October. American Edition. New-York: Leonard Scott & Co.

A New Edition of Tennyson. Boston: Ticknor & Co.

First Love.

Oh! precious is the flow'r that Passion brings
    To his first shrine of beauty, when the heart
    Runs o'er in devotion, and no art
Checks the free gush of the wild lay he sings;—
But the rapt eye, and the impetuous thought
    Declare the pure affection; and a speech,
    Such as the ever-tuned affections teach,
Delivers love's best confidence untaught;—
And all is glory in the o'er-arching sky,
    And all is beauty in the uplifting earth;
    And from the wood, and o'er the wave, a mirth
Such as mocks hope with immortality,
Declares that all the loved ones are at hand,
With still the turtle's voice the loudest in the land.
                                    W. GILMORE SIMMS.

Fig. 11: "To__," by Frances S. Osgood. *Broadway Journal* (November 22, 1845).

The speaker assures the star that it is not to blame for the myriad reflections it inadvertently produces. Though the wave energetically defends the star, however, the metaphor's limitations undermine its persuasive power, for both wave and star stand for people. While actual stars have no volition or intent, celebrities do, and therefore they may be accountable for the longing they produce in their fans. Because Osgood attributes to the star the signature quality of her own poetic opus – "flirtation" – she seems to defend her own lyric project, as she does in so many other poems. Here, however, the speaker places herself among the many waves. She therefore divests of her own flirtatious powers in order to succumb to the star's version of them. Poe resolves the gender ambiguity to his advantage by aligning his name, which appears at the end of a short story, with the blank in Osgood's title, identifying himself as the star. Poe harnesses Osgood's praise in order to promote his own poetic project by suggesting that his attractive powers have captivated the capricious, wayward poetess.

On November 29 Osgood's speaker performs the most radical divestment of lyric identity in order to express a preference for being possessed by Poe (fig. 12). The epigraph from "Israfel" ("In Heaven a spirit doth dwell / Whose heart-strings are a lute") strongly hints at the name that should fill the blank in "To __," even if Poe had not suspended his name above it.[82] With this preponderance of allusion, the reader cannot help but speculate that an enamored Osgood addresses Poe as if he were Israfel in order to reassure him that he can sing as "wildly well" as his celestial poet:

> I cannot tell *the world* how thrills my heart
> To every touch that flies thy lyre along;
> How the wild Nature and the wondrous Art,
> Blend into Beauty in thy passionate song –
>
> But this I know – in thine enchanted slumbers,
> Heaven's poet, Israfel, – with minstrel fire –
> Taught thee the music of his own sweet numbers,
> And tuned – to chord with *his* – thy glorious lyre!

If the reader refrains from filling in Poe's name, however, the blank generates a second scenario, in which the speaker addresses *herself* in order to meditate on her own apprenticeship to Poe's Israfel. In this case, the point of maximum captivation is also the point of full identification; if

318   THE BROADWAY JOURNAL.

We looked at the picture which he presented. I saw nothing in it of an extraordinary character; but its effect upon Bedloe was prodigious. He nearly fainted as he gazed. And yet it was but a miniature portrait—a miraculously accurate one, to be sure—of his own very remarkable features. At least this was my thought as I regarded it.

"You will perceive," said Templeton, "the date of this picture—it is here, scarcely visible, in this corner—1780. In this year was the portrait taken. It is the likeness of a dead friend—a Mr. Oldeb—to whom I became much attached at Calcutta, during the administration of Warren Hastings. I was then only twenty years old.—When I first saw you, Mr. Bedloe, at Saratoga, it was the miraculous similarity which existed between yourself and the painting, which induced me to accost you, to seek your friendship, and to bring about those arrangements which resulted in my becoming your constant companion. In accomplishing this point, I was urged partly, and perhaps principally, by a regretful memory of the deceased, but also, in part, by an uneasy, and not altogether horrorless curiosity respecting yourself.

"In your detail of the vision which presented itself to you amid the hills, you have described, with the minutest accuracy, the Indian city of Benares, upon the Holy River. The riots, the combats, the massacre, were the actual events of the insurrection of Cheyte Sing, which took place in 1780, when Hastings was put in imminent peril of his life. The man escaping by the string of turbans, was Cheyte Sing himself. The party in the kiosk were sepoys and British officers, headed by Hastings. Of this party I was one, and did all I could to prevent the rash and fatal sally of the officer who fell, in the crowded alleys, by the poisoned arrow of a Bengalee. That officer was my dearest friend. It was Oldeb. You will perceive by these manuscripts," (here the speaker produced a note-book in which several pages appeared to have been freshly written) "that at the very period in which you fancied these things amid the hills, I was engaged in detailing them upon paper here at home."

In about a week after this conversation, the following paragraphs appeared in a Charlottesville paper.

"We have the painful duty of announcing the death of Mr. AUGUSTUS BEDLO, a gentleman whose amiable manners and many virtues have long endeared him to the citizens of Charlottesville.

"Mr. B., for some years past, has been subject to neuralgia, which has often threatened to terminate fatally; but this can be regarded only as the mediate cause of his decease. The proximate cause was one of especial singularity. In an excursion to the Ragged Mountains, a few days since, a slight cold and fever were contracted, attended with great determination of blood to the head. To relieve this, Dr. Templeton resorted to topical bleeding. Leeches were applied to the temples. In a fearfully brief period the patient died, when it appeared that, in the jar containing the leeches, had been introduced, by accident, one of the venomous vermicular sangsues which are now and then found in the neighboring ponds. This creature fastened itself upon a small artery in the right temple. Its close resemblance to the medicinal leech caused the mistake to be overlooked until too late.

"N. B. The poisonous sangsue of Charlottesville may always be distinguished from the medicinal leech by its blackness, and especially by its writhing or vermicular motions, which very nearly resemble those of a snake."

I was speaking with the editor of the paper in question, upon the topic of this remarkable accident, when it occurred to me to ask how it happened that the name of the deceased had been given as Bedlo.

"I presume," said I, "you have authority for this spelling, but I have always supposed the name to be written with an *e* at the end."

"Authority?—no," he replied. "It is a mere typographical error. The name is Bedlo with an *e*, all the world over, and I never knew it to be spelt otherwise in my life."

"Then," said I mutteringly, as I turned upon my heel, "then indeed has it come to pass that one truth is stranger than any fiction—for Bedlo, without the *e*, what is it but Oldeb conversed? And this man tells me it is a typographical error."   EDGAR A. POE.

To ——

"In Heaven a spirit doth dwell,
Whose heart-strings are a lute."

I cannot tell *the world* how thrills my heart
  To every touch that flies thy lyre along;
How the wild Nature and the wondrous Art,
  Blend into Beauty in thy passionate song—

But this *I know*—in thine enchanted slumbers,
  Heaven's poet, Israfel,—with minstrel fire—
Taught thee the music of his own sweet numbers,
  And tuned—to chord with *his*—thy glorious lyre!
                              FRANCES S. OSGOOD.

Art-Singing and Heart-Singing.*

GREAT is the power of Music over a people! As for us of America, we have long enough followed obedient and child-like in the track of the Old World. We have received her tenors and her buffos, her operatic troupes and her vocalists, of all grades and complexions; listened to and applauded the songs made for a different state of society—made, perhaps, by royal genius, but made to please royal ears likewise; and it is time that such listening and receiving should cease. The subtlest spirit of a nation is expressed through its music—and the music acts reciprocally upon the nation's very soul. Its effects may not be seen in a day, or a year, and yet these effects are potent invisibly. They enter into religious feelings—they tinge the manners and morals—they are active even in the choice of legislators and high magistrates. Tariff can be varied to fit circumstances—bad laws be obliterated and good ones formed—those enactments which relate to commerce or national policy, built up or taken away, stretched or contracted, to suit the will of the government for the time being. But no human power can thoroughly suppress the spirit which lives in national lyrics, and sounds in the favorite melodies sung by high and low.

There are two kinds of singing—heart-singing and art-singing. That which touches the souls and sympathies of other communities may have no effect here—unless it appeals to the throbbings of the great heart of humanity

* The author desires us to say, for him, that he pretends to no scientific knowledge of music. He merely claims to appreciate so much of it (a sadly disdained department; just now) as affects, in the language of the deacons, "the natural heart of man." It is scarcely necessary to add that we agree with our correspondent throughout.   ED. B. J.

Israfel "tuned" both lyres "to chord with his," then Osgood is Poe. Poe intervenes in this equation by filling in the title's blank with his name, depriving Osgood of the possibility of self-address. In either case, however, Osgood's poem accrues under the sign of Poe, because Israfel is his creation, not hers.

With her cooperation, Poe dramatized what it meant to make copy out of Osgood while containing her circulation: he ultimately published twelve of her poems, and her name appeared more than thirty times in the brief period he had editorial control of the *Journal* (*EAP* 284). By claiming Osgood's poems as the property of a single recipient, Poe transformed their literary flirtation into a literal love affair in readers' minds that ultimately damaged his reputation. Though one might assume that greater strictures on women's public expressions of sexuality would have placed Osgood in greater peril than Poe, the exchange did not seriously compromise her reputation, nor did it seem to inhibit her poetics of circulation. In fact she published many of her most promiscuous poems in the years after the scandal. Just before her death in 1850, *Graham's* published "The Coquette's Vow" and "Lines to an Idea that Wouldn't 'Come,'" in which a poetess entices an idea into leaving the other poetesses he attends by offering him "a virgin page" and advertising her own sexual versatility: "take what route it pleases you / It's all the same to me."[83] Ironically, for Osgood to retain respectability she needed to maintain a maximum circulation, and her lyric promiscuity achieved the proper equilibrium between the figure of the author and the erotic voice of print.

What made Osgood appealing in her time made it difficult for anyone to extract her from the medium through which she moved so that she might become an Author that could move through the ages. Osgood's diffusion into her medium – contemporary critics note that she let her work run wild and uncollected through the magazines – helps to explain why her reputation was ephemeral. According to Poe, "Mrs. Osgood has taken no care whatever of her literary fame. A great number of her finest compositions, both in verse and prose, have been written anonymously, and are now lying *perdus* about the country" (*ER* 1188). But her twentieth-century disappearance may also be attributed to the legacy of Poe's strategies in the *Broadway Journal* exchange. In his childhood memoirs, Henry James challenges the "legend of the native neglect" of Poe by conjuring recollections of "forever mounting on little platforms at our infant schools to 'speak' The Raven and Lenore," and of visiting a neighbor at Christmastime, where I admired over the chimney-piece the full-length portrait of a lady seated on the ground in a Turkish dress, with hair flowing loose from a cap which was not as the caps of ladies known to me, and I think with a tambourine, who was somehow identified to my inquiring mind as the wife of the painter of the piece, Mr. Osgood, and the so ministering friend of the unhappy Mr. Poe. There she throned in honour, like Queen Constance on the "huge firm earth" – all for that and her tambourine; and surely we could none of us have done more for the connection.[84]

Osgood's portrait promotes the myth of Poe's allure. The remnant of her poetic legacy rests in the exotic, trivial image of the tambourine. James' portrayal of Osgood's presence supplants the memory of her lyric appeal rather than emblematizing it, as Whitman had in the 1860s. By the early nineteenth century, Osgood's function in cultural memory was to serve as "the connection" to Poe. Perhaps, then, it is appropriate that the portrait that James memorialized is actually not Osgood's at all, but her sister's.[85]

A broader dynamics of literary attribution enables James to remember numerous minor male authors decades after their deaths while lumping women into an indistinct, anonymous mass:

There were authors not less, some of them vague and female and . . . glossily ringletted and monumentally breast-pinned, but mostly frequent and familiar, after the manner of George Curtis and Parke Godwin and George Ripley and Charles Dana and N. P. Willis and, for brighter lights or those that in our then comparative obscurity almost deceived the morn, Mr. Bryant, Washington Irving and E. A. Poe – (59)

James remembers the men as bright lights and the women as a single, spectral female body, coiffed and bejeweled. While equally present in the literary scene, the "vague and female" authors serve as the amorphous atmosphere in which to articulate men's names, the list culminating with "E. A. Poe."

Poe's editorial experiments enforced an equation between the body of the poetess and the printed poem so that the poetess might serve as a medium for his lyric forms. His perverse literalism confirms that, like the work of actresses and singers, Osgood's poetry relied upon a fantasy of her living presence difficult to sustain after the death of the poetess. Ultimately, the close identification of the poetess with print media allowed not only for a corporeal understanding of her words, but also for the migration of poetic traits to her body. Marking his ambivalent relation to the seductive work of the poetess, Poe memorialized the process of forgetting Osgood in the act of paying tribute to her. Following his lead, critics have read Osgood's promiscuous poetics, or their historical resonance, as her literal body. Their participation in Poe's fantasy of female containment counters fears of female print proliferation. These impressionable fantasies, or fantasies of impression, help submerge the poetess in the antebellum sea of print, but they also testify to Osgood's continuing influence, important but unnamed.

CHAPTER 3

Sarah Helen Whitman, Spiritualist Poetics, and the "phantom voice" of Poe[1]

On November 19, 1875, George Eveleth, a Maine physician and literature buff, queried Sarah Helen Whitman about a spirit novel's authenticity:

I will ask you if you have read *the second part* of *Edwin Drood*, said to have been dictated by the spirit of Dickens through a Massachusetts medium? *I* have not met with it, but I have seen notices of it; and I have taken due account of the fact that the believers in spiritualism speak of its general manner as being almost identical with that of Dickens in the flesh; while, on the other hand, the *un*believers declare it a very bungling attempt (of an ignoramus) at an imitation. What say you?[2]

For Eveleth, convictions about the limits of identity so inform aesthetic evaluation that a circular logic is inescapable. Those who believe that identity is not constrained by corporeal boundaries entertain the possibility that a medium from Massachusetts might carry on Dickens' work. "Believers" take stylistic resemblance as proof of spirit visitation and predicate individual immortality on emulation. Dickens stays alive by circulating through others; his particularity endures through its replications. Those who think that the mind stops where the body ends, on the other hand, enforce a distinction between true genius and its pretenders; "*un*believers" take stylistic discrepancy as proof of the second-comer's inadequacy. The unbelievers predicate Dickens' longevity on his death; because his greatness cannot be reproduced, it must be preserved. In both cases, the aesthetic evaluation is a foregone conclusion, based on the reader's position on spirit visitation. Eveleth's intertwined questions about literary merit, the limits of individual consciousness, and the impact of critical ideology on aesthetic evaluation remain relevant in the study of American literary history, which is informed in crucial, yet unexplored ways by debates in his time.

Eveleth asked for Whitman's expert advice as a notable poet, but more importantly as a well-known spiritualist who believed in mental "telegraphy." Whitman actively valued poetic "echoes" as a sign of spirit visitation. An influential early defender of Poe, Whitman praised his poetry not for its originality but for its signs of ghostly inhabitance: "His mind was indeed a 'Haunted Palace,' echoing to the footfalls of angels and demons" (*EPC* 80). Her own elegies to Poe are haunted by "the echo of a harp whose tones / I never more may hear!" (*SHWP* 83). Her reiteration of Poe's "nevermore" – a ubiquitous word in the romantic period that Poe made his own through particularly insistent repetition – repeats his speaker's expression of sorrow over the lost Lenore in order to position herself as Poe's privileged mourner. Countering a model of lyric that prizes individual innovation, Whitman, along with other spiritualist poets, practiced mimicry as a mode of mystical affinity and spiritual communion.

Theories of spirit visitation bear a striking resemblance to romantic theories of inspiration, which claim that a broader power – nature, divinity, or "the people" – exerts an expansive influence on the poet's mind.[3] When Walt Whitman, for example, insists that "a bard is to be commensurate with a people," he not only stresses that he must be a man among men, but also that he must be able to "contain multitudes": a single bard should be equal to and exchangeable for the people he represents.[4] Or, as Mark Maslan puts it, "Although Whitman sees the common people as the source of democratic authority, he also believes that only representative mediation can realize that authority."[5] By absorbing what absorbs him, the American bard also "masters" what claims him: "His trust shall master the trust of everything he touches . . . and shall master all attachment."[6] Because he owns his experience of possession, the American bard's mediumship accrues to his name.

While Walt Whitman claimed mediumistic powers for the American bard, poet-mediums made a different bid for representative status. Mediums were possessed by visiting spirits without possessing them; therefore they were not considered to be the authors of the information they conveyed. Moreover, if Walt Whitman's bard could channel massive entities like "the people," poet-mediums claimed access only to particular writers – usually men – who had already proven their capacity for generalized inspiration. Though I mark a distinction for the sake of clarity, the relation between these two models – the first gendered masculine, the second feminine – is transactional. The exchanges between Poe and Whitman, and after Poe's death between Whitman and his fans and critics, offer an occasion to explore the mutually informing relation between romantic and spiritualist traditions of lyric inspiration.

Through their public romance, Poe and Whitman cultivated fantasies that lyric poetry enabled like minds to meet and mingle. The poems they exchanged in newspapers and magazines stressed spiritual twinship and formally registered this theme by blending signature traits of both authors: reciprocal mimicry signaled spiritual affinity. Extending this process of lyric mind-reading after Poe's death, Whitman forged an echoic poetry haunted by his ghost that reflected their initial mirroring practices. She and other spiritualist poets, primarily women, built a lyric telegraph whereby they could communicate with the dead poet and with others in his name. These networks served social processes of composing interiority. Lyric poetry functioned as the "inner life" itself, composed and held in common, its well-defined formal limits imitating the boundaries of the self-enclosed individual. In showcasing collective modes of poetic generation, Whitman and her circle promoted the myth of Poe's original genius. Their contributions have been obscured, however, because men converted women's spiritual revival of Poe into their critical biographies and literary studies by the end of the nineteenth century.

Whitman's work, like Osgood's, depends upon an understanding that the poetess personifies her medium of circulation. But whereas Osgood explored the erotics of female disembodiment in lyric form, Whitman sought to embody and transmit the spirit in the letter. If the poetics of sexual communion staged evacuations of corporeal presence, the poetics of spiritual communion offered the poem as material proof of spirit visitation. The divergence in practices cultivated different models of lyric reception. By figuring her reception as a series of anonymous, indiscriminate sexual encounters, Osgood advocated the maintenance of maximum circulation. Her public intimacy with Poe served as a dramatic counterpoint to her general print promiscuity. Whitman enforced exclusivity from the outset of her exchange with Poe, which she cast as a mystical, predestined encounter between two individuals with superior mental powers. Whereas Osgood stressed the inclusive elasticity of the coterie model of public lyric exchange, Whitman deployed Poe in public as a sign of intimate exchange among a circle of privileged insiders. Her poetic practice enforced distinctions between those who possessed secret knowledge and a larger circle of readers who looked on in mystified fascination.

POE'S HELEN, HELEN'S POE

Like Osgood, Whitman had earned a reputation as a fascinating literary figure long before she met Poe. By 1838, Sarah Josepha Hale, who had requested a year-long contract with Whitman for monthly poetic contributions to the *Ladies' Magazine* as early as 1829, named her, along with Felicia Hemans, as "one of the luminous stars of the poetic heavens"(quoted in

SP 108). An established poet by the 1840s, Whitman's verses were published in leading literary journals throughout her life and earned acclaim from such prestigious critics as George William Curtis and George Ripley (*SHWP* ix–xii). She also won respect as well as occasional criticism for her skilled philosophical reasoning and her willingness to participate in controversial debate. Her 1845 essay on Emerson, published in the *Democratic Review* with the by-line "By a disciple," caused Emerson to ask who the author was, and Thoreau to comment that it was not written "by a disciple in any ordinary sense"; George William Curtis wrote her that "it finds more of a system of philosophy than I think he [Emerson] is conscious of" (*SP* 200). Her review of Margaret Fuller's translation of Goethe (the two women were perhaps the leading female German experts in the country at the time) provoked Orestes Brownson to offer Whitman equal share of the profits of the editorial chair of the *Boston Quarterly* if she would write an article for every number (*EAP* 347; *SP* 218–219). An early supporter of the women's suffrage movement, Whitman wrote articles and poems in support of women's rights and became one of the vice presidents of the state suffrage association upon its formation in 1868 (*SP* 600). Her essays on various subjects – Shelley's unbelief, the whipping of tramps, the right of organ grinders to play in the streets, her European travels – were published regularly in *The Providence Journal* for many years (*SP* 218–219). She was also a valuable proponent of Modern Spiritualism, a popular, though controversial, religious and social movement. Fellow believers found Whitman's rational eloquence the perfect medium for a profession of faith, for it rendered the movement less easily dismissible.[7] Her correspondence provides a powerful impression of her influence on writers and intellectuals of a younger generation, including George William Curtis, John Hay, Louise Chandler Moulton, and W. D. O'Connor (Brown).

One of the most prominent American female intellectuals of her time, a highly respected literary critic, journalist, and poet, Whitman remains familiar today largely through her brief romance with Poe and as the inspiration of his second poem "To Helen" (*CWP* 441–448). While her cameo role in Poe's career has overshadowed Whitman's many accomplishments, she herself cultivated the terms in which she would be remembered, working hard to link her name with his in the public mind. Though their brief engagement collapsed before Poe's death; though Poe was engaged to at least one other woman (Elmira Shelton) and showed romantic interest of equal intensity in others (especially Nancy "Annie" Richmond and Fanny Osgood); though he wrote poems to other women after the death of his wife Virginia ("To Annie," "To M.L.S."), Sarah Helen Whitman alone is delivered to us across the ages packaged as Poe's possession. She is "Poe's Helen" largely because of her tremendous commitment to Poe's memory after his death. She worked to secure his place among the ranks of immortal geniuses through her extensive aid to almost every major and minor Poe biographer, most significantly John Henry Ingram, and through her own crucial work, *Edgar Poe and His Critics*, an early, influential defense of Poe against the slanderous attacks of his literary executor, Rufus Griswold.[8] Her prose defense and her poetic tributes – many of them composed and published after Poe's death – romanticized the relationship for a wide audience. A prominent spiritualist, Whitman publicly cultivated the fantasy that she was in contact with Poe's spirit after his death and that she and Poe would be united in a heavenly marriage rooted in spiritual and aesthetic twinship. To literary enthusiasts of the nineteenth century, her posthumous marriage was at least a mythic reality. Becoming Poe's Helen allowed Whitman to create Helen's Poe, an influential precursor of today's Poe, even if the icon's proprietor goes unnamed.

Even during her lifetime Whitman was a sacred figure for Poe worshippers. W. D. O'Connor, champion of Walt Whitman and author of *The Good Gray Poet*, showed her his Poe-inspired verses when he was young, hoping that she would confirm his vocation as a poet (*SP* 601). Girls and young ladies fascinated with Whitman's romantic relationship with Poe wanted to glean her first-hand knowledge.[9] They may have even wished to meet his spirit; his portrait presided over the seances that Whitman, dressed in black, with a tiny wooden coffin strung around her neck, conducted in her parlor on Saturday and Sunday evenings (fig. 13).[10] William Whitman Bailey (no relation) recalls in a memoir that Whitman "took utmost comfort in the communications of spirits, Edgar Poe and others, and promised if possible after death to reveal herself to me."[11] Mallarmé corresponded with her and sent her his translation of "The Raven" ("Le Corbeau") with the words, "Whatever is done to honor the memory of a genius the most truly divine the world has ever seen, ought it not at first to obtain your approval?" (quoted in *PH* 262). Around the memory of Poe orbited Whitman's well-known talents. As a poet, she wrote about him; as a literary critic, she defended him; as a spiritualist, she sought to communicate with him.

During their courtship, Whitman and Poe embodied their ethereal connection in a shared language of psychic rapport, which emerged from a mutual interest in the occult. Although their attitudes towards their objects of study diverged – one professed belief, the other skepticism – both were pioneer "investigators" of telepathy, transubstantiation, metempsychosis, and other forms of trans-identic experience. Before meeting each other

Fig. 13: Photograph depicting Sarah Helen Whitman as a medium. Inserted in Sarah Helen Whitman, *Hours of Life and Other Poems* (Providence: G. H. Whitney, 1853).

personally, they shared ties with prominent thinkers who were crucial to the rise of the Spiritualist movement in the 1850s. Andrew Jackson Davis, the "Poughkeepsie Seer," who claimed to be in communication with the spirit of Swedenborg, visited Whitman in Providence as early as 1845, and the two of them attended "the first effort to obtain manifestations in Providence" in September 1850. Poe visited Davis while conducting research for his mesmeric stories.[12] Robert Collyer, who made advances in anesthesiology through his experiments in mesmerism, and who credited Whitman for his introduction to animal magnetism, was also acquainted with Poe (*SP* 267). Poe also knew George Bush, the scholar of Hebrew and leading expert on Swedenborg who wrote to Whitman in 1847 that Andrew Jackson Davis was "the most astonishing prodigy the world has ever seen next to Swedenborg's oracles."[13] This common ground set the terms for the mystic language that the pair used during their courtship and that Whitman crafted into a poetic system of elegiac longing after Poe's death.

Whitman initiated communications conceived in telepathic terms with a valentine addressed to Poe that she included among those she and her sister wrote for Anne Lynch's party in February, 1848, attended by N. P. Willis, Margaret Fuller, Bayard Taylor, Grace Greenwood, Catherine Sedgwick, and Horace Greeley. Sending poetic representatives, the sisters did not attend, nor did Poe, who had not been invited because he had fallen out with the group. Poe had the opportunity to read the valentine, however, when it was published, apparently with Whitman's encouragement, in Willis' *Home Journal* on March 18.[14]

Drawing on Poe's own poetic intimations that he possessed supernatural powers, Whitman's speaker touts his ability to perform acts of transubstantiation whereby his spirit inhabits and enlivens his artistic creations. Incarnated as his Raven, Poe haunts the speaker's bedroom. Though he had not yet died, the speaker welcomes him back from the land of the dead as a sinister, vampiric lover:

> Oh! thou grim and ancient Raven,
> From the Night's Plutonian shore,
> Oft in dreams, thy ghastly pinions
> Wave and flutter round my door –
> Oft thy shadow dims the moonlight
> Sleeping on my chamber floor!
>> (quoted in *PH* 45)

Ventriloquizing Poe's gentleman speaker, a genteel lady envisions a seductive visit from the poet. Whitman's speaker performs her preoccupation with

Poe as a spiritual occupation of form. The metrical and sonic echoes of "The Raven" – in its book publication the poem even gained Poe's title, identical but for quotation marks – demonstrate Poe's haunting of the speaker's fantasies even while the poem takes spirit visitation as its subject. Whitman's mimicry signals affinity rather than inferiority, just as Poe's "The Raven" marks its affiliation with Elizabeth Barrett's "Lady Geraldine's Courtship," a fact Whitman would have been quick to notice, since Barrett was one of her favorite poets.

Her poem establishes a telegraphic system of communication whereby the poets pay spirit visits to each other's poetic worlds. Touring Poe's wonders, Whitman's speaker tells how he colonized her fantasies with the help of figures – the Raven, the Gold Bug, Lenore – that mediate between the land of the dead and the land of the living, coded in her mythology as Poe's and her own, respectively. Demonstrating her power to infiltrate and extend his dreamland, the speaker wanders on "Night's Plutonian shore," a place named but never shown in Poe's "The Raven":

> Oft like Proserpine I wander
> On the Night's Plutonian Shore
> Hoping, fearing, while I ponder
> On thy loved and lost Lenore,
> Till thy voice like distant thunder
> Sounds across the distant moor.
>
> *(PH* 45)

She casts Poe as both the Raven, messenger from the underworld, and as Pluto, its King. Her speaker is a would-be Proserpine, hoping to be plucked from her garden of flowers – the poetic landscape of an earlier phase of Whitman's writing – to be Pluto's queen. She tries out for the part by wandering on Night's Plutonian shore, pondering on Poe's Lenore (whom she equates with Proserpine), and hoping that a process of transubstantiation will install her in Lenore's place in Poe's mythology. She assumes that Poe's love is predicated upon a previous loss and, implicitly diagnosing him as a melancholic (as many have done since), she makes a bid to replace the original love object by growing to resemble it through dwelling upon it.[15] By equating Poe's Lenore with her Proserpine, and his Raven with her Pluto, Whitman creates a system of correspondences between their mythic realms that builds a bridge between Poe's work and her own.

Her valentine succeeded in invoking Poe's "voice" more clearly than "distant thunder." When Lynch sent him a copy, he responded by sending

Whitman his first poem "To Helen" on March 2 (*PL* 727–728). In June he sent her his second "To Helen," which was supposedly inspired by glimpsing her in her moonlit rose garden years earlier (*PL* 736).[16] Returning her visit to his "Plutonian shore" and confirming the permeability of the boundary between their imaginations, Poe's speaker enters Whitman's poetic garden. Finding her in a reverie among "the upturn'd faces of the roses," he is enchanted by an image familiar from Whitman's poetry of a solitary poetess pining among "the ungathered roses of our youth, / Pierced with strange pangs and longings infinite."[17] Crafting himself to fit the role of Whitman's fantasy companion, Poe answers her plea for mystic communion, attributing their meeting to "Fate (whose name is also Sorrow[.])" (*CWP* 445; 22).

Building on the mystical ideas set forth in Whitman's valentine, Poe's poem and his accompanying commentary suggest that people of like minds visit each other's dreams, and that fictional constructs channel the spirits of their human counterparts. Poe writes that the poem "contained all the events of *a dream* which occurred to me soon after I knew you . . . Ligeia was also suggested by a dream. Observe the eyes in both tale and poem" (*CWP* 444). According to Whitman, a message that Poe wrote on the manuscript copy (now lost) continues: "I regard these visions even as they arise, with an awe which in some measure moderates or tranquilizes the ecstacy – I so regard them through a conviction that this ecstacy, in itself, is of a character supernal to the human nature – is a glimpse of the spirit's outer world" (*CWP* 444). Linking his fictional women to spiritland, Poe claims that Ligeia is Whitman's supernal twin and suggests that he can establish a telegraphic connection that will translate Whitman from the terms of this world into those of the next. The mediumistic qualities of his fictional women and, at a second remove, Whitman, migrate to Poe when he offers her his services as medium for communication with other worlds.[18] His love letters to Whitman are saturated with references to mystical correspondences, coincidences, spiritual twinship, and other ideas that she took seriously and he sometimes embraced and other times ridiculed. Though in a posthumous tribute Whitman noted "how few his mystic language learned," here Poe learns Whitman's mystic language and mirrors it back to her (*SHWP* 87).

Taken as a pair, Whitman's valentine and Poe's answering poem create a tautological circuit whereby Poe dreams of Helen dreaming Poe, and Helen dreams of Poe dreaming of Helen. The mirrorlike nature of their interaction is captured in *Hours of Life*, Whitman's lyric autobiography:[19]

I heard a low voice breathe my name:
Was it the echo of my own, –
That weird and melancholy tone, –
That voice whose subtle sweetness came
Keen as the serpent's tongue of flame?
So near, its music seemed to me
The music of my heart to be.

(*SHWP* 112)

The speaker locates her seducer's appeal in his rhetorical resemblance to herself. Hearing a rendition of her own poetic music coming from outside herself creates a pleasurable sense of the uncanny, which she equates with love. The speaker compares the lover's emulation to the serpent's malevolent seduction of Eve, but even if he crafted his poetic resemblance with guile, it remains a proof of their mystic connection and holds the speaker captive "in a wild world of its own" (112).

Whitman seals this psychic fusion in "Stanzas," her response to Poe's tribute, which she published in the *Home Journal* on July 29, 1848 and afterwards sent directly to Poe (*PL* 745). The speaker demonstrates her immersion in his aesthetic principles by embedding a phrase from his poem within her own: "I dwell with 'Beauty, which is Hope' " (quoted in *PH* 52). This abstract domestic arrangement must have suggested a willingness to dwell with the poet, for the poem brought Poe to Whitman's door: gaining a letter of introduction, he went to Providence and proposed within one or two days.[20] Until that point, the two had exchanged nothing but poems. That they were more interested in dwelling together within an aesthetic realm is supported by the fact that their engagement lasted less than two months (*EAP* 388). Although she had little subsequent contact with Poe while he was alive, Whitman strengthened their mystical bond after his death, when the Spiritualist movement provided an idiom – that of spiritual telegraphy – that enabled her to develop and promote a collaborative aesthetic that centered on the solitary figure of Poe.

LYRIC TELEGRAPHY

While belief in spirits was not new, in the United States in the mid-nineteenth century it gained contours specific and fashionable enough to earn the name Modern Spiritualism. In 1849, four years after the first telegraphic message traveled instantaneously from Washington to Baltimore, the first mediums received messages from the land of the dead via the Spirit Telegraph. Maggie and Katie Fox, two girls from upstate New York, convinced their parents that disembodied raps delivered in the sisters' presence were the work of ghosts seeking to communicate. A neighbor decoded the messages according to a system of alphabetic correspondences inspired by the telegraph. This incident established the basic tenet of Modern Spiritualism, that the living may communicate with the dead through a human medium. The phenomenon received widespread publicity in November 1849, one month after Poe's death, when E. W. Capron publicly staged the Fox sisters' talents in Rochester, New York.[21] Mediums rapidly proliferated, forging a communications network through which phantom voices could speak. If Samuel B. Morse inaugurated the first telegraphic line with the words "What hath God wrought!," mediums responded literally to his query by conveying spirit messages that provided evidence of life beyond death.[22]

Discredited years later, the sisters admitted to making the mysterious sounds by cracking their toe joints.[23] The triviality of the scam, however, does not diminish the power of the religious movement it inaugurated. Historian R. Laurence Moore asserts that "scarcely another cultural phenomenon affected as many people or stimulated as much interest as did spiritualism in the ten years before the Civil War and, for that matter, through the subsequent decades of the nineteenth century."[24] In 1854, 13,000 people signed a petition asking the US Senate to appoint a scientific committee to investigate spirit communication.[25] People from all walks of life participated with varying degrees of skepticism, including many prominent writers: Harriet Beecher Stowe, Horace Greeley, Henry Wadsworth Longfellow, James Fenimore Cooper, John Greenleaf Whittier, and William Cullen Bryant were all spirit investigators.[26] In 1859 Oliver Wendell Holmes, Sr. attributed the movement's widespread influence to the respectable character of many adherents: "You cannot have people of cultivation, of pure character, sensible enough in common things, large-hearted women, grave judges, shrewd businessmen, men of science, professing to be in communication with the spiritual world and keeping up constant intercourse with it, without its gradually reacting on the whole conception of that other life."[27]

By demonstrating the empirical "fact" of spirit visitation, Modern Spiritualists hoped to secure a place for religious belief in an age that had experienced dramatic developments in science and technology.[28] Many commentators of the period, including Reverend T. W. Higginson, placed scientific empiricism and spiritualist prophecy firmly on the same continuum: "The progress of our age is remarkable for the quality of its facts. . . . What a step to steam from the brute muscle of horse! Then the imponderables – electricity, magnetism and their combinations and applications; then the discovery of a human power akin to this – a spiritual electricity – the power of man over man, of soul over soul."[29] According to Jeffrey Sconce, "American Spiritualism presented an early and most explicit intersection of technology and spirituality, of media and 'mediums.' "[30] If electricity was the force that bridged the gap between empiricism and mysticism, literati like Higginson were the apparatus through which a new version of heaven was articulated. The physical "proofs" of spirit communication were relatively banal and redundant: tables turned, raps sounded, trumpets and other musical instruments played in mid-air. Their significance lay in believers' (and skeptics') powers of interpretation. This new heaven was as potent as the words found to describe it, so it is no surprise that verbal performers – mystic writers and orators, spirit "translators" or mediums – took center-stage in the movement.

These writers challenged stark Calvinist alternatives of eternal damnation or heavenly election, which by the 1840s provoked heightened anxiety because of the increasing sense of individual responsibility in experiencing conversion. Spiritualists promoted a gradual system of Swedenborgian evolution in which everyone, retaining individual identity beyond death, ascended through a series of six spheres until they reached an idiosyncratic state of perfection (for some believers this state preceded a merger with an Absolute Identity).[31] The notion that the individual continued to evolve after death challenged Protestant doctrines of original sin, infant damnation, and Christ's saving grace.[32] Progressive social movements such as temperance, abolition, and suffrage drew strength from Spiritualism, arguing that people on earth could begin evolving in preparation for heaven. Imagining heaven in seances and in print provided both a social network and a symbolic location for collectively imagining intimate, selective, white, middle-class, often artistic or progressive communities within larger heterogeneous, anonymous communities such as the city and the nation.

Poetry's centrality to this process has rarely been noted or interpreted. Poets' ghosts were favored visitors to spirit circles: Poe, Shelley, Byron, Dante, Milton, Coleridge, Keats, Shakespeare, and Burns all made appearances. Mediums received spirits who were not poets, even Jesus Christ, speaking in rhyme.[33] Poets were mediums – the Cary sisters and Sarah Helen Whitman are prominent examples – and many mediums aspired to be poets in their own names as well as channeling the posthumous verse of others (*SP* 1–2). Achsa Sprague, a popular trance-lecturer, "spoke" her own lyric poems at an incredible rate of speed, which an amanuensis recorded.[34] Prominent mediums including Thomas Lake Harris and Lizzie

Doten published collections that contained both channeled and original verse, while their statements about poetic practice complicated the relation between these two categories.

The spiritualist notion that people retained their individuality beyond death raised the question of what form the posthumous identity assumed; the lyric poem offered an analogue for the shape humans took after shedding their "earthly garment[s]."[35] More ethereal than the human body, yet with clearly defined formal limits that mimic a bounded individual, the poem offered a celestial body that a human spirit might also occupy on earth. As "Embodied Thoughts," poetry lay claim to containing a purified identity, purged of accidental, inartistic, and organic characteristics: "the body of speech is prose, but the soul is poetry."[36] Writing in the years preceding the spiritualist movement, Poe's opus demonstrates this generic association in stark terms. His prose is dedicated to the intransigence of the material world, particularly the human body, which insists upon its physicality at the expense of the transcendent imagination, buried alive repeatedly within a corpse that cannot find a way to resurrect itself. Poe's poetry, on the other hand, explicates "Dreamland," a place where ethereal phantoms escape corporeality via symbolism. The two forms consistently allegorize their own fictional relations to language and thus their attitudes towards spirituality or materiality, causing spiritualists to imagine him as one of their mentors.[37]

Spiritualist poetry served contradictorily as both a telegraphic medium to bring heaven to its readers and writers, and a physical medium in which to create that place. Poetry's telegraphic capacities derived largely from its metrical and figurative aspects, which performed a transcendence of earthly language and offered a window to a place where celestial visions and harmonies replaced the imperfections of speech. "Heaven" inverted the status of materiality and ideality so that poetry gained the status of the real: "Poetry is a native flower of the Heavens. The language of the skies is lyrical. There thoughts are things; and the conceptions of the mind start before the vision into objective loveliness."[38] While earthly poetry intimated its heavenly ideal, however, it paled in relation to the luminous otherworld of living metaphor because it still relied on the physicality of printed letters on the page, or words from a human mouth. Describing his tour of Heaven with Dante, one of a host of "Lyric Angels," Thomas Lake Harris says that "the lovely regions" of this "ethereal abode" were "visited by the inmost spirit of the medium, and shadowed in the Poem."[39] Because the printed and spoken word have physical components, spirits demonstrated their purity by proving their independence from the material constraints of the poem; spirit voices traveled from one poem to another, or multiple voices occupied a single poem.[40]

Women's prominent engagement with spiritualist poetic practices is not surprising, considering that both mediumship and poetry-writing were identified with a "feminine" sensibility, characterized by a receptivity to outside influences. Soon after magazines began soliciting the contributions of poetesses, women, traditionally denied ministerial positions in institutionalized religions, were blessed with the powers of spirit mediumship.[41] In *History of Woman Suffrage*, Elizabeth Cady Stanton and Susan B. Anthony proclaimed that "the only religious sect that has recognized the equality of women is the Spiritualists."[42] Just as anthologist Caroline May remarked that poetry "has been freely employed among us to express the emotions of woman's heart," medium Cora Wilburn welcomed spirit communication "in the pervasive accents of inspired woman's tongue."[43] Other commentators distinguished between the feminine and the female in spirit communication, explaining that receptivity was the key to success: "the medium may be man or woman – woman or man – but in either case, the characteristics will be negative and passive."[44] These characteristics enabled "poetesses" to register and transmit beauty and mediums to transcribe spirits' dictations. On this assumption, feminist historian Ann Braude argues that mediumship gave women the license to speak in public only because they remained unconscious of their own volition.[45] In all their complex relations, both "passive" feminine values and women themselves were central to antebellum poetic production and mediumship, making spiritualist poetry a doubly feminine form.

While a form so thoroughly saturated with femininity would seem to connote an extreme weakening or loss of agency, poet-mediums made claims for both the originality of receptivity and the individuality of the spirit-medium. Retaining the category of volition, mediums conceived of meaning as the product of a transaction between two or more souls. The preface to *Asphodels* casts "healing medium" Sarah Gould as a translator while also insisting on her "Originality"; spirits re-present visual performances composed of symbolic gestures "whose right interpretation and rendering into current English, depend entirely upon the seer."[46] Gould's vision "seems to be the vagueness of poetical faculty elevated to the distinctness of actual sight. The language, rhythm, structure, and entire machinery of the expression, are as completely the speaker's as in the case of any author" (vi). The sensory basis of the encounters leaves the idea's origin indeterminable: "The ideas themselves, if ever pre-existent in the mind of another, and presented by a definite intention, are so presented through objects of the natural sense, symbols never preconcerted, that it demands as keen a perception to catch the meaning, as that by which ordinary poetry is made to interpret nature to the common mind" (vii). Gaining the status of natural objects, "ideas themselves" lose their associations with origin or ownership. Gould's verbal translation of her sensory perception of ideas makes her as innovative as any author, but it also makes all authors mediums of ideas that belong to no one in particular.

Trance speaker Lizzie Doten similarly declares that under the influence of "disembodied intelligences," "I have not necessarily lost my individuality, or become wholly unconscious." (*PIL* xii). She characterizes her mediumistic poetry as a cooperative effort between herself and the spirits:

I claim both a general and a particular inspiration. They do not, by any means, conflict. . . . For the very reason that I have natural poetic tendencies, I attract influences of a kindred nature. . . . It is often as difficult to decide what is the action of one's own intellect and what is the spirit-influence, as it is in our ordinary associations to determine what is original with ourselves and what we have received from circumstances or contact with the mind of others. (xi)

Because continuity between spirit and medium marks the act of poetic generation, attribution is both impossible to establish and irrelevant. Like-minded spirits validate Doten's "natural poetic tendencies" by choosing to communicate through her. While retaining the category of individual volition, she and other mediums conceived of meaning as a transaction between souls rather than an occurrence within a single consciousness.

Doten emphasized that lyric telegraphy likened minds to each other, forging bonds of sympathy. Configured as a linguistic rather than a corpo-real entity, the channeled spirit was both circulable and duplicable. Poet-mediums substantiated visits by reproducing the dead poets' stylistic ele-ments in new poems: Doten "translated" sonnets from the dead Shakespeare and Scottish dialect poems from the dead Burns ("For A' That," "Words O' Cheer"). An author's signature style conveyed to its human conduit the per-sonality contained within its contours, which the medium both absorbed and responded to. Doten claimed that Shakespeare's majestic influence "seemed to crush and overwhelm"; Burns' was "pleasant, easy and exhila-rating, and left me in a cheerful mood"; and Poe's "was neither pleasant nor easy. I can only describe it as a species of mental intoxication" (xx–xxii). Entertaining Poe, "I suffered the greatest exhaustion of vital energy, so much so, that after giving one of his poems, I was usually quite ill for several days" (xx–xxii). Doten absorbed his tell-tale metrics so convincingly that the *Springfield Republican* proclaimed "Resurrexi," "A Remarkable Poem": while "Miss Doten is, apparently, incapable of originating such a poem," "the poem is, nonetheless, wonderful as a reproduction of the singular music and alliteration of Poe's style, and as manifesting the same intensity of feeling" (quoted in *PIL* 104). Though equally cynical about the poem's otherworldly origins and Doten's reproductive capabilities, the critic agreed that "whoever wrote the poem must have been exceedingly familiar with Poe, and deeply in sympathy with his spirit." This accusation of plagiarism echoes the structure of spiritualist belief, for Doten herself claimed to be both the poem's author and its copier. The critic only substitutes someone else for Doten: "sympathy with spirit" is thus a secular synonym for spiritual telegraphy.

Instead of "suffer[ing] from a multiple personality disorder that precludes the development of a genuine poetic voice," as Shawn Rosenheim asserts, Doten challenges the very distinction between individual genius and collective identity that underpins such a diagnosis.[47] She imagined the poem as an internalized parlor for conversations among souls: "I have given to this work the title of *Poems From the Inner Life*; for . . . I have realized that in the mysterious depths of the Inner Life, all souls can hold communion with these invisible beings, who are our companions both in Time and Eternity" (*PIL* v–vi). Rather than a place of individual isolation, the Inner Life is a social utopia characterized by perfect understanding, a "Heaven within," for which the poem is an external marker (vi).

Doten's formulation raises questions about how to read poems spoken from two different perspectives simultaneously, a structure I will call the doubled lyric voice. Yopie Prins explores the question of a multiply constituted lyric voice by reading the Sapphic poetry of Katherine Bradley and Edith Cooper, who published jointly under the name of Michael Field. Prins characterizes their collaborative project as a "perfect mosaic of textual fragments rather than a living voice."[48] In spiritualist poetry, the living speaker performed her compatibility with the dead by overdubbing the spirit visitor's voice. The dead and the living exchange places: the spectral voice of the medium haunts the literal voice of the visiting spirit. Participants in the exchange – mediums, seance attendants, readers of published spirit verse – simultaneously imagined the living in the position of the phantom dead and the dead resurrected and embodied in linguistic form. Doten and Poe stand in this relation in a posthumous communication delivered in the style of his "Ulalume": "And there, as I shivered and waited, / I talked with the Souls of the Dead – / With those who the living call dead" (*PIL* 118).

Doten evokes a recurrent scenario from Poe's fiction in which the narrator tries to communicate across life's threshold; now that he is dead, Poe talks to souls with ease. His message doubles as the medium's description of her spirit conversations while waiting for Poe's spirit to arrive. By occupying his speaking position, Doten showcases her affinity with Poe and claims access to otherworldly powers. Her "phantom voice," which haunts his utterance, underscores the process by which textual signs project a ghostly subjectivity.

Retaining the magic properties of their birth, mediumistic poems converted readers into friends by establishing "spiritual rapport." The poems served as ambassadors of affection, extending the principle of private conversation outwards, forming communities of intimacy. Sarah Gould's preface describes the process whereby her "spontaneous effusions of the heart" emerge within a "friendly circle" of seance participants, which expands when the poems are published. Prolonging their unusually assertive beginnings, when they arose fully formed from the medium's trance state, the animated poems "select, by sympathy, a broader circle of friends, which, retaining something of the sanctity of personal relations, will be but a broader privacy."[49] The preface foregrounds the mimetic relation between the context of poetic generation and the poem's capacity to inspire spiritual communion with anyone it meets.

By literalizing poetic inspiration, spiritualist poets revised the romantic paradox that the most original poets are those who claim access to an extrapersonal power that descends in a lineage from earlier poetic geniuses. Susan Stewart discusses the "paradox of willed possession" in "romantic genius theory," using the example of Wimsatt and Beardsley: "In every case the claim of mastery relies upon an underlying claim of inspiration that from the outset will undermine intended consequences."[50] She constructs a "different picture of poetic-making" by exploring the ways in which earlier poetic structures "haunt" later poems. Claiming that the poetic unconscious is as important as authorial will, Stewart presents a case for a "conflicted – rather than unified – subjectivity" (37). While both romantic genius theory and Stewart's revision center on a single lyric subjectivity, however, spiritualist practices posit a more fluid relation between possessor and possessed, foregrounding the precursor's voice and arguing that the second-comer's imitative capabilities, rather than her innovations, make her notable. The spiritualist aesthetic valorizes what antebellum readers might call a "feminine" or what Harold Bloom might call a "weak" poetics, which blurs the distinction between poet and precursor, individual psychology and intersubjectivity. Governed by metaphors of translation and telegraphy rather than possession or origination, the spiritualist aesthetic values secondary, echoic utterances as the most profound and universal. According to this logic, if the greatest poets are great mediums, then the greatest mediums are great poets, since they entertain spirit visits from multiple geniuses who choose their posthumous representatives on the basis of affinity.[51] Steeped in femininity, spiritualist poetry defines an aesthetic characterized by "sympathy of spirit," an evaluative term for the conflation of the medium with her message. In the process, it offers an important commentary both on critical definitions of original genius as the basis of poetic achievement, as well as recent critiques of genius, originality, and literary authority. An analysis of the posthumous circulation of Poe's spirit voice within a community of women poets helps develop such a commentary.

POE'S "PHANTOM VOICE"

Soon after Poe's death in 1849 he began to make posthumous appearances in print. In a letter to the *New York Tribune* on March 26, 1851, Sarah Helen Whitman claimed that he initiated communications within twenty-four hours of his death. As if to encourage her publication of the event, his raps kept Whitman company as she wrote: "Even now, while I am writing to you, I hear a succession of slight sounds, which seem to proceed from the center of a table which stands at the distance of four or five feet from the desk at which I am seated." Thomas Lake Harris received poems transmitted by the dead Poe in the mid-1850s (*SP* 463). Later, Sarah Gould and Lizzie Doten also published his posthumous communications. Poe's friend Thomas Holly Chivers was disgruntled when the medium Lydia Tenney attempted to add "Message from the Spirit of Edgar A. Poe" to Poe's collected works, not because such messages were impossible, but because Poe "had done nothing like it while alive, and . . . his spirit would never stoop to plagiarizing such bad lines."[52]

Because Poe cultivated telegraphic capabilities during his lifetime, particularly with respect to women poets, he became a medium, in the dual sense of mystical conduit and artist's materials, for female poet-mediums after his death. In 1864 Lizzie Doten proclaimed Poe, already dead for fifteen years, a colleague:

Edgar A. Poe was a medium. "A medium!" you say. "He himself would scorn the name; and we, who knew him, deny it". . . . He was a medium for the general inspiration that sets like a current of living fire through the universe. No special, no individual spirit wrought directly upon him, but he felt the might and majesty of occult forces from the world of causes, and trembled beneath their influence. (*PIL* 145)

According to Doten, Poe does not achieve the status of pre-eminent medium by virtue of his originality. To the contrary, precisely because his poems are void of particularity, "Poe" becomes the name for "general inspiration," which mediums seek to harness by replicating his formal structures. Rather than a creator, Poe was conceived as a poetic transmitter that, according to Sarah Helen Whitman, conveyed early reports of "Shadow-Land, which, through a class of phenomena unprecedented in the world's history, was about to attest itself as an actual plane of conscious and progressive life."[53]

The number of women poets claiming Poe as an inspiration of varying degrees of literal presence – ranging from muse to visiting spirit – confirms his significance as a source of female inspiration. Although Thomas Lake Harris first entertained Poe's spirit, Lizzie Doten soon intercepted communications and claimed to have established a better connection. She recorded Poe's first visit in "Resurrexi," in which he justifies his shift in venue by arguing for the superiority of the feminine vessel. His preference for Doten reflects his progress in the afterlife. The spirit Poe contrasts his domination of Harris with his collaboration with Doten:

> Once before I found a mortal
> Waiting at the heavenly portal –
> Waiting but to catch an echo from that ever-opening door;
> Then I seized his quickened being,
> And through all his inward seeing,
> Caused my burning inspiration in a fiery flood to pour!
>
> Now I come more meekly human,
> And the weak lips of a woman
> Touch with fire from off the altar, not with burnings as of yore;
> But in holy love descending,
> With her chastened being blending,
> I would fill your souls with music from the bright celestial shore.
>
> (*PIL* 105)

"Poe" casts his visit to Harris as a rape that manifests the untempered violence of his overly passionate nature. His peaceful, cooperative visit to Doten marks his spiritual evolution, cast in terms of feminization. "Blending" with Doten's "chastened being" and speaking with "the weak lips of a woman" fosters his religious conversion. The shift from a fiery and forceful invasion to holy love's descent suggests that Poe has evolved from a satanic figure into one that resembles or represents Jesus Christ.

The exemplar of an individual damned under the old system, Poe's emotional sensitivity towards women while he was alive ripened him for redemption under the newly feminized religious outlook. Poe implicitly pleaded for female aid by dramatizing his doomed condition in poems like "Israfel," in which the flawed poet longs to become a lyric angel, or "The Raven," in which the speaker remains forever in the shadow of his loss of Lenore. Answering his plea, spirit-mediums reported his posthumous transformation from the troubled earth-being ravaged by sin – he started off by all accounts in the lowest "sphere," still indulging in his crippling earthly behaviors, including heavy drinking – into an inversion of himself that espouses the spiritualists' optimistic vision of heaven as a place where every sinner may become a luminous angel. As Doten "translates" Poe's posthumous revision of "The Raven": "And my soul from out that shadow / Hath been lifted Evermore!" (*PIL* frontispiece). Poe's pioneer journey mapped out the posthumous landscape, simultaneously shaping and proving its existence. While they recuperated Poe's tarnished image and perpetuated his memory, spiritualist poets gained the sanction of a "genius" whose opinion was rendered further unassailable through his otherworldly ascension; Alfred Russell Wallace said that Doten's renditions of Poe's poems were "finer and deeper and grander . . . than any written by him in the earth-life."[54] In a reciprocal dynamic, mediums helped Poe gain a foothold in the realm of immortal fame, while his visitations lent credentials to mediumistic literary performances.

"TWIN STARS"

In contrast to Doten's collegial relationship with the posthumous Poe, Sarah Helen Whitman emphasized her exclusive romantic connection. The fiction of lyric telegraphy forged during their courtship provided Whitman with a personal channel for communication after Poe's translation to the other side. Her engagements with a single spirit lover diverged from the practices of Doten and other poet-mediums who based their professional reputations upon their versatility and entertained a wider circle of visitors. Whereas Doten drew upon Poe's posthumous authority to preach spiritualist gospel, Whitman circulated Poe as a kind of calling card to forge intimate communities on the model of a salon gathering.

This process began before Poe's death, when Whitman published "Our Island of Dreams" in the *American Metropolitan* after the rupture of their engagement. She wrote to John Ingram that she published the poem because she "had not dared to answer" personally a letter Poe had written, and the lines were "so eloquent of all that I would have wished to express" (*PHR* 35). The poem begins with the female speaker's plea to her readership to convey a message to her ex-lover who has fled from the island where she remains:

"Tell him I lingered alone on the shore / Where we parted, in sorrow, to meet never more" (*SHWP* 76). As in other phases of the poetic courtship, the readership of "Our Island of Dreams" stands in a curious relation to the designated recipient of the poem's message, as if communication between Whitman and Poe depended upon the participation of a sympathetic audience, or as if Poe were a conduit for the communication that Whitman wished to initiate with a larger readership, whose fantasies promoted their reputations.

Surrounded by waves that "ever murmur" variations of Poe's word, ("no more, never more") the speaker suggests that his evacuation from the mutually created space – "Our Island of Dreams" – allows her to fill his absence with a nostalgic reverie of longing. Though she has sole possession, she figures the island as a personal repository of shared poetic discourse. The word "nevermore" was ubiquitous long before Poe embedded it within a metrical scheme with sticking power. By repeating a common word over and over again in a literally unforgettable and imitable poem, Poe inscribed his name in readers' memories. Whitman attached her own reputation to the word by evoking it to mourn the end of her relationship with Poe, reminding readers of her fidelity while advertising him as her unforgettable love (her "Lenore"). A common predicament, Poe's "nevermore" sticking in the reader's mind, took on a specific, personal meaning when Whitman claimed it because she cultivated an internally consistent autobiographical mythology in her poetry that centered on her relationship with Poe.

Though "nevermore" resonates with a death knell to their particular relationship (and later to Poe himself), Whitman claimed that she wrote the poem "four or five years before for an Italian gentleman to accompany a wild, monotonous, dirge-like air which he had composed for the guitar" (*PHR* 35). This estimate places the poem's date of composition *before* the publication of "The Raven." Given the echoic quality of Whitman's poem, the story seems somewhat unlikely, but it makes her the creator of a Raven-like resonance which "The Raven" then imitates unknowingly, since "Our Island" was published after "The Raven," though it may have been written before. The unconscious imitation posited in Whitman's tale of composition, by Poe of Whitman, by Whitman of Poe, by the poem of the situation, invests each participant with a telepathic, premonitory perception. The idea that she had written her poem before she knew Poe, and that it nevertheless accurately recorded the current mood and circumstance, signaled for Whitman the prophetic qualities of lyric itself and the presence of a guiding hand. She recounted that discovering the unpublished verses among her manuscripts "was an indication of what Macbeth calls 'fate and metaphysical aid.'"[55]

Publicly uniting their reputations after Poe's death, Whitman staged posthumous marriage ceremonies in her poetry that prepared for their heavenly reunion. Retaining continuity from poem to poem, her lyric speaker leads a poetic life that parallels Poe's passage to spiritual rebirth. In *Hours of Life*, she prepares for resurrection by burying her living heart in Poe's "narrow casket" (*SHWP* 112). In the fifth sonnet of the cycle to Poe, she encases her image within her tomblike poem, lily at her breast, a sleeping beauty awaiting an awakening kiss:

> Where stately, storied cenotaphs inurn
> Sweet human hopes, too fair on earth to bloom, –
> Was the bud reaped, whose petals, pure and cold,
> Sleep on my heart till Heaven the flower unfold.
>
> (*SHWP* 94)

The "stately, storied cenotaphs" evoke both graveyard tombs and Whitman's sonnets, markers of poetic possibility that "inurn" "human hopes" and foreshadow spiritual rebirth. Imagining her death in terms of poetic composition rather than physical decomposition, Whitman scripts and re-scripts the "sad dawn of love in realms of death revealed." The live burial motif sets the stage for a joint resurrection that places Poe in spiritland and Whitman in the center of a spiritualist poetic practice.

Whitman's speakers foreground the cooperative nature of the aesthetic that enables joint resurrection. In "Resurgemus," for example, the speaker enacts a ceremony with Catholic overtones that borders on the Satanic – part wedding, part funeral, part profane worship – in which the speaker walks down "cloistral aisles" over "solemn sounding graves" in a cathedral setting until, "kneeling by a lampless shrine," she consecrates her devotion to "Poe":

> My erring spirit pleads for thine
> Till light along the Orient blooms.
> Oh, when thy faults are all forgiven,
> The vigil of my life outwrought,
> In some calm altitude of heaven, –
> The dream of thy prophetic thought, –
> Forever near thee, soul in soul,
> Near thee forever, yet how far,
> May our lives reach love's perfect goal
> In the high order of thy star!
>
> (*SHWP* 87–89)

Emphasizing her role in Poe's resurrection, the speaker worships his haughty "altitude" even while she prays for its realization. His heaven is as much the product "outwrought" by her vigil as "the dream of [his] prophetic thought." Jointly created, the heaven can be jointly inhabited, a utopian domicile as well as an aesthetic accomplishment for two artists who wish to dwell within their created world.

Whitman extended and perpetuated this cooperative aesthetic by establishing Poe's absence as a conduit in a system of telegraphic communication. She included "Resurgemus" in a memorial volume dedicated to her friend and rival for Poe's affection, Frances Sargent Osgood.[56] Osgood followed Whitman's unfolding relationship with Poe after her own flirtation had ended; the publication of Whitman's valentine elicited Osgood's response: "I see by the *Home Journal* that your beautiful invocation has reached 'the Raven' in his eyrie and I suppose, ere this, he has *swooped* upon your little *dove-cote* in Providence" (quoted in *PH* 48). While Whitman's selection for Osgood's memorial volume might suggest romantic rivalry, her poem also encourages readers to identify both women as the poem's speaker, since they both could be plausibly cast in the role of mourning lover. Superimposed in a common voice, identified in their loss of Poe, they share a single set of sentiments. The elegy that marks Poe as conduit examines the process of sympathetic identification:

> Those melancholy eyes that seemed
> To look beyond all time, or, turned
> On eyes they loved, so softly beamed, –
> How few their mystic language learned.
> How few could read their depths, or know
> The proud, high heart that dwelt alone
> In gorgeous palaces of woe,
> Like Eblis on his burning throne.
> (*SHWP* 87–89)

The "mystic language" of Poe's eyes initiates readers into a common realm of unearthly knowledge by affording a view into the spatial geography of Poe's soul. Those who have glimpsed his "proud high heart" are drawn into a community of the "few" who can "read" his "depths." Whitman's fantasy of Poe's catalytic gaze recalls his poetic tribute to her eyes ("What wild heart-histories seem to be enwritten / Upon those crystalline, celestial spheres"), as well as his insistence that observing his visions obliterates identic and temporal boundaries (*CWP* 446; 42–43). Here Poe and his female vision change places, so that Whitman now showcases his gaze.

Drawing on cues from their love affair, Whitman disseminated a style of reading in which readers found themselves in Poe and believed that he found himself in them. By perpetuating the mimic structure of reciprocal admiration, she helped to install the apparatus through which his memory survived. Out of her involvement with Poe, Whitman developed a highly sociable poetic system, characterized by exchange more than self-containment, in which participants crafted themselves interactively while their poetry dramatized the event. Their practices generated generic intimacies, exchangeable personalities, and "inner lives" coextensive with literary celebrity.

Whitman structured this community as a mystic kinship system founded upon her spiritual affinity with Poe. Two trends in her opus bear an inverse relation to each other: her reticence to pay tribute to family members (or even to write about daily life within the home), and her willingness to pay tribute to friends. While Whitman's work was primarily lyric, and while she wrote an extended autobiographical poem, *Hours of Life*, she almost never mentioned her immediate family members: her husband, who died of consumption after five years of marriage; her mother and mentally unstable sister, with whom she lived before and after her marriage; her father, who deserted the family when she was ten, and who returned nineteen years later to live in a hotel in the same city as his family and have affairs with actresses (*EAP* 356). Sarah's sister Susan Power wrote of their father's odyssey: "Mr. Nicholas Power left home in a sailing vessel bound for Saint Kitts / When he returned, he frightened his family out of their wits" (quoted in *PH* 10). While her family life seems intriguing enough to write about, Whitman wrote only one poem to her sister after her death ("In Memoriam"), one to her husband's memory ("In April's Dim and Showery Nights"), and none to her father or mother (*SHWP* 201, 34).

Although she barely mentioned family relationships in her poetry, Whitman wrote a series of sonnets to Elizabeth Barrett Browning, two poems to Elizabeth Oakes Smith, and many others to friends and fellow poets. Most significantly, she wrote eighteen poems to Poe, who also serves as the cornerstone of *Hours of Life*. Taken together, these two tendencies suggest that, rather than providing a source of inspiration, the familial sphere of relationships shut down or resisted lyric expression; for Whitman, as for Osgood and other poetesses, the print public sphere was the main location for the production and circulation of the personal. Dematerializing the family by materializing the word, Whitman replaced or supplemented genetic and situational terms of identity offered within the family in order to form lyric identity within a utopian family forged through literary exchange. Whitman's lyric identity was not absolute or inviolable, but provisional and transactional, defined in terms of her relative position in this mythic family system.

With a mystic faith in the power of the letter to offer proof of spiritual connection, Whitman discovered relation in the resemblance of surnames. Claiming that "Power" (her maiden name) and "Poe" had a common root, she linked them both to a common noble ancestor, Roger Le Poer, the Norman Chaplin of Henry the First (*PHR* 183). By deleting the unlike letters in their names, Whitman created family resemblance, so that Poe became "another cousin, or 'twin star' / We drop the W, he the R"(quoted in *EAP* 361). Poe apparently helped to construct this dubious genealogy, for Whitman wrote to John Ingram:

> You ask how I know, or how I found out, that Poe was descended from the Le Poers. I "found it out," in the first place . . . by *instinct*. I am as sure of it as if his descent in a direct line from the "high and mighty Baron" with whom I claim kinship had been traced out for him at the Herald's office by Sir Bernard Burke himself, but I know about it only what I am going to tell you. One evening he had been speaking of the strange sympathies and correspondence in our tastes, feelings and habits of thought, when I said suddenly, "Do you know, I think we must be related and that your name, like my own, was once spelled Le Poer." He looked up with a surprised and radiant look, and said, "Helen, you startle me! I know that certain members of my grandfather's family did so spell their name." (*PHR* 182)

Whitman replaces genetic terms of identity with lineages of common feeling concretized in verbal similarities, which retroactively confirm racial and familial status. While forging imaginative lineages based on elective affinities might serve as a strategy to overcome the racialized distinctions underpinning slavery, the practice reinforced whiteness as a trait shared by writers to whom Whitman bequeathed British and French origins. In a letter to James Wood Davidson, for example, when speaking of the "transfusion of mind through mind," Whitman says: "I am inclined to think it will be found oftener between persons of the same race or country – and more especially between remote branches of the same family" (Brown, folder 40). Nevertheless, spiritual kinship makes Poe a blood relative, rather than the reverse. His metaphoric twinship combines almost every major family role: cousin, sibling, father, and husband. Again manipulating the letters in their names, Whitman found in her "true" name, Sarah Helen Poer, the anagram "Ah! Seraph Lenore," proof that she was destined to be Poe's wife in the spirit world. In a symbolic gesture of union, Whitman published this anagram with one of Poe's name (Edgar Poe), "A God Peer," in *The New York Evening Post* in the 1860s (*PHR* 204).

Whitman's search for the spirit in the letter caused her to locate talismanic power in her maiden name, "Power," which she repeatedly converted into a common noun, and then bequeathed to Poe, as in the final lines of this sonnet: "*Thou* wert my Destiny – thy song, thy fame, / The wild enchantments clustering round thy name, / Were my soul's heritage, its royal dower; / Its glory and its kingdom and its power" (*SHWP* 90).[57] Whitman no sooner makes Poe the site of "power" than she has him transmit it to her, his rightful heir, as her "soul's heritage." In an incestuous circuit, Poe is the "dower" which the speaker brings to her marriage with Poe, a process that cycles her power through him to make it available to herself. The "Thou" of Poe to which Whitman proclaims her devotion is made up solely of secondary characteristics, his corporeal presence evacuated. Poe's "name," "song," and "fame" are all verbal constructs that circulate independently from Poe among a community of readers so that they may become the signature properties of shared poetic discourse. Poe's name becomes the sign of the telegraphic capacity of language to forge kinship between readers and writers.

In her correspondence, Whitman adopted fellow poets and Poe fans into her utopian community through an associative logic. By placing her dead lover in a mediating position, Whitman injected her epistolary exchanges, particularly with other women, with romance. She and poet Mary Forrest, for example, carried on an extensive correspondence that mimicked Whitman's spiritual romance with Poe. According to John Grier Varner, the two women "found their soul wanderings made easier by the fact that they were both attracted by that same star which Poe had called Mrs. Whitman's attention to in 1848" (*SP* 464). That star was Arcturus, a sign of guardianship. Suspended in the heavens, Poe became a sharable symbol of artistic guidance that presided over Whitman's poetic exchanges and enabled her to cultivate mystic kinship.[58] Forrest writes to Whitman in July, 1856:

I must commune with you, while our dear Arcturus is telling, in soft, ruby whispers, the memories of our deepest loves. What a divine light it is between us! I never see its red gleam now, but, with holy and beautiful dreams comes an endearing *thought* of the newly-found – the long-affined. . . . And when your spirit is with bygones – when you sit in twilight, with memory – Arcturus, do not pass over the sign of my spirit, as it meets you. (Brown, folder 133)

Under the sign of Arcturus, Forrest conflates "the newly found" with "the long-affined," her present friendship with Whitman and Whitman's past romance with Poe. Whitman does the same: "I know that you will be interested dear Mary in all that I have told you of Edgar Poe and it is very pleasant to speak of him to you. . . . It is not often that I can speak with such a sweet assurance of sympathy. And now, dear, *goodnight*. Your 'Proserpine'" (Brown, folder 47). In signing the letter "Proserpine," Whitman declares herself Forrest's as well as Poe's. Forrest in turn assumes Poe's place by writing a poem to Whitman entitled "Proserpine," which Whitman presented to "The Phalanstery," a Providence literary circle.

Whitman's association with Sarah Gould, a young Quaker medium specializing in "healing poems," highlights the ways that Poe's mediating spirit promoted both intimacy and publicity through contagious modes of poetic circulation. Gould transmitted posthumous messages from Poe to Whitman.[59] Elizabeth Oakes Smith recalled overhearing one occasion while "stopping at the Gorham House" during a vacation in the White Mountains:

Mrs. Whitman and Miss Gould occupied a room adjoining mine . . . and I heard some fragments of what passed, which were more fully explained in the morning. Mrs. Whitman had been . . . impressed with the presence of Poe. . . . He seemed eager to say something, as if he had importuned her to do for him a kindness, extend some aid, which she could not understand, when Miss Gould turned in her sleep, and murmured distinctly, "Pray for me, Helen; pray for me," the medium being able to interpret the meaning of the spirit urgency. (quoted in *SP* 393)

Retelling what she could not quite hear, Oakes Smith mirrors the event back to its participants, demonstrating the social nature of these communications. Although the women collectively decided that Poe sought Whitman's aid in ascending through the heavenly spheres, the words "Pray for me, Helen" also hold a personal appeal from the younger poet to her mentor figure. The doubled lyric voice, in which the ghostly poet's literal voice is overlaid with the living poet's spectral voice, forges triangulated bonds of intimacy.

Gould's "The Serpent Horror," a 136-line poem in the style of "The Raven," supports both textual and paratextual readings, so that we may trace her symbolic quest to become a poet alongside Poe's spirit journey. She and Whitman were crossing Long Island Sound on their way to New York City when Gould delivered a message from Poe, "still in the throes of serpent agony and chiding [Whitman] for neglect" (*SP* 391). The speaker characterizes the poem as an animated dream that intrudes upon consciousness:

> I with pain had wrestled fiercely,
> Void of slumber, through the night,
> When there came a dream to pierce me
> Through and through, with wild affright.[60]

Identified doubly from the outset, the speaker is both a reluctant medium resisting the spirit's rape of consciousness, and a disoriented Poe, unable to distinguish sleep from waking in the afterlife where such dichotomies are an illusion ("there is no death but only Life!"). Speaking alongside the medium, Poe both inhabits her dreams and dreams himself. In a fiction of perfect sympathy, his tortured inhabitance doubles as Gould's painful struggle with poetic inspiration.

While Poe recounts a drunken bout of self-unravelling in the poem, the medium traces the fall from her own bright poetic world of faith into his world of doubt and disbelief. Struggling to wake up or die, the speaker moves from an Edenic garden replete with talking flowers to its Satanic inversion, full of "dark and scentless flowers / Which had sprung in noxious bowers" (161). In a rendition of Adam and Eve's fall from grace, a "bright serpent" emerges "from a crevice" near a violet, entrances the speaker, strangles him/her "with its circlets icy cold," and then, in typically redundant Poe fashion, also poisons him/her with its venomous breath. This infectious, hypnotic contact transports the speaker to a place where everything has grown serpentine: trees, their branches, brooks, rivers, oceans, clouds. Finally the horrified speaker discovers that s/he too has succumbed:

> "Oh, ye heavens!" I shuddering moan,
> "I too, am a serpent grown.
> Hissing, twining, coiling, rattling,
> With the hideous serpents battling . . ."
>
> (161)

Demonstrating the dangers of a porous identity, the heavenly garden of sympathetic exchange mutates into hellish paranoia and self-alienation. Sympathy transforms into its fearful double, identic dissolution, as the lyric speaker becomes the serpentine subject of the poem. Even while the speaker narrates a process of identic disintegration, however, textual and paratextual readings remain intact. The "hissing, twining, coiling, rattling" of Poe's sonic word play (recall his "bells, bells, bells, bells, bells, bells, bells") threatens to render his message nonsense while it attacks Gould's ability to maintain a reasonable narrative.

Just as the self becomes totally other, into "serpent grown," the lyric "I" disappears. Instead the speaker addresses a "Thou" who resembles the former "I" in every aspect, a shift in perspective which nonetheless retains a doubled aspect:

> Thou didst forget to call last night
> Upon thy guardian angel bright,
> Who hitherto has watched thy sleep,
> Its dreamings pure and high to keep.
>
> (162)

Chastised for not praying to the good angels and thus letting "strange guests into thy spirit come," "Thou" is in an analogous position to the "I" who previously recounted the tortuous hallucinations. Thou's "pure and peaceful thoughts serene" are supplanted by "wild forms" that "swept across thy vision" (162). Depending on whether we wish to imagine that a new "I" addresses the previous speaker, or that the same speaker addresses someone in an identical circumstance, Gould may chastise Poe for forgetting to pay tribute to the higher power that can extract him from his suffering after he has learned to resist temptation; or Poe chastises Gould for leaving her consciousness unprotected from his sinister invasion by forgetting to pray. In either case, I and Thou mirror each other, the structure of their experience identical. Gould and Whitman opted for another interpretation, that Poe accuses Whitman of forgetting to pray for him, so that Whitman's neglect is the source of the nightmare visions that Gould absorbs and articulates for her. Ultimately all three figures become interchangeable through their shared experience of hallucinatory suffering. Channeling the emotional response of spectators and participants alike through a single poetic form renders suffering not only analogous, but structurally identical.

Through her lyric mediumship, Gould gained not only the skills, but also the poetic consciousness of the more established poets. She paid tribute to her apprenticeship in her poem "To Sarah Helen Whitman." The mentor poet's superiority resides in the collective quality of her soul's composition:

> And every utterance of thy simplest song
> Finds, in my soul, an echo warm and true,
> And clearly opens, to my mental view,
> Thy spirit's quiet and exalted home,
> Whither good angels love so well to come,
> And often, lady, from the realms of thought,
> A votive offering I to thee have brought,
> But when, all trembling, I approached the shrine
> Where burned a fire so lofty and divine,
> I feared my gift too simple was to place
> Beside the first-fruits which that altar grace . . .
>
> (65)

Whitman's inner life is a pastiche, made up of visiting angels and others' poetic tributes (the intimidating "first-fruits" left before the altar). Gould characterizes Whitman's personal charisma as a textual inner space – "the pages of thy heart" – that holds entities imported from outside herself. For Gould, Whitman's superior powers derive from social activity that disperses lyric identity into an internal community of spirits that constitutes personal amplitude.

Responding to Whitman's soul "echo, true and warm," Gould's speaker aspires to structure her interiority through analogous strategies of inspired mimicry. Having only recently refined her talents enough to dare approach her mentor's shrine, the speaker fuels her aesthetic ascension by communing with both the angels and Whitman, their earthly kin. The angels furnish the speaker with poetic powers to overcome her lower social status and educational deficiencies, first "stringing" her heart to make it an instrument, and then teaching her "all the beatific skill, / To wake its numbers whensoe'er I will" (66). Whitman's apparition motivates the speaker to emulation. Enacting her artistic evolution within the poem, the speaker's "mental view," initially obscured, opens onto "revelations so exceeding clear" that she can "read the pages" of Whitman's heart and "plainly trace" her "spirit features" (66). "To trace" suggests both to copy an original and to touch a physical presence; ultimately, the poem materializes what it invokes, and the poet stands back to view a creation that has gained a life of its own, a life that is Whitman's. This final dissociative act, whereby the speaker ceases to be a poet and becomes a seer, legitimizes her artistic power by negating it. Lyric mimicry twins the women – they become "sister soul[s]" – and allows Gould to absorb Whitman in a way that leaves them both more ample (66).

Whitman cultivated a family network of Poe admirers who imagined her as his guardian. Mary Forrest's romantic "twin star" and Sarah Gould's "sister soul," Whitman concluded that Poe biographer John Ingram was part of the family circle when he noted that his last name meant "son of the Raven" in Scottish; she occasionally referred to him as "MacRaven" (*PHR* 372). She also decided that Poe's spirit governed W. D. O'Connor's lifetime loyalty towards her.[61] It may seem curious that Poe, who was obsessed with originality and phobic about plagiarism, even while he was a compulsive imitator and plagiarizer, would be the patron saint of a circle of poets that blithely circulated and recycled the words, ideas, and styles of others in a way that rendered plagiarism irrelevant. But while the cult of Poe posthumously revised his living presentation, that revision drew on Poe's own poetic practices. His personal, critical, and poetic attention and attraction to women poets enabled his "phantom voice" to haunt their works after his death. Whitman and other women put the finishing touches on Poe's mystic portrait in the decade after his death before presenting it to the biographers who became the official keepers of his memory. Productive of female community, Poe's reputation disseminated so effectively by virtue of what it could do for women poets.

In the years after the Civil War, a new generation of male literary critics and biographers reinterpreted the feminine spirit of Poe and poetry that earlier fans had produced. This later group sought vicarious intimacy with Poe through the women who had known him. Sarah Helen Whitman's recollections and artifacts were crucial to this reclamation project. Almost every Poe biographer and Poe-inspired poet contacted her, seeking information and sanction for their work: Thomas Cottrell Clarke, James Wood Davidson, Eugene Didier, George Eveleth, William Fearing Gill, William Gowans, John Henry Ingram, Stéphane Mallarmé, W. D. O'Connor, and Richard Henry Stoddard.[62] Their studies simultaneously denied and reiterated the spiritualist poetics that informed Whitman's accounts of her relationship with Poe. While rejecting the premise that spirit visitation was literally possible, their writings embedded mediumistic structures within rational forms of academic inquiry. Insisting on their objectivity, these critics were nevertheless guided by the conviction that they had a privileged, inspired understanding of Poe. Possessed by Poe, they sought to make him their unique possession. The basis of their critical aesthetic was a disavowed yet structurally embedded feminine mysticism. By both replicating and denying feminine forms of lyric mediumship, these scholars reproduced the dynamics of Poe's own engagement with the poetic practices of his female contemporaries, through which he both claimed and discounted their influence.

Sarah Helen Whitman's correspondence with George Eveleth demonstrates the ways in which spiritualism and skepticism, and feminine and masculine literary practices, are non-opposed aspects of a single cultural dynamic, for which Poe serves as a historical channel. Eveleth's fascination with Poe fueled a correspondence that persisted for many years. Skeptical of Poe's death, Eveleth initially contacted Whitman because he thought she was pretending to communicate with Poe's spirit while actually harboring his person. By hiding Poe, she was helping him pull off his ultimate joke on the public, in the style of the balloon hoax and Valdemar's return from the dead. Eveleth voiced this suspicion in an early letter to Whitman: "once more, I am forced back upon my original ground – namely, upon the belief that you are at the other end of the wire, assisting Poe to lead the multitude (myself among the number) by the nose!"[63] In spite of Whitman's protests,

Eveleth kept a tenacious grip on his interpretation for at least a year, sending messages through Whitman to the "living" Poe, including critical commentaries on his final visionary work, *Eureka*. Eveleth preserved the tenets of Spiritualism even while rejecting them by trying to use a material version of its telegraphic apparatus and designating Whitman as the operator. By literalizing Whitman's symbolic communication system, Eveleth demonstrates the convertibility of mysticism and skepticism: if Poe were alive, and Whitman were helping him dupe the public, they would be mocking a naïve belief in spiritual telegraphy. Because Poe is dead, however, Eveleth's insistence on an ironic relation to spiritualism is naïve: he accepts Whitman's mediating role, but insists upon Poe's literal presence. In either case, the structure of communications remains the same.

Underscoring the convertibility of seemingly opposed perspectives and belief systems, Eveleth changed his mind about Spiritualism. Whitman became so offended at his insinuation of fraud that she threatened to return his letters unopened on at least two occasions.[64] Her angry rebuttal caused him to reconsider and then accept the possibility of spirit communication. During his subsequent correspondence with Whitman, he requested that she visit him posthumously, and that she bequeath to him her unpublished accounts of her interactions with Poe and other spirits.[65] He also asked if the definitive biography of Poe would in reality be an autobiography, dictated from the spirit world: "Will not the *authorised memoir* of the poet be an autobiography, given through an unknown medium?"[66] Speculating that biographers are spirit telegraphs who remain unconscious of their mediumship, Eveleth stressed the force of critical identification that underpins author studies.

Preoccupied with agency, Eveleth equated spiritual power with unconscious mimicry as the force that propels a plot in life or art. He asked Whitman if she thought spirits, not Booth, assassinated President Lincoln:

What a deep-meaning affair is this assassination of the President, isn't it? . . . I can't help running it over in my mind, that the perpetrator of the horrid act was some other than Booth himself – it seems to me that the evidences pointing to him, such as his hat left in the President's Box, his spur dropped, and the papers in his trunk, are put *a little too obtrusively in the way*. – What say you to the suggestion, that the same incomprehensible, hidden forces which move in the manifestations of Spiritualism, have a part also in this *motley drama with Horror for the soul of the plot?*[67]

Just as Poe's disappearance was too literal a rendition of his death, the material signs of Booth's guilt add up too well, and the plot makes too much sense to be true. Whereas Eveleth had earlier accused Whitman of cloaking banality in an aura of mysticism, here he imagines a spiritual master hand that engineers the "motley drama." He borrows his characterization from Poe's "The Conqueror Worm," in which human "mimes, in the form of God on high" are marionettes manipulated by "vast formless things" for the pleasure of angels (*CWP* 325–326). At stake in both Poe's poem and Eveleth's theory of spirit assassination is a question of human agency: do people possess the power to originate a plot, or do they merely reiterate a pre-scripted fate? While a scenario in which dark forces manipulate people for their entertainment diminishes human control and creativity, the notion that spirits scripted the assassination of Lincoln for larger, inscrutable purposes lends amplitude and significance to a tragedy that threatens to evacuate national meanings.

In later letters Eveleth equated spiritual and print media in their capacity for conduction. Casting words as both the containers of character and vehicles of its dissemination, Eveleth wrote Whitman that he wished to absorb her literary electricity:

I am much obliged for the two print letters enclosed. They are characteristic, therefore interesting to me. There is a glow about their descriptions which impels me right into the poetical heart of the matter described. I wish some spirit would steal your power and transfer it to me – not lessening yours in the stealing though.[68]

Eveleth admires Whitman's ability to transport him beyond his identic boundaries. Like Sarah Gould, he fantasizes that a spiritual transfer of poetic power might convert his attraction to Whitman's glowing "print letters" into his own force without diminishing her store. Whitman, after all, had received her power through her own identification with Poe, the initial source of Eveleth's admiration. He and Whitman repeatedly returned to the concept of a spiritual talent transfer. Whitman noted the resemblance of Eveleth's handwriting to Poe's, and Eveleth noted that the affinity could be gained or lost, since it was rooted in material forms; he told Whitman that his fatigue had caused his handwriting to lose its resemblance in that particular letter.[69] Speaking of J. W. Davidson's request for a submission to his *Living Writers of the South*, Eveleth recounted: "I informed him at once that I could lay no claim to being Southern, whether as a writer or not, unless I was born of Poe, through reading the productions of his genius."[70]

Eveleth applied the spiritual logic of poetic conduction to the issue of plagiarism. Writing of a case where a Mr. Ball acknowledged "borrowing" from Whitman, Eveleth explored questions about the relation between imitation and originality, inspiration and plagiarism:

I saw, by the *Round Table* and other journals dated some weeks since, that Mr. Ball, of New Jersey, had written you acknowledging that he had borrowed from you in the letting out of one of his poetical inspirations, but that he was at the time unconscious of the borrowing. How does he account for the passage of the thoughts and words from your own mind to his own?[71]

A conflict between two characterizations of Mr. Ball's act generates Eveleth's questions. Within a system of possessive individualism valuing private ownership of intellectual property, Mr. Ball would be condemned as a plagiarist. Within a system of spiritualist poetics valuing communal activities governed by rapport, however, his unconscious duplication would be a sign of mystical affinity. A logic of scarcity governs the individualist aesthetic: the theft depletes the owner's work and the plagiarizer's work is derivative. A logic of surplus, on the other hand, governs the spiritualist aesthetic: supernatural power grows and multiplies when it is shared.

Sarah Helen Whitman and George William Curtis, an influential literary critic and shaper of genteel American taste (he was *Harper's* "Easy Chair," among other things), debated questions of literary value from these different perspectives. Whitman's fascination with telegraphic writing matches Curtis' antagonism. Twenty years her junior, Curtis discovered a mentor in Whitman when he was twenty-one and asked her advice about his poems. The pair debated aesthetic issues for many years, including the merits of W. D. O'Connor's poetry (*PH* 20). Known for championing Walt Whitman, at the age of nineteen O'Connor showed Sarah Helen Whitman poems redolent of Poe's influence, hoping that she would confirm his genius. She sent them to Curtis, who dismissed them as imitative in a letter dated August 1, 1853:

The poems of our friend O'Connor are, to my mind, too exclusively rich echoes of Poe, to be of real benefit to himself in their publication. All the phraseology of Poe, the nepenthe – the mandrake – the romantic terms for familiar objects, recur in O'Connor and not in new or individual forms which would be agreeable. . . . They are the masquerades of Fancy in guises which were gorgeous when they were original, as with Poe, but are painful and poor, when assumed by another *for the reason* that they were fine upon Poe. (Brown, folder 122)

Curtis labels derivative the echoic element that enables Whitman to identify O'Connor as Poe's kindred spirit. He condemns O'Connor's work for what he commends in Poe's, acknowledging that the primary difference is chronological. Because Poe marked certain poetic practices with his signature, they appear false when used by another: Poe is better because he was first.

This contradiction emerges from Curtis' attempt to shift the terms of aesthetic judgement from a reader-response basis to one that privileges and protects intellectual invention.[72] Responding to Whitman's assertion that "poetic power is the power of exciting poetic emotion," Curtis protests that "the excitation of the emotion is due to him who first develops that power":

That is to say if I move you as no other poet has moved you, I have shown in me the presence of that power. But if I move you only by the use of the same means that Milton or Keats have employed . . . with such slight modifications as are inevitable in all echoes and imitations then, although the poetic emotion may be excited in you, the praise is not mine but the other poet's. . . . Thus, also, if a passage in a poet is Shakespearean or Miltonic, it is no glory of that poet's because we don't want what is less in quality, but what is different. . . . It is this individuality, this something that does not refer to others, but is strictly peculiar, that passes, I suppose, under the name "creative power."[73]

Curtis discounts the reader's response in order to distinguish between authors even as he predicates the idea of original genius on the certainty of reproducibility. Because Poe and O'Connor inspire the same "poetic emotion" in the reader, Curtis fears a mass production of Poes or Miltons and wants to ensure that the author gets credit for the invention. Curtis stops circulation at the site of romantic genius, naming and forming that originary place. Curbing the system of poetic exchange that Whitman promotes, he designates certain authors as fonts of originality, and the rest as imitators.

Curtis' argument, however, did not convince Whitman, who wrote against the margin of the letter, along with exclamation points at crucial passages, "Is not *all* poetry full of echoes?" Early, influential literary critics like O'Connor, Curtis, and Ingram suppressed this question when they buried their imitations of Poe and their admiration for the echoic Sarah Helen Whitman, and advanced the cause of originality in the form of Walt Whitman, or a renovated Poe, stripped of his indebtedness to women.

These questions of possession inform early Poe criticism, which transfers Poe's spiritual legacy from the women who knew him to the men who canonized him. John Henry Ingram was key figure in this process. Ingram made his lifelong mission the recuperation of Poe's reputation from the slanders of Rufus Griswold. He obsessively tracked down the people who knew Poe and collected their memories as well as their material keepsakes. Poe's friends exported their letters, photographs, and memorabilia of all kinds to England, most of which only returned in 1921, when the University of Virginia acquired Ingram's collection after his death; by that time he had acquired, as he put it, "a room-full of Poe."[74] Convinced that Poe was a displaced British citizen unappreciated by uncivilized Americans, Ingram tried to reconstitute him archivally in England: the more property Ingram accumulated, the more British Poe became.

Judging from *Poe's Helen Remembers* and *Building Poe Biography*, John Carl Miller's informative collections of source materials for Ingram's landmark writings on Poe, women were among the most voluble and valuable contributors to his recuperative project. Ingram's contacts included Elizabeth and Anna Blackwell, Marie Louise Shew Houghton, Stella Lewis, Mary Gove Nichols, Annie Richmond, Elizabeth Oakes Smith, and others. Sarah Helen Whitman's contributions were by far the most significant, rivaling Ingram's own. His "Providence" (as he addressed her in their extensive correspondence), Whitman provided Ingram with Poe's manuscripts; she recounted conversations and interactions with Poe; she offered interpretations of his work and of events in his personal and professional life; she also evaluated information from other sources. Her pivotal defense of Poe, *Edgar Poe and His Critics*, written in response to Griswold's slander, "strengthened and confirmed" Ingram's desire to vindicate Poe.[75] Since he never knew Poe, Ingram coveted Whitman's first-hand knowledge. At the same time he claimed greater authority through a wider sphere of knowledge – he interviewed more people and amassed more information – and through greater sympathetic understanding. Suggesting that knowing Poe through his poems was superior to knowing him personally, Ingram substituted poetic identification for personal acquaintance.

In their exchange, the question of who possessed true knowledge of Poe hinged on the question of who was most possessed by him. When Ingram initiated contact in December 1873, as part of his quest to build a definitive biography, he proffered Poe-inspired poems as tokens of psychic inhabitance: "I enclose you two of my juvenile poems inspired by Poe . . . I send these verses to show you how long I have been under the weird influence of Poe" (*PHR* 10). Seeking Whitman's confidence in order to glean her knowledge, Ingram stressed his passionate identification with Poe in order to distinguish himself from mere academics: "I have asked these questions hurriedly and apparently coldly and businesslike, but you must not deem that I am unsympathetic, or want the information for mercantile purposes. I admire and reverence Edgar Poe to an extent that makes me quite a scoff among the many, who think I am somewhat crazy on the point: but you, and those who study him with kindred feeling, cannot avoid the glamour of his masterly influence" (*PHR* 14). Equating his enchantment with Whitman's, Ingram succeeded in appealing to her "kindred feeling," for she wrote that she found his interest in Poe authentic, citing the "genuine poetic feeling" evident in Ingram's early Poe-inspired poems (20).

Encouraged, Ingram recounted the story of the poems' genesis, which confirmed his vocation as a poet:

One night, when I was still a boy, I went into my own room and for the 500th time, began to read out of Routledge's little volume of Edgar Poe's poems. Suddenly, something stirred me till I shuddered and quivered with intense excitement. "I felt as if a star had burst within my brain." I fell on my knees and prayed as I could only pray then, and thanked my Creator for having made me a poet! I seized a pencil and wrote a wild lyric, "The Imprisoned Soul." (62)

Brought to his knees by the high-voltage shock of transmission, Ingram thanks an unspecified Creator, who could be God or Poe, for "having made [him] a poet." While not precisely a translation from the spirit world, the resulting poem retains the traces of Poe's influence, confirming him as Ingram's inspiration, and validating Ingram as Poe's spokesman.[76] Poe's influence makes itself felt with the intensity of a spirit visitation, and justifies the Poe scholar precisely as if he were a spirit medium.

Whereas Whitman's affinity with Poe underwrote collective poetic practices, Ingram's affinity with Poe justifies private accumulation. He envisions himself as an intellectual miner who extracts knowledge from women and then becomes sole owner, as if memory were transferable, physical property. He writes to Whitman:

My material is accumulating largely. *Mrs. Houghton is invaluable* – but everything will be duly weighed and "*recast*" before it is embodied in the biography definitive. My correspondents send me much that is worthless – some think that I only want marvellous anecdotes – some sentimental fancies and others *their* ideas. Mrs. E. O. Smith has sent me a paper on E. A. Poe which contains some striking thoughts and admirable criticism but, as regards biographical value, not worth a single page of Mrs. Houghton's. (283)

Ingram imagines that the only valuable information women can provide is raw material that he can "*recast*" as if it were molten metal and he were the sculptor who could definitively "embod[y]" Poe. The certainty with which he distinguishes between "anecdotes," "ideas," and "criticism" that can be scraped away and discarded, and the precious "material" that remains, raises questions about how the process of separation occurs. He imagines that he can reduce women's memoirs to their vital elements and extract Poe's true nature, purged of its feminine conduit: through alchemy, women's recollections become Ingram's facts.

The more information and artifacts Ingram acquired, the more possessed by Poe he became. Though he initially referred to the biography as an enterprise he shared with Whitman – "I have just returned the proofs of the engravings of E. A. Poe for *our* life" – by October 13, 1874 he was referring to Poe's life as his own: "I do long for you to get my 'memoir' . . . and get your opinion on it" (165, 216).[77] While writing Poe's biography, Ingram took on Poe-like characteristics: paranoia, obsession with plagiarism, contentiousness, and delusions of abjection and grandeur. His personification of Poe culminated in a public attack on Whitman in 1877 in which he asserted sole claim over the Poe dynasty. On February 10, Ingram drew her attention to a review in the *London Athenaeum* of "The Life and Poems of Edgar Allan Poe; and Additional Poems. Ed. by E. L. Didier," a copy of which Whitman had recently sent him. Though Ingram said the review was written by a friend, to whom he had lent Didier's book, he himself wrote the "severe 'skull dragging,'" in which he said this about his "Providence" (474):

An "Introductory Letter" by Mrs. Whitman, whose "Edgar Poe and his Critics" is laid under heavy contribution, follows the Preface: it is, of course, written in an authoritative tone, but, in following out some such subtle researches in the domain of "antenatal influences" as those which inclined Mr. Shandy to forebode misfortunes for Tristram, the lady has been somewhat out in her reckoning; it would scarcely be safe to carry such delicate investigations back further than nine months, even for such a phenomenal person as Poe, who was born on the 19th of January, 1809, just 276 days after his parents appeared as the leading characters in an English version of Schiller's "Robbers." (477)

In order to claim Poe, Ingram dispossesses Whitman by discrediting her ideas about spiritual possession. Though he does so under the rubric of rational inquiry, his academic persona is recognizable as a personification of Poe, whose critical signature was the clever hatchet job, frequently inflicted upon his friends without warning.

Whitman assumed that Ingram knew that she would identify his authorship. She responded by disavowing their friendship, addressing her letter "To one who calls himself my 'friend'" (482). She was less shocked by the criticism than by its tone: "The matter itself was of little moment, but the *animus* of it gave a rude shock to all my previous impressions" (483). She was further struck by Ingram's staging of the attack: "That you should have drawn attention to this singular performance surprises me. . . . I have re-read the virulent article with astonishment" (483). Ingram disavowed his action in his letter of April 26, 1877: "*I here declare that the words are not mine*" (487). In a way he was right: both his initial attack and subsequent denial bear Poe's signature.

The competition to be Poe's legitimate heir played out as a battle over national integrity. Just as Ingram completed what he believed to be the definitive Poe biography, American biographers attacked Ingram and worked to reclaim the American poet.[78] Eugene Didier accused Ingram of stealing keepsakes from Poe's friends by borrowing and not returning them:

Every schoolboy knows who discovered America, but many intelligent men and women do not know who "discovered" Edgar A. Poe. Some years ago an obscure Englishman claimed to have discovered Poe and made him known to the American people. Not only did this obscure Englishman claim to have introduced Poe to American readers, but he attempted to belittle and read out of court all Americans who presumed to write about their own countryman. But while attempting to undervalue their work, he did not hesitate to appropriate, – I like a gentle word, – their material. I was a student of Poe's life and works before this presumptuous Englishman had emerged from his original obscurity. . . . I confess I have been astonished at what I have heard regarding the peculiar methods this "Discoverer" has used in adding to his Poeana. (quoted in *PH* 256–257)

Whether or not Ingram literally stole the materials that were eventually restored to American soil, the situation provides an allegory of critical possession. Recent Poe studies have re-enacted this international drama, in which foreign critics "steal" him and American critics seek to "restore" him to his legitimate owners. In the introduction to *The American Face of Edgar Allan Poe*, for example, Shawn Rosenheim and Steven Rachman assert that "there is a growing impulse to resist Poe's wholesale assimilation to the realm of psycholinguistic universals, and to restore his writings to the cultural milieu from which they appear to have been wrenched."[79] And Terence Whalen designates "the French appropriations of Poe by Baudelaire, Lacan, and Derrida" "critical and cultural sediment which threatens to distort Poe's historical situation."[80]

Ingram worked hard not to let the Americans take Poe back and grew increasingly hostile towards anyone who had a claim on Poe. Despite the impossibility of stopping Poe's circulation, he wanted to be the sole interpreter and transmitter of his legacy. In a final, audacious gesture after Whitman's death, Ingram requested custody of her literary remains, particularly her private correspondence with Poe, only to discover that she had made provisions so that he would not get his hands on any of it. In response to his inquiry, Whitman's friend Rose Peckham wrote Ingram that Whitman had her own plans for a posthumous memoir, and that "all Mrs. Whitman's correspondence in reference to Poe would be carefully guarded for future use," so that even Ingram's own letters could not be returned to him (*PHR* 504). Peckham moreover stressed that Whitman had only provided Ingram with portions of materials that came from a much larger store from which Whitman's executors would create the definitive memoir:

> The letters of which you have copies . . . form a part of the manuscript from which the executors will get their facts. They have never been given in their entirety to any person yet, the *copies* you have being only *extracts*. Mrs. Whitman was very cautious and prudent, with all her amiability and generosity, and as this memoir has long been one of her cherished plans, I dare to say any information she gave other writers was duly noted, and will probably be supplemented by unsuspected reserves. (504)

Whitman had the last laugh, retaining materials in the hopes that another critic would give her more credit and Poe his due.

If Whitman related herself to Poe in order to be remembered in her own right, she was successful according to Virginia Woolf, who identified this trajectory and found Whitman the more interesting figure. In her review of Caroline Ticknor's *Poe's Helen* in the *Times Literary Supplement* of 1917, Woolf proclaimed:

> The real interest of Miss Ticknor's volume lies in the figure of Mrs. Whitman, and not in the love letters of Poe, which have already been published. It is true that if it had not been for her connexion with Poe we should never have heard of Helen Whitman; but it is also true that Poe's connexion with Mrs. Whitman was neither much to his credit nor a matter of moment to the world at large. . . . Mrs. Whitman, on the other hand, comes very well out of the ordeal, and was evidently, apart from Poe, a curious and interesting person.[81]

Although I have claimed that *Poe's Helen* has bequeathed to us Helen's Poe, there is every possibility that interest in Sarah Helen Whitman will expand to take into account her other impressive accomplishments.[82] A case study in critical possession, Poe criticism has inherited the dynamics already established in the exchange between John Ingram and Sarah Helen Whitman. Although Ingram frequently is credited with founding traditions of Poe scholarship, early Poe biography and criticism, whose mythologizing tendencies have profoundly influenced traditions of Poe studies, is to an unexamined degree a product of women's memories, fantasies, and desires.

We can learn much from exploring how they have shaped Poe's reception, and how Poe shaped his own reception by appealing to a female readership. In spite of Ingram's attempt to stop Poe's circulation, Poe continues to convey much that does not belong to him, nor to any particular critic.

Recent studies of Poe, two incompatible models of literary history – one acknowledged, the other submerged – frequently compete, register a disjunction between portrayals of the exceptional individual's influence and of the cultural transmission of ideas. In *Reading at the Social Limit: Affect, Mass Culture, and Edgar Allan Poe*, for example, Jonathan Elmer explores Poe's ambivalent relation to mass and elite literary culture. He argues that when Poe figures mass culture, mass culture inevitably figures Poe (20). Though Elmer formulates an interactive relation between Poe and mass culture, however, he centers his reading almost exclusively upon Poe's work. Poe stands alone at the center of anonymous and amorphous social currents, which the anxiety generated by his exceptional self-awareness renders legible (29). Instead of exploring the ways that meaning occurs in transactions between individuals or entities, Elmer designates Poe as the site of a dramatic, internalized tension between the individual and the social.

If Elmer's study focuses on the figure of Poe, Shawn Rosenheim's *The Cryptographic Imagination: Secret Writing from Poe to the Internet* traces the multivalent dispersion of Poe's influence in American culture and beyond. While Rosenheim's study offers an ideal opportunity for examining the ways in which meanings take shape in processes of exchange and circulation that are not controlled by any single individual, he defines Poe's "telegraphic writing" as a unidirectional transfer of influence whereby "Poe's writing reproduces itself in his readers" (121). Rosenheim's astute analysis of the ways in which ideas are transmitted and transmuted directs readers to conclude, rather contradictorily, that the only person who is not a telegraphic medium for influence is Poe himself. "Genius" is therefore a power station that transmits but does not receive cultural signals, that has transformative powers but cannot itself be transformed.

I have suggested that Poe's imitation of women poets encouraged them to adopt him as their medium of choice after his death, thus perpetuating their practices in his name. In attributing common strategies to Poe, Elmer, Rosenheim, and others reinscribe a historical elision that perpetuates the myth of isolated genius. While Poe helped write the terms of his own reception, the Poe that survives is a collective creation, memorable not because he single-handedly forged a prophetic "pathway to our twentieth-century imagination," as Rosenheim suggests, but because he personified mediumship.[83] Rather than a unidirectional system of transmission, lyric telegraphy is a bidirectional system of communication, one that forges meaning in the transactions between individuals, shaping cultural modes of interpretation in the process. Though the question of who came first, Poe or the poetesses, may be both indeterminable and impertinent, literary history persists in crediting him alone. It is therefore worth emphasizing the priority of the poetesses in mimic modes of cultural transmission.

CHAPTER 4

Elizabeth Oakes Smith's "unspeakable eloquence"

In the mid-1850s, Sarah Helen Whitman and Elizabeth Oakes Smith playfully debated the terms of their fame in an exchange of manuscript poems.
Their banter offers insight into the conditions of reception that enforce
continuities in the quite various work of the women poets treated in this
study. The friends compete for poetic prowess by displaying precision and
wit in diagnosing their poetic demise. Whitman begins, however, by boasting about her celebrity status in response to Oakes Smith's request for her
autograph:

> The Gods decree that you shall have,
> Dear lady, whatso'er you crave –
> But if you sell my autograph
> Remember, you're to give me "half" –
> And should your silver tongue persuade
> Some verdant youth to "make a trade,"
> As fast as you find fools to buy
> I promise you a new supply.
>
> Say, though I never wrote a book
> I occupy a cozy nook
> In Dr. Griswold's – That's his name
> Endorses all my drafts of Fame –
> That in his preface, hand in hand
> With you and Mrs. Brooks, I stand;
> Three pensive Caryatides,
> Supporting the emblazoned frieze
> Of his fair Pantheon – Say, in short who –
> Ever don't know me doubtless ought to.
>
> (quoted in *SP* 414)

Mocking the market for poetesses, Whitman praises Oakes Smith's "silver
tongue" not for its melodic purity but for its huckster's eloquence. She pictures her friend tricking green youngsters into mistaking current fashion

for enduring value so that they pay for the most efficient kind of signature collectible, the signature itself. In his "Autography" series, Poe explores
the question of the signature's saleability; according to Meredith McGill,
the woodcut reproduction of the author's signature belies handwriting's
uniqueness but nevertheless "*produces* th[e] mass-produced magazine as
an original."[1] Bypassing the magazine's reproductive capabilities, Whitman
offers to mass produce the signature by hand if it will turn a profit. In doing
so she succinctly diagnoses the way that the sign of the poetess stands in for
and supplants her poetic output. If her poems' fiction of transparent communication is successful, it negates the mediation by which readers came
to love the writer they never knew, and the poems disappear in the process.
The autograph then replaces the poem as the sign of intimate connection.

In the second stanza the poetess' collectibility re-emerges in a comic
image of three quite different poetesses – Maria Brooks, Oakes Smith,
and Whitman – as interchangeable columnar figures, assigned to support-
ing roles in Griswold's shrine, *The Female Poets of America*. The idealized
body of woman stands in for the body of work; enshrinement purges the
poetesses of particularities. According to the Roman architectural writer
Vitruvius, caryatid columns originally represented the women of Caryae,
who were forced into hard labor because their town sided with the Persians
during their invasion of Greece in the fifth century BC.[2] Whitman slyly
suggests that the literary labors of women poets have glorified not themselves, but Griswold, who earns credit for collecting them. Pressed into
service, the columnar women support their canonizer's creation, composed
of themselves. Whitman's architectural rendering of Griswold's anthology
comically contrasts a symbol of European literary foundations with his
ephemeral Pantheon of poetesses by foregrounding the difference between
marble, which endures, and paper, which is more easily subject to decay.[3]

Not to be outdone, Oakes Smith responds by lightly suggesting that the
plight of the poetess is more dismal than Whitman imagines. If Whitman
suggests that their fame is of dubious merit (her "doubtless" cuts both ways)
and contingent on male patronage, Oakes Smith suggests that it has already
been eclipsed. Bored, the fickle Griswold has moved on to champion Alice
and Phoebe Cary, whom Oakes Smith figures as chickens in a stylized
performance of female cattiness:

> . . . I would like to tell the story
> Of our eclipsed Griswold glory,
> No more the Dr. walks in dreams
> Where Grecian marble coldly gleams.
> Near flowing brooks he's not the fit man

To wander by, and Mrs. Whitman
May go alone, in joy or woe
He thinks no more of her or Poe –
No acorn germ nor oak tree myth
Can lure him back to Mistress Smith –
He prates no more of Fanny, fairy,
But keeps abroad of Mother Cary,
Her chickens, and one (I tell the common tale)
He takes to be a Nightingale,
Indeed he thinks he may inveigle,
The chicken, to a very eagle.
                    (quoted in *SP* 414)

Oakes Smith suggests that a new generation of writers has lured Griswold away from his earlier loves. Though he once took pleasure in dwelling within Maria Brooks' pastoral landscapes, sympathizing with Whitman's romantic attachments to Poe, succumbing to Oakes Smith's enchanted auto-mythologies, or submitting to Fanny Osgood's spritely spells, Griswold has tuned into an earthier strain of singing. He now champions the sisters from rural Ohio, who were raised on a farm and educated at home (thus their incarnation as barnyard chickens).[4] This regionalist duo has supplanted the earlier, more refined female monument and stranded the Caryatides:

. . . we are left
All high and dry like crafts bereft
Of tide, to carry us to sea –
Poor Mrs. Brooks and you and me,
I'm so bereft of heart this letter
Must go in absence of a better –
I have not strength to sign my name,
And send without as your note came.
                    (quoted in *SP* 414–415)

Recasting the trio of poetesses as a set of waterless boats, Oakes Smith mourns the loss of their ability to circulate. Ironically assuming the persona of a female invalid whose romantic misfortune consumes her, she confides that the lack of an outlet for her work has generated despondency about revising even her private correspondence; the joke here is that the private letter doesn't require the same revision as a published piece, unless one is competing with one's correspondent for poetic mastery. Oakes Smith then reiterates Griswold's act of erasure and expedites her predicted eclipse by withholding her signature. Her refusal to sign is a more extreme version of Whitman's decision to enclose her signature on a separate sheet for

Oakes Smith to sell (that gesture is implied by Oakes Smith's response). Circulation generates celebrity by proliferating signature images of the author as currency; these in turn exhaust the reader, who turns away and willfully forgets, ensuring celebrity's decline.

Whitman's final sally in this mock war of words distinguishes between Oakes Smith's strategies and prospects and her own:

> 'Tis very well for you to jest
> So lightly of this new-found nest,
> But if this be not all a fiction
> About the Doctor's dereliction
> Alas for me! If he doth lack me
> I've not another friend to back me.
>
> You, perched upon your oak-tree bough
> (A pretty rookery, I trow)
> Look gaily down on all below,
> Sipping nepenthe from your scorn
> And caring little how I take on
> At this desertion but in sooth,
> Fair lady, 'tis a sober truth
> That "Mistress Smith" without the Oaks
> Is hardly known from other folks.
>
> (quoted in *SP* 416)

Whitman complains that while her own fame depends upon Griswold's patronage, Oakes Smith has greater potential longevity because she has cultivated a mythology of self-sufficiency. Oakes Smith planted a signature seed in her popular early poem "The Acorn," which tells the story of a "monarch" oak tree from its tiny beginnings.[5] The poem references her self-made family tree, a genealogy that she initiated by appending "Oakes," a male ancestor's family name, to her married name. Oakes Smith adopted the double name after the success of her narrative poem *The Sinless Child,* which features an innocent version of a post-lapsarian Eve. She extended her mythical genealogy by legally changing her sons' names to "Oaksmith" and tried unsuccessfully to get her husband to do the same. She also gave one of her sons the name "Appleton," designating him fruit from a woman's sinless Tree of Knowledge.[6]

Whitman pokes fun at Oakes Smith's bid for lasting fame that hybridizes feminine authorship with a masculine strain. That Oakes Smith's pen name is not floral, like many poetesses of her generation, but arboreal suggests a competitive desire to rise above and overshadow all the other pen names. Whitman levels this charge when she depicts the oak tree as the poetess' haughty perch. She identifies none other but Poe as Oakes Smith's proto-type by portraying her as a raven, "sipping nepenthe from her scorn," as Poe's lyric speaker also unsuccessfully attempted to do ("Quaff, oh quaff this kind nepenthe and forget this lost Lenore"). To underscore the allusion, Whitman shifts from iambic tetrameter to the trochaic meter of "The Raven" (the four-beat line suggests half of Poe's octameter lines, which are broken in the middle by strong caesuras). Whitman recasts Oakes Smith's bid for longevity as wishful playacting, however, when she identifies her generic married name, "Smith," as the untransformable core of her fantas-tical myth-making. Try as they might, Whitman suggests, women poets' ability to recast reception on their own terms is limited by forces beyond their control.

Whitman and Oakes Smith's self-deprecating characterizations are com-ically exaggerated. In the previous chapter I traced the ways that Whitman ingeniously takes advantage of coterie conventions to cultivate, albeit in the terms of Poe's genius, a lasting image of herself as Poe's protector. Both writers held public attention long after Griswold turned his attention to other writers, and even after he died in 1857; he may have promoted their celebrity, but he did not control it to the degree that they suggest. Indeed, their exchange pokes fun at Griswold's inflated sense of his significance and his parasitic exploitation of their work for his profit. Whitman identifies an enabling source of this gender injustice when she concludes her analysis by reversing herself once again and signing her name:

> You hint that I'm unknown to fame, –
> At least "I write without a name."
> Now if you think that such credential
> Is to this document essential,
> Below, as plain as ever writ man,
> You'll find it –
> > Sarah Helen Whitman
> > (quoted in *SP* 416)

Whitman indicates the paradoxical plight she shares with Oakes Smith and other antebelllum women writers, who "'write without a name'" even when they sign their names just like any man. She attributes their dilemma to a disparity in legal protections when she mockingly signs the letter as if it were a legally binding contract, and she were a naïve woman who could not distinguish between the two. Her "confusion" indicates that a woman's signature on a contract only counts as a personal greeting because coverture laws disable its legal force.[7] Even while the two friends mock their desire for a lasting audience, they critique the limitations of their reception. Their self-conscious ingenuity depends upon generic constraints that they astutely delineate but cannot remove. Rather than subverting or transcending limitation, their critical ingenuity depends upon the full force of their received identity as lyric mediums.[8]

This epistolary exchange articulates key differences between these poetesses' outlooks as well as their shared position. While nineteenth-century terms of reception required that the poetess assume the guise of consumer or commodity in her lyrics, Oakes Smith tried to claim the status of lyric producer. While Whitman and Osgood (who had died by the time of this exchange) accepted the plastic forms of feminine generic identity, Oakes Smith argued against them. Rather than embracing print mediumship, like Osgood, or spiritual mediumship, like Whitman, and dispersing herself via erotic or spiritual communion, Oakes Smith sought to evade the terms of the poetess' reception and set herself up as a rival to Poe and other prominent male writers like Emerson and Coleridge. In recognizing and lamenting her failure, Oakes Smith acknowledged the inevitable fall of the poetess into silence that Tricia Lootens relates to Christian models of sainthood and Yopie Prins locates within a Sapphic tradition of Victorian poetry. Both claim that the poetess can only rise in public estimation by aspiring to an abstract and glorious ideal of womanhood that precludes earthly particularity. Recognizing the inevitability of this transaction, Oakes Smith offered a critical reading of the poetess figure she could not avoid inhabiting.

Virginia Jackson and Yopie Prins locate the specificity of Oakes Smith's rehearsals of the poetess' fall in the extremity of her idealization of the figure: "The poems of Oakes Smith seem to lift the type of the poetess so free of social gravity that it spins in midair. In fact, Oakes Smith's work so idealized the lyrical type that its very abstraction may have consigned it to history."[9] That lyrical type, they assert, emphatically countering feminist critics who seek to recover the woman from the work, is "not a speaker, not an 'I,' not a consciousness, not a subjectivity, not a voice, not a persona, not a self"; rather she is a figure through which women writers explored their "outside position on subjectivity" (523). Such a provocative assertion leaves unanswered the question of why, if the poetess is not the lyric speaker, readers have so long suffered from a case of mistaken identity. Moreover the problem of the poetess, her simultaneous absence and surplus of imagined presence, is not, or not merely, a problem of her own. Rather it is an intensified version of the problem of lyric in an age when the idea of genius held sway. Certainly the tension that M. H. Abrams identifies between mimesis and inspired self-expression, the mirror and the lamp, bears a family resemblance. Though her extreme typicality renders the poetess most vulnerable to oblivion, a broader dynamic of celebrity culture marked popular poets as mediums of exchange whose successful circulation erased their particularity in cultural memory; their collective practices constituted the figures of genius who carried them forward under their individual signatures. Rather than marginal or distinctly separate, the poetess' problems of specificity come, at least in part, from the extreme typicality of her situation, a typicality that makes her worthy of study.[10]

Oakes Smith identified the poetess' problem as one of sameness rather than difference. She noted that Poe's performance of inconsolable sorrow echoed the nightingale tradition in women's poetry, causing women to respond with solace. Because Poe mimicked poetesses, it perplexed Oakes Smith that he did not suffer the same fate of obscurity. Moreover, if poetic genius was predicated on the mimicry of the poetess, then why couldn't a poetess earn the reception of an original? Oakes Smith rehearsed a range of lyric types, both feminine and masculine – she also published under the name Ernest Helfenstein – conducting an algebraic study of the gendered terrain of nineteenth-century poetic possibilities and limitations. In doing so she diagnosed the obstacles to the poetess' survival in cultural memory and demonstrated the ways that masculine romantic forms absorb the feminine types they deny.

Like Poe, Osgood, and Whitman, Oakes Smith was fully immersed in antebellum coterie and print cultures, settings that served as the platform for her advocacy of women's rights and aesthetic reformation. In the 1840s, seeking both critical acclaim and financial gain – her husband's failed business dealings had left their large family bankrupt – she published in a variety of forms and forums, often shrewdly anticipating the reading public's interests (*HL* 2, 259). She contributed to an array of genteel magazines, including *Graham's Magazine*, *Southern Literary Messenger*, and *Godey's Lady's Book*. The publication of *The Sinless Child* in 1842 established her as one of the most talented poetesses of her time. She earned a reputation as a women's rights activist when she took over Margaret Fuller's position at Greeley's *Tribune* in 1849 and wrote a series of influential essays that were issued as a popular pamphlet entitled *Woman and Her Needs* (1851). One of the first women to lecture on the lyceum circuit, she traveled throughout the country from 1851–1857, speaking primarily on women's rights. Her many novels include an early paperback, *The Western Captive* (1842), which sold over 2000 copies in four days; *The Newsboy* (1854), which spurred discussion of child labor reform; and *Bertha and Lily* (1854), a feminist story admired by Susan B. Anthony about an unwed mother who becomes a minister.[11] In the early 1850s she published two plays, *The Roman Tribute*, and *Old New*

York; or Democracy in 1689, which were moderate stage successes. In the 1860s and 1870s, her reputation in decline, she published memoirs about the antebellum New York literary scene and her peers, including Sarah Helen Whitman, Jane Ermina Locke, William Cullen Bryant, N. P. Willis, and Poe. Poverty required her to work even in her seventies, and she sold encyclopedias door to door. She also served as pastor of the Independent Church in Canestota, NY in 1877.[12] Oakes Smith lived long enough to witness the eclipse of her once significant reputation. An avid preserver of her own archives, she clipped for her scrapbook an article written in 1885 by Susan E. Dickinson entitled "Women Writers. A Chapter on Their Ephemeral Reputations. Hopes and Ambitions That Have Faded in Sad Disappointment." Evoking Oakes Smith as one of the last living antebellum literary stars, Dickinson pays homage to her dying memory: "Let us hope that her setting sun . . . may linger in its going down and be beautiful and radiant to the last."[13] In her final years, Oakes Smith positioned herself as the last witness of a dying age and of the death of her own aspirations.

Oakes Smith's sustained contemplation of the poetess' decline and Poe's ascent serves as an appropriate conclusion for this study because such nineteenth-century feminist attempts to critique and transform the gendered terms of reception continue to shape contemporary modes of feminist literary history. Reading Oakes Smith's thoughtful, inventive, but largely unsuccessful experiments in modifying recalcitrant forms in order to craft a female lyric subjectivity affords insight into the ways that critics are also bound to repeat the terms we inherit. Analyzing the terms and conditions of repetition provides insights into nineteenth-century American poetic practices and their legacy that searching for successful innovations cannot. The chapter begins with an analysis of *The Sinless Child*, which proposes a model of feminine genius that cannot resolve the problem of its own reception. In order to purify Eva's mental capacity, Oakes Smith portrays her as God's favorite medium; this portrayal, however, undermines Oakes Smith's authority as her character's creator. Like her author, Eva must relinquish her claim on intellectual reserves in order to gain her reader's admiration. Adopting the pen name Ernest Helfenstein, Oakes Smith then wrote as a man who could not determine how to both retain his mental reserves and share them with his readers. In the late 1840s and 1850s, in her own name, Oakes Smith rewrote the poems of prominent male writers such as Poe and Coleridge in order to expose and condemn their simultaneous appropriation and denial of the feminine. The formal vengeance her poems enact is destructive rather than creative, confirming that the terms of lyric representation are recalcitrant without a shift in the terms of reception.

Giving up on the curative potential of formal experimentation alone, Oakes Smith turned to social criticism in order to challenge the inevitability of feminine dissolution and masculine absorption, positing a utopian ideal of "woman yet to be" that would correct gender inequities. Finally, in her unfinished autobiography and some brief poems, Oakes Smith conducted paradoxical exercises in articulating muteness as a way of claiming lyric identity at her reader's expense. Acknowledging their self-canceling formulations and proffering a conundrum to an uncertain reader, these writings suggest that though the poetess cannot write her way out of her problems of reception, she can identify and diagnose the terms under which she labors.

THE SINLESS CHILD IN SEARCH OF A READER

The Sinless Child stakes a claim for female genius by grafting a masculine capacity for philosophical contemplation on to the figure of a female child that in every other regard is an exaggerated ideal of antebellum femininity. First published in the *Southern Literary Messenger* in 1842 and popular throughout the 1840s, this long verse narrative tells the story of a Christ-like child named Eva whose knowledge is the source of untainted morality rather than a mark of original sin.[14] With a chaste kiss, Eva converts her sinful lover to goodness before she "ceases to be present" and returns to heaven, a place better suited to her ethereal perfection. The story may sound familiar to those who have read *Uncle Tom's Cabin*, whose Little Eva is a direct descendant of Oakes Smith's creation, as is Longfellow's Evangeline. At the time of publication, however, this poem about a holy female child, part angel, part human, was hailed as a unique creation, "a rare work of genius" and "a fresh and original poem, whose inspiration seems drawn from the purest well-springs of thought and fancy."[15] Charles Fenno Hoffman proclaimed that the poem was "so perfect and so pleasurable . . . that we are half-disposed to cry 'Eureka!' and declare that The American Poem has at length been produced by our fair countrywoman."[16]

Although Oakes Smith published many other poems, recent critics of nineteenth-century women's literature consider *The Sinless Child* to be the most important poetic accomplishment of a woman whose talents lay primarily in the realms of political activism and prose, and they have usually restricted their analyses of Oakes Smith's poetry to this early work.[17] Perhaps they have focused upon *The Sinless Child* in part because it most easily fits Jane Tompkins' delineation of a sentimental literature, "not as an artifice of eternity answerable to certain formal criteria, but as a political enterprise, halfway between sermon and social theory, that both codifies and attempts to mold the values of its time."[18] While the poem may be regarded as popular rather than elite and religiously didactic rather than artistic, however, it more precisely dramatizes a struggle between these terms rather than affirming one side of the equation.

In a generally laudatory review, Poe asserts that a conflict between Christian proselytism and secular aestheticism afflicts the poem at its source:

> At one time we fancy her . . . attempting to show that the condition of absolute sanctity is one through which mortality may know all things and hold converse with the angels; at another we suppose it her purpose to "create" (in critical language) an entirely novel being, a something that is neither angel nor mortal, nor yet fairy in the ordinary sense – in a word, an original *ens*. (*ER* 907–908)

According to Poe, Oakes Smith should choose between promoting spiritual communion via the figure of Eva and showcasing her own ability to create an unprecedented "being." Poe elides the distinction between Eva's novelty and the poet's originality, so that Oakes Smith's failure to develop fully the personification of genius results in her poem's failure to be a work of genius. Her conflicting aims cost her nothing less than immortality, in his estimation: "she has very narrowly missed one of those happy 'creations' which now and then immortalise the poet" (911). He does not feel that she has earned his removal of the quotes from around "creation" that would transfer creative powers from God to the poetess. If she had been surer that she was Eva's creator rather than God's mediator, she could have received due credit.

While deeming the poem a promising failure (it *could* have been "one of the best, if not the best, of American poems"), Poe neglects to specu- late about the reasons behind its dual focus. Claiming female powers of poetic origination, Poe as well as Oakes Smith must have known, had little precedent, and he seldom assigned those powers to the poetesses he praised. Seeking to establish the ground for such a claim, Oakes Smith turned to the established presumption that women are more proximate to divinity. *The Sinless Child* embarks on the pedagogic enterprise of intro- ducing the public to a model of inventive female authorship by showcasing that model as a divine invention. That assertion bestows credit on God for creating Woman, which in turn undermines Oakes Smith's claim to origi- nary powers. If the Christ-like child's mystical force of religious conversion seems compelling, then that is because Oakes Smith was God's medium, and the credit should accrue to Him, not her. In other words, Oakes Smith's bid for artistic success erases the figure of the author. As Poe suggests, *The*

Sinless Child is shaped by dual, conflicting ends that undo it in fascinating and informative ways.

The conflict is informed by the legacy of the biblical Eve's original transgression, which underpins the association of sin with "Woman Thought," the phrase Oakes Smith uses in her later writings to evoke a philosophical mode that does not yet exist. She diagnoses a public suspicion of female accomplishment:

> Genius and beauty, God's crowning gifts, are looked upon with distrust, if not with dread. The fear that a woman may deviate the slightest from conventionalism in any way, has become a nervous disease with the public. Indeed, so little is she trusted as a creation, that one would think she were made marvellously beautiful, and endowed with gifts of thought and emotion only for the purpose of endangering her safety – a sort of spiritual locomotive with no check-wheel.[19]

Oakes Smith argues for the positive potential of female deviance by claiming that God sanctions the use of his gifts. Her defense may have aggravated the public concerns she sought to assuage, however, by reminding readers that the Bible depicts the thinking woman as "a spiritual locomotive with no check-wheel," and that the contemporary thinking woman has inherited a potent strain of Eve's sinful rebelliousness.

Oakes Smith is not alone in expressing this concern, of course. Lydia Sigourney also explores intellectual anxieties associated with Eve's legacy in "Thought," one of several poems she wrote about the dangers of thinking. The speaker begins familiarly enough by addressing a muse: "Stay, winged thought!" Rather than inviting the thought to inspire her, however, she interrogates it as an intruder that seeks to seduce and betray her:

> "Thou'rt a subtle husbandman,
> Sowing thy little seed, of good or ill,
> In the moist, unsunn'd surface of the heart.
> But what thou there in secrecy dost plant
> Stands with its ripe fruit at the judgment-day."[20]

The speaker casts Thought as a man who impregnates the female mind indiscriminately with ideas whose growth lies hidden from the bearer. Worried about unwittingly nurturing evil, the speaker instructs readers to "Beware of thoughts. They whisper to the heavens / Though mute to thee." She presents a quandary: composing poems requires entertaining thoughts, but the thoughts will almost certainly mutiny: inseminate the poet with sin, and then "prompt the diamond pen of the recording angel." Sigourney's inventive solution is to write a poem about the problem of thinking in which the speaker hails then rejects the muse without ever inviting him in. Her poem prefaces a poem that remains unwritten.

Oakes Smith's revision of the story of Eve champions her "gifts of thought and emotion" by showing their peaceful inhabitance within a sanctified female mind (*PW* 16). Ultimately, however, no one, including Eva, can sustain the possibility that she can both think and remain sinless. Eva is that "fond Ideal! vital made," blessed with "the gift of thought," whose holiness the narrator frequently reiterates, anticipating a reader's difficulty accepting that she could be both thoughtful and good: "And O! her face was pale and sweet / Though deep, deep thought was there" (38, 40). "Though" underscores the perceived contradiction between sweetness and profundity in a girl. Eva herself fears the "stain" of her own thought, which is supposed to be indisputably holy:

> "The human eye I may not fear,
> It is the light within,
> That traces on the growing soul
> All thought, and every sin.
> That mystic book, the human soul,
> Where every trace remains,
> The record of all thoughts and deeds,
> The record of all stains."   (37)

Like Sigourney's speaker, Eva imagines that a holy pen perpetually traces unconscious thoughts in the soul's "mystic book" for God to read on Judgment Day. Thinking is a form of unwilling writing – and writing is a form of unwilled thought – that results in self-incriminating confession (this recalls Osgood's quite different portrayal of compulsory confession in "To My Pen"). The poem exchanges scenes of Eva's pleasurable reading of the divine book of nature – "Each tiny leaf became a scroll / Inscribed with holy truth" – for scenes of self-exposure before the scathing gaze of the divine critic (21). When Eva the reader becomes God's text, her terror culminates in a vision, cast in the language of Revelation, that collapses thinking, reading, and writing into one searing epiphany:[21]

> "I may not scorn the spirit's rights,
> For I have seen it rise,
> All written o'er with thought, thought, thought,
> As with a thousand eyes!
> The records dark of other years,
> All uneffaced remain;
> The unchecked wish forgotten long,
> With its eternal stain."   (*PW* 48)

Multiplied to sublimity, the spirit's thousand written thoughts read themselves with horrific scrutiny. The collapsed distinction between reader and
writer portrays not sympathetic communion, but the threat of eternal suffering. As in the work of earlier Puritan "saints," Eva's attunement to God's
works also sensitizes her to His judgment. Anticipating her reception precludes her from imagining a mental sanctuary free from an omnipotent
gaze and therefore precludes thought itself, so that Eva's intellectual gifts
ultimately work against mental ambition. *The Sinless Child* presents a double bind in which Eva's attempts to think recall original sin, yet erasing
sin threatens the very capacity for thought, prerequisite for a figure of
genius.

Underscoring this dilemma is Eva's resemblance to the romantic figure,
familiar from the work of Rousseau and Wordsworth, of a prescient, sensitive child of nature who holds the seeds of greatness within him. While
noting the poem's striking newness, Oakes Smith's contemporaries found
its doctrines reminiscent of Wordsworth. One critic writes that "the abstract
theory developed, partakes largely of Wordsworth's philosophy, but in its
details, the story displays a fancifulness and glow wholly distinct from the
bard of Rydal Mount."[22] Central to the poetry of both Wordsworth and
Oakes Smith is the proposition that the child is closer to God than man
because he has recollections of spirit life before birth: "trailing clouds of
glory do we come / From God, who is our home."[23] Wordsworth's adult
poet aims to return to that inspired state via the "philosophic mind," experiencing and overcoming sin in his quest for greatness. Eva's innocence,
however, is the poem's central premise; her problem is trying not to fall
from grace. If the romantic quester tries to return to innocence through
a self-conscious scrutiny of experience, a sinless quester has nowhere to
go.[24] The "absolute sanctity" of the poem's protagonist is antithetical to the
"growth of the poet's mind" even as the poem introduces Eva as an ideal
Poet as well as God's perfect medium.

Unable to assume a lyric subjectivity, Eva is the object rather than the
subject of Oakes Smith's third-person narrative poem. Indeed, Eva's problems with purity impede her ability to generate any narrative, not just
her own. She cannot tell stories about sinners because she cannot comprehend sinful thoughts. Her mother wishes to know, for example, if an
acquaintance murdered his child, and Eva answers: "If thou the story wilt
relate / A light will on me grow / That I shall feel if guilt were his / Or only
common wo" (*PW* 50). Though "thought" is Eva's peculiar talent, she feels
rather than thinks about the father's guilt, and glows with the knowledge
rather than arriving at it through any stipulated mental process. "Thought"

appears in the static rather than the active form; "deep, deep thought was there," in Eva's mind, yet its origins and development remain unclear. Rather than thinking her own thoughts, Eva reads "that mystic book – the human soul – upon which, thoughts, shaped into deeds, whether externally, or only in its own secret chambers, inscribe a character that must be eternal" (46). In other words, she reads others' works rather than writing one herself.

While Eva confirms the character of others by registering their thoughts, she lacks an audience that would validate her own acts of perception. The poem establishes the problem of the non-existent human reader from the outset. Just as Eva fears God's assessment of the text of human souls, her acquaintances, including her own mother, fear her ability to perceive and report their transgressions. Eva addresses her mother:

> "Such gift is mine, the gift of thought,
> Whence all will shrink away,
> E'en thou from thy poor child dost turn,
> With doubting and dismay."   (38)

Rather than reassuring Eva, her mother confirms Eva's perception:

> "The glances of thine eye
> Are such as make me turn away,
> E'en with a shuddering dread,
> As if my very soul might be
> By thy pure spirit read."
>
>   (36–37)

Repulsed by her daughter's awareness, Eva's mother begs her to "leave these solemn words" and "deck thy hair" instead, to care for feminine surfaces rather than depths. Instead of winning an audience with her talents, Eva must sacrifice her admirers to her gift: "Alas! That to assimilate to the good and beautiful should debar us from human sympathy!" (34).

The question of how to command sympathy sharpens into the more pressing question of how to stave off violation. Although powerlessness strengthens the female child's sympathetic purity, it disables her from defending against predatory adults. The poem's embedded narratives offer case studies of perverted domestic relationships in which parental figures abuse the children they should protect simply because they can: a stepmother tortures her husband's children from a first marriage until their mother's ghost forces her to stop; a man apparently rapes and certainly kills his illegitimate son, while the child's mother grieves herself to death. In the story proper, Albert Linne's untempered sexual desire threatens to destroy Eva. A young man who "panted for action and renown," Albert enjoys taking pleasure from women against their will – the "ravished kiss," the "stolen joy" – and that is his desire when he encounters Eva sleeping in the forest. Whereas the narrator has stressed Eva's intellectual gifts as her primary claim on the reader's attention, her unconscious purity rather than her conscious perception stops Albert in his tracks:

> He looks, yet stays his eager foot;
> For, on that spotless brow,
> And that closed lid, a something rests
> He never saw till now;   (73)

Instead of watching Eva read his soul, the scene logically required by the poem's argument for the power of female thought, Albert scans Eva's inert countenance. Neither glowing with the force of awareness nor offering material for Albert's interpretation, Eva's "spotless brow" lacks a legible imprint; an empty page stays Albert's foot. Moreover, though Eva's inscrutable interiority has been the poem's mystical subject, Albert notes that "a something rests" "on" her "brow" and "lid," not within her head. A talisman of purity, Eva's status as visible object, not thinking subject, protects her from attack.

Rather than commanding sympathy, Eva enables self-knowledge. Even after she awakens, the transparent light of her sinlessness lets Albert read his own soul while hers remains invisible. Her purity redirects his energies inward, enabling him to comprehend his criminal past:

> He looked within his very soul,
> Its hidden chamber saw
> Inscribed with records dark and deep
> Of many a broken law.   (74)

Eva's alleged interiority resolves into a mirroring surface that motions others inward by displaying their reflection, a process that resembles psychoanalysis.

By the end of the story, the double binds that vex "Woman Thought" distill into an absolute paradox: in order for Eva to gain a sympathetic audience for her mental talents, she must renounce them. Before Albert, Eva abided by a nun-like vow of solitude, "For who will clasp a maiden's hand / In grot or sheltering grove / If one unearthly gift debar / From sympathy and love!" (38). After she meets Albert, however, a seraph instructs her to be "'Content to feel – care not to know, / The sacred source whence Love arise'" (82). Eva obeys, annulling her philosophical potential:

> . . . Eva doubted, questioned not,
> Content only to feel,
> The music of a manly voice,
> Upon her senses steal –
> To find one heart instinctive learn
> The beatings of her own,
> And read afar unuttered thought
> Known unto his alone.   (82)

Until this point, Eva's interpretive abilities had prevented her from being the subject of human exegesis. In order to experience human communion, she has to give up interpretation altogether. Consecrating her devotion to Albert, Eva not only ceases to think but also "cease[d] to be present" (86). She tempers the sinful reader's invasive desire by dissolving into Albert so completely that "in every voice of prayer or praise / Was heard young Eva's tone" (89). Exchanging voice for inflection, Eva now tinges another's words.[25] Once understood she is absorbed: the act of appreciation consumes the artwork that is also figure of the female artist.[26]

While this final scene of liquidation might seem to annul the poem's attempt to establish a prototype for "Woman Thought," Eva becomes a martyr for the cause, "the lost pleiad in the sky of womanhood," who inspires people to read women writers in general and Oakes Smith in particular (*PW* 86). In the prefatory "Inscription," Oakes Smith sends Eva "forth, to other hearts to speak"; in making her way into the heart of the public, this fictive proselytizer opened a path for the philosopher-poet to follow (15). By embracing Eva as her offspring – "my spirit's cherished dream, its pure ideal birth" – Oakes Smith laid claim to her poetic child's sinlessness (15). Her friends renamed her "Eva" after her creation. Oakes Smith's affiliation with "the pure virgin of the soul" allowed her to taste forbidden pleasures:

The Sinless Child brought me not only favorable critiques from the Press, but, also, a vast number of beautiful letters from both men and women. . . . My husband used to read these letters and poems, and exclaim, "They write like lovers" and so they were: beautiful lovers of the best in our woman nature. After the publication of the Sinless Child my friends called me Eva, and I was having the delights of authorship without the penalties. (*HL* 303)

Oakes Smith figures her new-found celebrity as a pleasurable and unpunishable form of adultery. Providing her with a broad audience and a new public identity, the sinless child sanctions readers' passionate adulation of the author that inspires her husband's jealous admiration. (Seba Smith was a well-known humorist whose reputation declined as Oakes Smith's grew.)

The poem's success spurred her to assert authorial independence from her husband by changing her literary signature from "Mrs. Seba Smith" to "Elizabeth Oakes Smith."

After *The Sinless Child* galvanized the author's feminine credentials, Oakes Smith began experimenting with masculine conventions of authorship under the name Ernest Helfenstein. In the 1840s and 1850s her poems (and occasional short stories) regularly appeared over his and her signatures, often in the same issue of *Graham's Magazine*.[27] In 1848, both Caroline May and Rufus Griswold unveiled the author's identity, which was no secret by then, in their anthologies of women's poetry. Helfenstein's poems appeared in Oakes Smith's collected works as early as 1843, and she published her popular Christmas fable for adults, *The Salamander* (1848), with the subtitle "Found amongst the papers of the late Ernest Helfenstein. Edited by Elizabeth Oakes Smith"; though she killed him off then, poems continued to appear in his name at least into the 1850s, in *The United States Magazine*.[28] Contrasting feminine charm with masculine philosophical rigor, a reviewer recognized that the difference in the signature's gender connoted a difference in writing style: "Mrs. Smith, in her own name, has long been known as a charming writer both of prose and verse, and 'Ernest Helfenstein' has won as high fame in the line of metaphysical speculation."[29] Adopting a male pseudonym was less common for an antebellum woman writer than taking a botanical name that emphasized the affinities of woman with nature and promised a dramatic performance of ultra-femininity. Oakes Smith's choice of a German man's name positioned the woman writer as an apprentice to a masculine romantic tradition by gesturing to one of its most eminent national sources. The name "Helfenstein" – "helping stone" – advertises the pseudonym's function as an aid to understanding masculine structures of poetic expression. Oakes Smith's suggestion that she writes in a dead man's name foregrounds her ventriloquism of an empty conceit.

By writing as a man, Oakes Smith demonstrated the interdependence of gendered conventions rather than enforcing separate spheres of poetic discourse. In Helfenstein's name, she wrote chivalric works with titles such as "Thoughts Before a Duel" and "Stanzas For Julia" that promote feminine powers of purification from a man's point of view.[30] In "The Soul's Ideal," for example, Helfenstein entertains an Eva-like muse who inspires him to quest after spiritual and artistic ascension. Ernest could just as well be Albert appraising the after-effects of absorbing Eva:

> There was a dream, a dream of life and youth,
> That came to me, I know not when the time;
> A creature made of loveliness and youth,
> With form and feature tranquil yet sublime:
> No angel was it, but a thing half real,
> And soon I loved her, as my soul's ideal.
>
> . . . .
>
> She led me where all shapes of beauty dwelt;
> She gave to sense a something more than earth,
> And when my soul its strange unquiet felt,
> She whispered promise of a higher birth:
> She gave me strength the inner life to trace,
> And thus more real grew her own fair face.[31]

Like Albert and many poet-figures before him, Ernest pictures his soul's ideal as a woman whose divinity sustains and reflects his spiritual purification. Whereas Eva dissolves into Albert, this feminine muse becomes increasingly vivid under the pressure of scrutiny. Vividness is not to be mistaken for presence, however: Ernest makes clear that her apparitional nature is the impetus for his spiritual ascent. If she were really there, she would no longer possess purifying powers:

> She taught me faith and constancy to know,
> To meekly wait for the appointed one,
> Despite the yearning felt for evermoe
> While dwells the soul companionless and lone.
> And when at length content upon me came,
> Love and the Soul's Ideal were the same.

Imagining posthumous and post-corporeal Eva's audience, Oakes Smith conjures an ideal reader for her ideal poetess. If Poe can make women readers love the man who cannot stop mourning his Soul's Ideal, Oakes Smith suggests, she can make male readers recognize their indebtedness to their female muses. In the same volume of *Graham's*, she underscores Helfenstein's debt by cross-referencing his "Soul's Ideal" with a poem written in her own name entitled "Mental Solitude," in which a female speaker reminds a soaring male eagle to acknowledge his feminine muse, which she calls his "'Soul's Ideal,'" in quotes.[32]

A partner in Eva's missionary project, Helfenstein lends a portable shape to her liquid purity and sends her out to readers. In a poem entitled "To ___" in *Graham's* and "The Gift" in *The Home Journal*, he describes the contents of his poem, which is itself the gift, to its recipient. Equating it with a diamond-like gem, Helfenstein claims that a static form contains an enlivening liquid center:[33]

> The crystal gem I send to thee
> Is cold, and hard, and bright,
> And valueless the gift will be
> If pondered not aright.
> It changeth not its mystic hue;
> Though storm and flame surround,
> 'Twill gleam as when the miner drew
> Its splendor from the ground.
>
> For deep within its secret core
> A liquid fount is sleeping,
> An uncongealed and hallowed store
> The gem is freshly keeping;
> And thus, ah! thus, for thee I keep
> A fountain sealed and pure,
> Where holiest memories sacred sleep
> And crystal-like endure.
>
> Though many a year of sorrow veil
> The hope that once was ours,
> And I but seem more cold and pale,
> Like nun in cloister bowers,
> Yet will thy memory live unchanged
> A fountain deep concealed,
> Live, though by weary years estranged,
> All else, though cold, congealed.

The poem's impenetrable exterior informs and protects the sensitive center from the reader to whom it is proffered. The beloved may gaze into the crystal but cannot see nor touch the animating core that Helfenstein describes. That core is redundantly composed of the essence of the one whom Helfenstein addresses. He speaks to his love of his love, distilled by memory and preserved through encryption. The "gift" is predicated on the inability to give it, for giving it would defile it.

In the final stanza Helfenstein shifts from talking about his poem to talking about himself, confirming that poem and persona are not only analogous but interchangeable. Both Helfenstein, a poem's personification, and his poem, personified as a poet, are bi-gendered: a masculine stoicism provides an impenetrable receptacle for a feminine essence that is imprisoned and adored. The poem's genderings become even more convoluted when Helfenstein, a woman's conceit of a male poet, likens himself to a cloistered nun. Oakes Smith persistently attempts to purge gender from all but its generic significance in order to argue that women and men can equally inhabit and ventriloquize bi-gendered poetic forms. Her Helfenstein, a woman's impersonation of a man, is the converse of her Poe, whom she casts as a man's impersonation of a woman (see chapter 1 and the coda). In her feminist novel *Bertha and Lily* (1854), Bertha, a grown version of Eva, describes herself as "a woman, a man, if you choose, in intellect, but less than a child in knowledge of the heart."[34] Bertha, who gave birth to an illegitimate sinless child, supercedes a male minister whose name is Ernest Helfenstein and gains a congregation of her own. Understanding that male poets appropriate and ventriloquize female forms to positive effect, Oakes Smith reverses the valence of gendered appropriations. That she recurrently revivifies Helfenstein to rehearse his demise, however, suggests that the dynamics of genius are not as symmetrical and exchangeable as she would like. Though Helfenstein may expand the poetess' repertoire, he leaves the masculine configuration of solids and liquids intact, so that Oakes Smith must reiterate in a man's voice the Poet's absorption of the poetess.

POETIC JUSTICE

Though masculine captivation, absorption, and circumscription of the feminine may be inevitable in *The Sinless Child* and the poems of Ernest Helfenstein, other poems project feminine speakers that seek to disengage their attention from masculine figures, with little success. Oakes Smith turned to the Gothic mode for these experiments. If sympathetic feeling leads to feminine entrapment, converting women from speakers to listeners, from writers to readers, and from producers to consumers, one might posit that the process could be reversed by abnegating the "tender sentiments": love, pathos, and elegiac melancholy. In a rendition of "The Raven" entitled "Love Dead" (1848) the speaker goes one step further and murders Love at its source. The poem's epigraph serves as an epitaph for the poem's contents, delivered dead to a man's door:

The lady sent him an image of Cupid, one wing veiling his face. He was pleased thereat, thinking it to be Love sleeping, and betokened the tenderness of the sentiment. He looked again, and saw that it was Love dead and laid upon his bier.[35]

Expecting tender sentiments from his "lady," "he" is taken aback by her cruel joke. Her message, easily mistaken for a token of regard, signifies the death of her love for him. The male reader, not the female writer, is the sentimentalist whose search for female tokens that validate his significance is frustrated by her vengeful negation. The lyric speaker simultaneously decries a tradition that bestows upon women's poetry the status of biological emission, and masculine configurations of genius that replicate the practices of poetesses while denying any relation.[36] The image of the dead Cupid embodies two inseparable traditions: the poetic melancholy of Sigourney – the insatiable longing for a dead infant – and the poetic melancholy of Poe – the insatiable longing for a beautiful dead woman. Both formulations present the woman poet with a single obstacle: the conversion of a woman speaker into a captive audience. The first tradition insists upon an empathic identification with the lost child that arrests and encompasses the maternal mourner's attention. The second tradition relies upon a woman's death to nourish the poem's "Mournful and Never-ending Remembrance." If "the death of a beautiful woman is unquestionably the most poetical topic in the world," and "the lips best suited for such a topic are those of a bereaved lover," as Poe absurdly codifies in "The Philosophy of Composition," then how is a woman poet convincingly to claim the role of lyric subject (*ER* 19)? Oakes Smith suggests the recalcitrance of the problem in the extremity of her proposed solution: she stages the death not only of the loved one, but also of the poetic tableaux of Love itself.

Identifying the source of her dilemma, the speaker kills love in the symbolic presence of a rival poem: a specter of Poe's Raven wafts through the poem's initial lines:

> Flapping came a heavy wing, sounding pinions o'er my head,
> Beating down the blessed air with a weight of chilling dread –
> Felt I then the presence of a doom
> That an Evil occupied the room.[37]

A bird's "heavy" "flapping" oppresses the speaker and informs her utterance. The trochaic octameter and frequent use of identical "ing" rhymes formally echo "The Raven," with the difference that Oakes Smith's lines cut off Poe's feminine endings. Oakes Smith's formal emulation identifies the bird as Poe's, but the word "pinions" suggests that the Raven arrived in Oakes Smith's poem via Sarah Helen Whitman's valentine to Poe ("Oft in dreams, thy ghastly pinions / Wave and flutter round my door–"). Whereas Whitman's speaker welcomes the Raven's visitation and embraces the glamour of Poe's influence, Oakes Smith's speaker resents his intrusive omnipresence. The "sounding pinions" that flap through the poem evoke not so much the overshadowing problem of genius, but of an insinuating rhythm that forces the speaker to write to the "beating pulse" of Poe's contagious meter. In "The Raven" Poe's speaker writes beneath the shadow of Elizabeth Barrett Browning's *Lady Geraldine's Courtship*. Now Oakes Smith evokes her metrical anxiety via the figure of Poe, suggesting that his Raven dooms her poem before it begins by determining its reactive make-up.

Restaging the epigraph in the poem proper, the speaker diagnoses herself as suffering from a suffocating intimacy with the figure of Love, and seeks to resolve the problem by murdering the infant Cupid nestled close to her heart. Though the title "Love Dead" implies a passive end to Cupid, the speaker confesses to murder while dissociating herself – like Poe's first-person narrators – from the meaning of her actions:

> I knew that Love could never change –
> That Love should die seems yet more strange –
> Lifting up the downy veil, screening Love within my heart,
> Beating there as beat my pulse, moving like myself a part –
> I had kept him cherished there so deep,
> Heart-rocked kept him in his balmy sleep,
> That till now I never knew
> How his fibres round me grew –
> Could not know how deep the sorrow
> Where Hope bringeth no tomorrow.
>
> I struggled, knowing we must part;
> I grieved to lift him from my heart;
> Grieving much and struggling much, forth I brought him sorrowing;
> Drooping hung his fainting head, all adown his dainty wing,
> Shrieked I with a wild and dark surprise –
> For I saw the marble in Love's eyes;
> Yet I hoped his soul would wait
> As he oft had waited there,
> Hovering, though at Heaven's gate –
> Could he leave me to despair?

"Love" is a sinister fetus, at once alien and intimate, that parasitically nourishes itself from the speaker's heart's blood. "Moving like myself a part," Love is not a wholly convincing rendition of a human child or a personal feeling: a foreign body may be mimicking the motions of the host in order to stay unchallenged. The speaker responds ambivalently by "screening" – both protecting and interrogating – this potential intruder. Its "fibres," evocative of paper as well as plantlike tendrils, threaten to contract not only "round" the heart, but also round the speaker's identity, her "me." "Love" is a poem of ambiguous origin: its "beating" echoes both the speaker's pulse and Poe's poem. The lines that most closely mimic "The Raven" are those in which Cupid seems to thrive, and cutting off his oxygen supply disrupts the poem's rhythm: the lines "I struggled . . ." and "I grieved . . ." switch from trochaic to iambic meter, jarring the heart's rocking; the lines contract from eight beats, to six beats, to four beats and then fluctuate, as if gasping for air. The speaker confesses to aborting her body's inhabitant even while the poem's dissociative logic denies cause and effect. "Knowing we must part," she uproots Love's constricting "fibres"; "grieving much and struggling much," she "lift[s] him from my heart." Her ambiguous reaction to discovering the "marble in Love's eyes" – she "shriek'd with wild and dark surprise" – registers incomprehension that severing the blood supply would cause Love's death, or that she would do such a thing, even while she has already admitted to it.

The speaker marks her own survival by underscoring the death of Love:

> Unfolded they the crystal door,
> Where love shall languish never more.
> Weeping love, thy days are o'er. Lo! I lay thee on thy bier,
> Wiping thus from thy dead cheek every vestige of a tear.
> Love has perished: hist, hist, how they tell,
> Beating pulse of mine, his funeral knell!
> Love is dead – ay, dead and gone!
> Why should I be living on? –
> Why be in this chamber sitting,
> With but phantoms round me flitting?

"Beating pulse of mine, his funeral knell!" doubles as an exultant confession of murder and a celebration of survival. The speaker negates Love's languishing by using its own sign, Poe's "never more," against itself. According to the poem's logic the speaker can only survive by murdering communion. Although "Love Dead" prepares the ground for a lyric subject by extinguishing an empathic model of femininity, the speaker discovers too late that she needs a listener in order to speak, and the poem concludes with uncertainty about how to fill the space it has cleared. In offering up murdered sentiments, "Love Dead" forcibly denies female sympathy to the male recipient in order to make the female speaker the center of attention. Her figural violence commands the reader's attention via affront: shock, perplexity, and aversion supplant identification. Oakes Smith counters Poe's portrayal of a narcissistic man obsessed with his own suffering with a narcissistic woman who mourns the death not of a man, but of sympathetic attraction. What is left at the end of the poem is not mournful and never-ending remembrance, but the question of how to engage the reader at all, and whether there is any possibility of speech beyond the generic constraints that "Love Dead" tried to destroy. Just as Poe's speaker sits under the shadow of the raven, Oakes Smith's "Love Dead" sits under the shadow of "The Raven" while dramatizing its dilemma.

The number of Oakes Smith's poems that enact female vengeance towards recalcitrant traditions testifies to a discontinuity between fantasies of apocalypse and a modified vision. In "Love Dead" the first does not result in the second, and the poem voices frustration at the unregenerative outcome of the experiment. "The Drowned Mariner," published in *The Poetical Writings of Elizabeth Oakes Smith* (1845), again dramatizes female invisibility by directing the reader's attention towards a familiar point of poetic visibility, Coleridge's "The Rime of the Ancient Mariner": the titles alone indicate a murderous relation between Oakes Smith's poem and its predecessor (*PW* 187–189). "The Drowned Mariner" proposes that the solitary quester, another commanding figure of suffering masculine genius, has literally submerged his feminine relations, and that the murdered albatross stands in for an unconfessed crime against women. In "The Rime," a female specter of "Life-in-death" metes out the Mariner's punishment.[38] When she departs, the moon rises in her place to illuminate his crime. Oakes Smith's poem is also illuminated by "moonlight pale," and the lunar speaker uses her omniscient perspective to orchestrate the feminine powers of sea, ship, and storm to punish the mariner for killing his betrothed.

Oakes Smith's mariner sets out on his solitary sea voyage confident of his heroic stature and blithely unaware that he is caught up in a psychic storm of channeled rage:

> The mariner swayed and rocked on the mast,
> But the tumult pleased him well,
> Down the yawning wave his eye he cast,
> And the monsters watched as they hurried past,
> Or lightly rose and fell;
> For their broad, damp fins were under the tide,
> And they lashed as they passed the vessel's side,
> And their filmy eyes, all huge and grim,
> Glared fiercely up, and they glared at him.[39]

The sea creatures hover just beneath the surface of the water like submerged thoughts. Part of the landscape that the mariner oversees, they glare back with malice at being overlooked. He, however, is too complacent – "pleased" with the "tumult" – to notice the threat. Oakes Smith's turn on the romantic ballad suggests that she levels charges against poetic form. She underscores her poem's secondary and recursive status by retracing and doubling the ballad stanza – a form that already troubles the relation between folk art and individual accomplishment – lingering on rhymes for two lines before moving on to the next. Delaying narrative progression, the speaker broods on the form itself. This stationary motion echoes the "yawning wave" that sways and rocks the boat within the poem, suggesting that Oakes Smith's formal disruptions joggle the mariner, but he little suspects that they foreshadow narrative revenge.

The invisible wrath reveals itself to be explicitly feminine in the fourth stanza. Feminine boat, ocean, and speaker collude to conjure up the mariner's moment of judgment:

> Wildly she rocks, but he swingeth at ease,
> And holds him by the shroud;
> And as she careens to the crowding breeze,
> The gaping deep the mariner sees,
> And the surging heareth loud.
> Was that a face, looking up at him,
> With its pallid cheek, and its cold eyes dim?
> Did it beckon him down? Did it call his name?
> Now rolleth the ship the way whence it came.
>
> The mariner looked, and he saw with dread,
> A face he knew too well;
> And the cold eyes glared, the eye of the dead,
> And its long hair out on the wave was spread,
> Was there a tale to tell?
> The stout ship rocked with a reeling speed,
> And the mariner groaned, as well he need,
> For ever down, as she plunged on her side,
> The dead face gleamed from the briny tide.
>
> Bethink thee, mariner, well of the past,
> A voice calls loud for thee –
> There's a stifled prayer, the first, the last,
> The plunging ship on her beam is cast,
> Oh, where shall thy burial be?
> Bethink thee of oaths that were lightly spoken,
> Bethink thee of vows that were lightly broken,
> Bethink thee of all that is dear to thee, –
> For thou art alone on the raging sea.   (45–46)

Now "she" rather than the mariner "rocks," and he begins to feel implicated: he not only "looked" but also finally "saw with dread." His dawning recognition accompanies the metamorphosis of the glaring monsters into a single corpse of a drowned woman that charges the mariner with an unspoken crime. The narrator's precise series of interrogatives suggest that she knows of a criminal secret in the mariner's past, one that he hoped to bury at sea but that now resurfaces. Instruments of vengeance, the "raging sea" and the ship that rocks ever more "wildly" "with a reeling speed," disrupt his solitary adventure and force him to confront his shadowy past by rejoining a wronged woman in her watery grave. Oakes Smith's narrator suggests that "The Rime's" tale of a crime against an albatross covers up another story of a crime the mariner has committed against the drowned woman, one that leaves him free to roam the earth divested of family ties. The true "tale to tell," according to Oakes Smith's revisionary poem, would be about the dubious value of the "oaths" and "vows" the mariner made to others before he ever boarded the ship.

The dead woman's interrogation – "And the cold eyes glared, the eye of the dead, / And its long hair out on the wave was spread" – echoes the description of the inspired poet in "Kubla Khan" – "His flashing eyes, his floating hair!" – marking the crime as one of poetic appropriation.[40] The inspired man seems to have drawn his extraordinary electrical charge from the dead woman, leaving her enraged corpse to bear witness. Exacting punishment for poetic abandonment, Oakes Smith's narrator drains the mariner of resistance and extinguishes his electric gleam:

> The stout limbs yield, for their strength is past,
> The trembling hands on the deep are cast,
> The white brow gleams a moment more,
> Then slowly sinks – the struggle is o'er.   (46)

She then sends him to the ocean floor where he must reunite with the family realm, and the domestic verse forms, that his quest had submerged.

Affirming the democratizing powers of death, the descent strips away layers of distinction until the mariner rests on the ground upon which principles of exclusion are built:

> Down, down, where the storm is hushed to sleep,
> Where the sea its dirge shall swell,
> Where the amber drops for thee shall weep,
> And the rose-lipped shell her music keep,
> There thou shalt slumber well.
> The gem and the pearl lie heaped at thy side,
> They fell from the neck of a beautiful bride,
> From the strong man's hand, from the maiden's brow,
> As they slowly sunk to the wave below.
> A peopled home is the ocean bed,

> The mother and child are there –
> The fervent youth and the hoary head,
> The maid, with her floating locks outspread,
> The babe with its silken hair,
> As the water moveth they lightly sway,
> And the tranquil lights on their features play;
> And there is each cherished and beautiful form,
> Away from decay, and away from the storm.
>
> (46)

A specific charge is finally leveled against the mariner upon his arrival at the ocean's floor, and evidence of his crimes, perfectly preserved if not fully explicit, is finally arrayed against him. "A beautiful bride," the first in a list of generic types and the one the speaker dwells upon longest, has been raped and strangled. The description underscores the theft's redundancy: "The strong man's hand" took all her pearls, both the symbols of purity strung around her neck and her actual virginity. Oakes Smith's story explains Coleridge's Mariner's compulsive need to speak to the Wedding Guest. The crime has ceased to matter by the time it is revealed, however, because now the mariner has joined the crowd. A gem-like realm of petrified humanity where the dead sleep in domestic harmony, the "peopled home" of "the ocean bed" embodies a sentimental aesthetic so often placed in opposition to Romanticism, the "low" to its "high." The props of sentimental poetry – tears preserved in "amber drops" and elegiac music from a "rose-lipped shell" – indoctrinate the drowned mariner into a poetic culture where he is one of many citizens, and "each cherished and beautiful form" finds a preserve "away from decay and away from the storm." Drowning the mariner reveals a buried multiplicity of forms, one for each group previously represented by the representative man. This utopian landscape of poetic multiplicity, however, is coded as irrecoverable, for it exists out of sight and beyond the reach of the living in a lost city of the enshrined poetic dead. Oakes Smith portrays this alternative landscape as a place that can be imagined but not conveyed. She submits to her readers a buried, irrecoverable vision. Her Gothic poems of the 1840s level formal charges of appropriation but again run up against the recalcitrance of gendered poetic traditions.

"FEMININE TERMINATION"

Finding no formal remedy for poetic injustices, Oakes Smith broadened her scope in the 1850s to examine the social underpinnings of gender inequities.

While she continued to publish poems, she also began diagnosing wrongs against women in lectures and prose writings. She was a delegate and speaker at the women's rights conventions of the 1850s, shared lecture platforms with Emerson and abolitionist Wendell Philips, and met with success on the public lecture circuit while also generating controversy: a number of her friends and acquaintances did not approve of women speaking in public and ceased relations with her.[41] In addition to *Woman and Her Needs*, she published many other polemical pieces in magazines and newspapers that diagnosed and prescribed remedies for social injustices against women. Impressed by Oakes Smith's feminist novel *Bertha and Lily*, Susan B. Anthony wrote to say that while she was normally too practical to enjoy romances, this one "will do a glorious work for women."[42] Underscoring the importance of mass media for the success of the women's rights movement, Anthony stressed that the work should be "published in a form so cheap that the poorest serving women might be able to buy a copy of it."

Rather than dismissing aesthetic aspirations in favor of political activism, Oakes Smith insisted that the two were inextricably linked: "I speak upon literary as well as reformatory grounds," she informed the editor of the *Evening Mirror*.[43] She articulated a rather fluid and inconsistent social theory of poetry in which the horizon of aesthetic accomplishment is dependent upon the conditions of social justice. Oakes Smith located the origins of women's literary limitations in undue social constraints. In an article entitled "Inequality of the Sexes," she asserted that the "poetry of woman is always of a melancholy cast" because "she is too large for the sphere in which society compels her to move" (quoted in *HL* 296). Because she rarely has "magnanimity enough to . . . grasp any sceptre of power; therefore it is that she beats her wings against her barriers, and fills the air with her sad complainings."[44] Under the stress of containment, writing and publishing poetry serve as therapy: "Women poets pour out their sorrows in rhythm, and are thus more cheerful in their daily walk than the discontented wife and fretting mother who have no such resources." Meter offers the solace to women that rocking offers crying children, but the home remedy is unsuited for the name of Poetry, for women are rendered inarticulate with grief over the loss of their proper dimensions: "We are by no means content with our women poets. Because the good Father works no miracle in their relief, they will not see that the same voice, so full of melancholy power in its wailings, is the sign of a force no less potent in redemption" (*HL* 296). Although Oakes Smith exhorts women to convert their collective grief into redemptive potency, she also implies that accomplishing the transition would take a miracle, one the Father chooses not to work. In order for women to be capable of producing great art they must expand to their proper social and spiritual circumference, but the way to achieve this is elusive.

Expanding circumference was a central preoccupation of one of the era's most prominent personifications of genius, Ralph Waldo Emerson, who stresses both the poet's receptive capabilities and his ability to stand alone: "The Poet is the man without impediment, who sees and handles that which others dream of, traverses the whole scale of experience, and is representative of man, in virtue of being the largest power to receive and to impart."[45] In "Experience," he attributes this ability to himself:

My reception has been so large, that I am not annoyed by receiving this or that superabundantly. I say to the Genius, if he will pardon the proverb, In for a mill, in for a million. When I receive a new gift, I do not macerate my body to make the account square, for, if I should die, I could not make the account square. (*RWE* 233)

Emerson's infinitely expansive receptivity enables him to become as large as anything Genius offers. He makes the insights of others his own not by claiming sole ownership, but by absorbing what also belongs to others without thinking less of himself. The poet has a strong enough hold on his "I" that he can receive everything that comes from outside without losing himself. As in other formulations of his time, Emerson's vision of "the great man" doubles as a prescription for producing a great poem. Coleridge succinctly articulates the intimate relation: "What is poetry? Is so nearly the same question with, what is a poet? That the answer to one is involved with the solution of the other."[46]

Oakes Smith shares Emerson's perspective without sharing his ability to evoke a subject that can "receive and impart" under his own name even while naming his relation to a larger measure. If Emerson's Representative Man, like Walt Whitman's Walt, is not complete in himself but contains multitudes, Oakes Smith's woman has difficulty assembling the fragments of particular relational identities into a whole: "We live in fragments – daughter, wife, mother, friend – no woman's life is rounded unless she fills these relations" (*HL* 73). Instead of "receiving this or that superabundantly," like Emerson's Man, Oakes Smith's Woman "fills . . . relations" to others: her identity is incidental, not immanent, and she cannot hope to forge a receptive circle until she assembles all the pieces into a rounded life.

In *Woman and Her Needs*, Oakes Smith locates the source of the difference between Emerson's ever-completing Poet and her own fragmented poetess in a system of governance that makes Man a citizen and Woman a subject of his laws. Marriage, the institution that enforces this hierarchy, is the single greatest obstacle to female subjectivity, on a par with death itself. In the "marriage relation," a woman's "very existence is merged with that of her husband; the children of her blood are not hers; her property is not hers; she is legally dead."[47] Marriage is morally bankrupt as a purported social contract, for while the groom is a fully consenting party, the bride is "an infant in law, whose pen to a commercial contract would be worthless; who might indeed be hung for murder, or imprisoned for theft, but whose name in a contract is nothing."[48] Man's superior, expansive integrity is contingent on subsuming "the Puritan woman," who, "with here and there a revolt, as in the case of Anna Hutchinson, looked up to men in the Miltonic style: 'He for God only, She for God in *him*'" (*HL* 180).

Arguing for women's property rights sensitized Oakes Smith to the possibility that writers without legal recourse may lose their work to better-positioned authors without a trace. Just as the husband's legal advantage allows him to take his wife's property, Emerson's literary pre-eminence enables him to posit an absorptive poetics in which the representative man may "receive and impart" the thoughts and feelings of others while augmenting his identity. Reporting a conversation with the sage, she complains that "Emerson defends this practice of taking material wherever it may be found"; Oakes Smith takes issue with his assertion that " 'Thought is common property; all have a right to the best' " (*HL* 283).[49] Emerson argues, as Harold Bloom does after him, that "The greatest genius is the most indebted man" who makes others' thoughts his own.[50] In such a formulation, Oakes Smith sees only "a wholesale defense of plagiarism" (*HL* 283).[51] Emerson's model of the artist as representative man threatens to drain a precariously defended supply of thoughts:

Emerson has defined the poet as "a man without impediment." The modern idea of art opens a wide field for laborious endeavor and a great sluiceway to plagiarism. A writer finds a thought full of artistic suggestion, and straightway he makes artistic use of it. I remember Mr. Emerson, in a conversation with me, justified the so doing; but to me it seems an ill use of another's property.[52]

Identifying with the forgotten more than the remembered, Oakes Smith wishes to protect the anonymous writers whose work nourishes the Representative Man so that he can grow to superhuman proportions. While both poetesses and the Poet were credited with receptive powers, then, poetesses were unable to claim the insights that nourished the Poet's expansion.

Oakes Smith personalized the issue when she expressed the wish that her social activism would some day result in a great poem. Writing to E. P. Whipple in 1851 about her "wonderful success" as a lecturer, Oakes Smith says she is "happier in being thus a voice to my kind than I ever could be in any mere Artistic effort." She aligns the "mere Artistic" with the selfishly personal, against the Woman who could represent the griefs of her "kind." Finding artistry divorced from public duty insufficient, she hopes that social activism will prepare her to write a great poem: "In the meanwhile I do not neglect literature, and hope this may be part of the discipline that is to prepare me for a great Poem hereafter – if I do not write it the conception grows beautiful and grand before me, and seems a point to be obtained – if not it upholds me now."[53] On Heaven or on a more perfect earth, accomplishing the "great Poem hereafter" would reward her service as the voice of her kind. Milton is her example:

Nothing can live that is not en-vased. The form must be beautiful, or the creation sinks with the old chimeras of rude chaos and dull night. Milton lived a life of achievement, nursing in his great heart the desire at some time to write "something which his countrymen would not willingly let die." Here was the true soul of the artist. Paradise Lost realized the hope.[54]

Living an admirable life converts mortal body to immortal soul, and poems replicate the beautiful human form that generates them. The public man and the "en-vased" poem are identical; because the pathways to an effective public life are closed to women her poems necessarily emerge deformed and her countrymen let them die.

Oakes Smith repeatedly insists that the contemporary woman is a man-made substitute for the non-existent True Woman: "Men have written for us, thought for us, legislated for us; and they have constructed from their own consciousness an effigy of a woman, to which we are expected to conform."[55] Woman has had to be the object of man's ventriloquy – to "see and hear through his senses, and believe according to his dogmas" (27). While "men seem resolved to have but one type in our sex," Oakes Smith asserts "our right to individuality" (27). In asserting that right, however, she encounters a circular problem. The individual woman cannot emerge before the public has ratified an ideal to which she can aspire: "the idea of a true noble womanhood is yet to be created. It does not live in the public mind."[56] In order to establish that ideal, however, a worthy female individual must prove its plausibility. Lacking both an individual and a type, Oakes Smith tries to write both into being, even while she notes the futility of the task: Woman "must cast herself down amid the aridness of thought – hungry and thirsty for the truth."[57]

Oakes Smith debated the terms of women's poetic achievement with poetess Mary Forrest (who appeared in the previous chapter as Sarah

Helen Whitman's intimate correspondent) in an exchange of letters published in *The Evening Mirror* in 1855. Forrest wrote to the *Mirror's* editor, Hiram Fuller, to chastise him for condemning Oakes Smith's willingness to display herself on the lecture circuit: "you are merciless towards her as a lecturer."[58] She later asked Fuller for an introduction: "I *like* her and want to shake hands with her. May I do so through your paper?"[59] In the letter of greeting that followed, Forrest reassured Oakes Smith that while some may find her "'strong-minded' thought" unnatural in a woman, Forrest is certain that her womanhood is intact: "If, then, through the medium of strong, deep thoughts, written or spoken, seasonably, you achieve a noble purpose you are no less a woman – no less a God-commissioned woman!"[60] While affirming Oakes Smith's gender, Forrest is "not yet a convert to your peculiar theory" that women should yoke their artistic and spiritual energies to public advocacy of social causes. In her response Oakes Smith suggests that Forrest is more like her than she lets on by drawing attention to the fictive nature of Forrest's "private" plea: "your object was not to say all this to me personally – you desired that your whole-souled utterance should be broadcast, like the book which called it forth."[61] (Forrest had noted that she admired Oakes Smith's social protest novel *The Newsboy*.) The two women, assuming the roles of ultra-feminine poetess and ambiguously gendered philosopher-poet, go on to debate the contours and content of womanhood, with Forrest playing the resisting potential convert, Oakes Smith the proselytizer for a public ideal of womanhood.

Younger than Oakes Smith and apparently unfamiliar with her 1840s incarnation as "Eva" the sinless poetess, Forrest says that Oakes Smith's "idea is 'bodied forth' so softly, I quite suspect you of being a poetess, though I do not remember to have seen anything in the poetical vein over your signature. Tell me, do you write poetry?"[62] When Forrest claims to intuit Oakes Smith's purely feminine poetic sensibility, Oakes Smith dissociates herself from inherent femininity and claims that true art is sexless:

You say you suspect me to be a "Poetess." Shall we not drop the feminine termination? There should be no sex in the world of Art. Milton and Shakespeare and Michael Angelo were Poets. Elizabeth Browning is a Poet. It is a term not to be highly arrogated. Verse-writing is too common to be entitled to my especial notice, and I am utterly nauseated with the cool conceit with which these writers assume the term. Grasshoppers chirp, and beetles whirr, and crickets are said to sing, and so I suppose these insects in the realm of Poesy must be called poets, Gerald Massey, and all, who flaunt their domesticity before the public like a sort of Barnum baby show put into rhythm.[63]

After the style of Emerson, Oakes Smith strives through oracular pro-nouncements to enact a new set of relations that "drop the feminine termination." While Emerson derides the "female poetasters" as "the anti-poetic influences of Massachusetts," Oakes Smith condemns a male practitioner for the domestic exhibitionism usually charged to poetesses.[64] In place of appellations like "songbird" and "nightingale" that naturalize the relation between women and light verse and endow the poetess with a compensatory glamour, Oakes Smith substitutes the vaguely masculine and demeaning metaphors of beetle, grasshopper, and cricket, creatures associated with mechanical monotony rather than sentimental expressiveness. On a second front, she challenges the exclusive alignment of men with high art by placing Elizabeth Barrett in the company of Milton, Shakespeare, and Michelangelo, a move that Barrett had made before her.

Oakes Smith finally responds to Forrest's query after rephrasing it in acceptable terms:

Yes, I "lisped in numbers, for the numbers came," if that is to be a Poet. If to feel a soul in all the great universe of God, to leap at the record of good and noble deeds, to weep at human suffering and pray for human redemption . . . constitute a Poet, I must be one. I say it reverently and modestly, "magnifying mine office," "not as if I had already attained," but in view of intimations, and hope for the future; for, as Milton said, I have wished at some time "to write something, which my country men would not willingly let die."[65]

Oakes Smith's testimonial to poetic genius is composed largely of her male predecessors' words. Her verbal bricolage seems strangely superfluous because the expressed sentiments are so unremarkable: "to feel a soul," "to weep at human suffering" are appropriate aspirations for any poet or poetess. Because the sentiments are the same, great men's words take on a fetishistic power to remove Oakes Smith from one category and insert her in the other. The quotes alone mark both the proximity and the distance between them. She punctuates her proclamation of future greatness with a sonnet addressed to Forrest that both asserts and cancels its poetic claim. Its first words – "Not yet, not yet!" – begin by declining to begin, and the speaker continues by refusing to join Forrest in the "sylvan shade" and "mountain glade" of the woodland "where, tunefully, ye wile the hours along." She chooses instead to help the needy: "I in aid of these must pass ye by!" Oakes Smith simultaneously confirms and denies Forrest's suspicion of her ambition by offering a poem that defers poetic accomplishment.

In a poetic oratory delivered in Boston at a women's rights convention for which Emerson was the main speaker, Oakes Smith expands on ideas about gender and genius that are implicit in her exchange with Forrest. "Thoughts on Woman," a long philosophical contemplation in blank verse, argues that gender categories are in fact moral designations, distinct from biological sex. Milton and Tennyson don't realize this, but Shakespeare gets it right:

> We talk too much of sex, as Milton did –
> And Tennyson does now – and all weak men;
> But mighty Shakespeare better read the truth,
> And framed a murderous Macbeth, woman weak
> And manish bad; bound to a tiger wife –
> A manish woman, cruel, keen – who longed
> For pomp and power, nor scrupled at the means,
> So she could rule.[66]

"Woman" means weak and good, "man" means powerful and bad. Womanish man and "manish woman," Macbeth and his Lady are gender hybrids whose biological assignations have little to do with their moral character or capabilities.

In an eclectic vision combining Platonic and Christian elements, the record of earthly deeds determines gender in the afterlife. Initially, the perfect celestial form seems to be asexual: "True man and woman true but represent / A soul, where sex is not." But then Oakes Smith distinguishes between biological sex and conceptual gender; while the soul has no sex, it is gendered feminine: "All fairest forms / Will take the woman shape; the finer sense / Take hers. Poets are women in disguise – ." The divine light will reveal that Milton, Shakespeare, and the rest are really women who visited this earth disguised in transgendered form, or who transcended their male bodies to achieve womanly perfection. The body of woman is the spiritual form that the morally pure individual will assume in the afterlife:

> The resurrection light will show that men,
> The truest, noblest types of manly worth,
> Have all been women: she, if base and vile,
> Unchaste and sensual, proves herself a man.
> The woman type is higher far than she –
> The highest of her sex, who sits apart
> In her white folds over her snowy breast
> And sighs at her own beauty –

This formulation retains and even intensifies a claim for the female form's superiority while also rendering gender designation arbitrary. Good men can be women and bad women can be men in the afterlife, and women who assume masculine roles in this life – speaking in public and showing concern for civic duties – are preparing for true womanhood in the celestial sphere.

Even while Oakes Smith insists on the arbitrariness of earthly gender, she reaffirms woman's spiritual superiority. Because the female form is the divine shape of moral purity, then earthly women cannot help but hold premonitory significance:

> In the great archetype there is no sex.
> The revelator on his lonely isle
> The woman yet to be, beheld – and saw
> In vision, gorgeous and sublime, a shape
> More grand and beautiful than earth has seen . . .

The "woman yet to be" is a non-existent ideal that earthly women nevertheless resemble. If true poets are future women, then the Great Archetype is a Poetess in which the feminine is not a termination but a foundation. At the peak of optimism, Oakes Smith summons a prophetic vision of what is yet to be that leaves unanswered the question of how earthly women get from here to there. Her later writings indicate that she never discerned a way.

"UNSPEAKABLE ELOQUENCE"

Oakes Smith introduces her autobiography as a project of recording what has already been forgotten: "I will now write a book in which I will figure as the principal personage. . . . I belong now to a past period, the memory of which it may be well to retain" (*HL* 72). The fate she predicted in her poetic exchange with Whitman fulfilled, Oakes Smith casts herself as a ghost of a forgotten age to which her autobiography will bear witness. Contemplated as early as 1848, promoted in a series of "Autobiographic Notes" published in *Beadle's Monthly* in 1867, her *Human Life: Being the Autobiography of Elizabeth Oakes Smith* remained unfinished and unpublished when she died in 1893.[67] As if she were not fully willing to live in the present, she disrupts her attempts at retrospective synthesis with newspaper clippings from the 1840s, 1850s, and 1860s that are pasted into the text; sometimes she attempts to integrate them into the manuscript, sometimes they stand alone without comment. Her collage approach to autobiography blurs distinctions between middle and late periods of her work and generates tensions between her earlier celebrity and her almost complete obscurity at the time of the autobiography's final writing. Though she asserts a wish to preserve the past and to claim some measure of personal significance, she never fulfills her repeated promise to publish the work. In her later writings Oakes Smith characterizes her future obscurity as a near certainty, but she nevertheless writes as if she will be read, as if it were necessary, even when impossible, to compose subjectivity in relation to a comprehending reader.

Reflecting this self-cancelling situation, Oakes Smith's later work explores an abortive poetics that counters Emerson's absorptive poetics. If an absorptive aesthetic is the counterpart of the man who remains fully self-possessed in marriage, an abortive aesthetic is the counterpart of the woman who must give herself away. Oakes Smith locates women's lost capacity for greatness in her maidenhood, "the most beautiful and the most suggestive period of a woman's life" (*HL* 174). The young virgin approximates the profile of the romantic genius as the "complete man." Virginity signifies productive and alluring self-enclosure for Oakes Smith: "To me the Puritan maiden seems a creature of exquisite grace, sweetness and purity, suggesting only a lovely remoteness, the seclusion of Oriental symbolism – 'A garden enclosed – a spring shut up – a fountain sealed.'"[68] Marriage violates the spiritual integrity upon which intellectual and artistic accomplishments are based: "Oh! the beautiful world that once faded from view. . . . Where was the sacred inner consciousness that allies the maiden to the angels?" (*HL* 179). In the unequal marriage contract, the loss of virginity signifies the violation not only of body, but of the mental place from which great thoughts emerge: "The girl who has sacrificed this by a premature marriage will carry in her breast, to the end of her life, the sense of a loss – the sense of desecration": marriage is "the great life-long mistake" (*HL* 174). Oakes Smith casts her own marriage at the age of sixteen to a man twice her age, exacted by her mother to remedy her daughter's desire for a college education, as a tragedy: "That was a terrible day of storms and wind that saw me taken away from my Mother" (179).

A sonnet commemorating marital "desecration" punctuates Oakes Smith's comments on maidenhood: "The following bon-mot may perhaps better express my meaning, as the uttered feelings of a girl, when the exigencies of life press heavily upon her, and she cannot recall the sweetness of untasted maidenhood" (*HL* 174). The speaker accuses her husband of stealing her youth:

> Thou didst bereave me of my golden days:
> My heart calls backward for those girlish hours,
> With which dear nature Maidenhood endowers –
> Upon my head the pang of wrong always,

Burns like the noon-day sun's all-scorching rays
Oh! the crushed garlands, and the withered flowers!
The blighting damp that hung o'er rose-deck'd bowers!
The frost that hushed the wood-bird's morning lays!
Oh! Lost, lost joys of youth! I wear the Cross
Like some pale Nun, but not her vestal fire –
Grow moody dull like Miser o'er his loss,
And o'er perverted duties vainly tire; –
Curse the vile Crime, and the worldly dross –
That lays dear Love upon his fun'ral pyre.[69]

The speaker implicitly contrasts Nature's dowry of "girlish hours" with the marriage dowry: the first gives and the second takes away female integrity. In the poem's logic, virginity is natural and matrimony is an obscenity that imposes "perverted duties." The speaker reverses the commonplace that a Nun's pallor comes from sexual deprivation; this ruined Nun's blanched complexion derives from having sex rather than abstaining from it. Depleted of her "vestal fire" she has no way to rekindle her passionate self-enclosure, and can only brood over her loss. The miserly moody dullness replicates the maiden's uplifting self-enclosure, however. Imitating lost maidenhood, Oakes Smith's later speakers seal themselves off, presenting the reader with a reticent exterior that signifies a traumatized withdrawal that is structurally analogous to maidenhood.

In the mythology of Oakes Smith's later work, if maidenhood could have generated inviolate poems, marriage's "desecration" results in a damaged poetic output. Explicating the violated writing process and its flawed result, Oakes dramatizes the impossibility of poetic articulation by comparing the daughters she never had, the poems she never wrote, and her "arrested beautiful development," all brought on by marriage:

I knew of my hunger and thirst for knowledge, and how imperfectly this had been gratified – how prematurely abridged by marriage. More than this I had a sad consciousness of a sweet beautiful life – buried away – smothered out – lieing like the statue in marble – never to be brought forth – it was not dead, for spasmodically expression sprang to the surface in the shape of essay or poem – and even gave moral and political theses, which attracted a certain local interest. I felt painfully that had I been a boy, time and space would have been given me to fill up this arrested beautiful development, while marriage, which a girl must not refuse, was the annihilation of her. I saw no just reason for this, but the fact remained, and I was secretly glad not to add to the number of human beings who must be from necessity curtailed of so much that was desirable in life; who must be arrested, abridged, engulfed in the tasteless actual. (*HL* 190)

Oakes Smith's buried female poet echoes Poe's somnambulant lyric women, as if the marmoreal "sleeper" or the statue-like Helens were struggling to throw off their trance and speak. She – or "it" – is also akin to the prematurely entombed women of Poe's fiction, who try to make their presence known to their male doubles, like Roderick Usher's sister, who claws her way out of the tomb. Oakes Smith locates her "arrested" double, at once more intimate and more alien than Poe's, within her own body, like an unborn child; yet she does not give it a fully human shape or claim it as her own. As if even contemplating the concept of marriage deprived Oakes Smith of her subject position, she begins a sentence with "Had I been a boy," but concludes in the third person: "marriage . . . was the annihilation of her." Not quite stillborn, the woman poet, "buried away – smothered out" remains in a state of suspended animation – "lieing like the statue in marble – never to be brought forth." The figure reiterates Oakes Smith's earlier figures of poetic impossibility: the sinister Cupid in "Love Dead" and the "cherished and beautiful" dead forms in "The Drowned Mariner." Oakes Smith's elegiac relation to her unborn poet and poems contrasts with her lack of regret over the daughters she never had. She implies that non-existence is the only way to avoid witnessing the "arrested beautiful development" that gasps for air, unequal to the task of eloquence.

If the absorptive aesthetic requires external sustenance, the abortive aesthetic functions according to a self-consuming logic. Self-consumption mimics Emersonian self-reliance while showcasing its damaged aspect. Instead of shaping a perfect whole, Oakes Smith advocates self-annihilation. Burning her words and even her own flesh to inculcate stoicism is a recurrent theme in Oakes Smith's later writings. Portraying herself as an aspiring martyr in childhood, she tells in her autobiography of holding her hands over candle flames and applying a mustard poultice to her leg to see how much burning pain she could secretly endure. She burned her diaries as quickly as she filled them, and from the ages of five to ten, she would "print" her poems and stories "in miniature volumes" and "delight my friends by reading them"; but "books written with zest, would soon revolt my growing taste, and were resigned to the flames" (*HL* 115). Rather than a sign of the young girl's failure, the burnt books marked artistic progress towards the elusive moment when she could write one "good enough to keep."

Positing self-immolation as a potential solution for women's lack of an inner space, Oakes Smith suggests that mental fire could hollow out a depth beneath the fragmentary and superficial figure of womanhood that is the sum of her social relations. *Woman and Her Needs* optimistically evokes the rejuvenating effects of self-consumption:

We are not happy in a half-utterance; for the wealth struggles for its power; the smothered fire burns and consumes till it find room for its healthful glow. A thousand women are ill-natured and miserable, not from positive ills about them, but from compression; they have that within, demanding space and indulgence, and they pine for its freedom. (89)

In the first chapter, I claimed that Poe imagined women as an ore to mine; here Oakes Smith posits a way for women to mine themselves: "the wealth" itself "struggles for its power." The very women who suffer from "compression" serve as the fuel for their "smothered fire." It "consumes" them in order to create "space and indulgence" for "that within." This self-damaging self-consumption has the unpredictably positive result of producing a "healthful glow." The inner space burned into being is *not* subjectivity, though it may be a prerequisite: "it" is the thing that cannot be named because it has been too compressed to identify. Fire generates a void that waits to be filled rather than a positive place for mental contemplation. Indeed, the rhetorical progression of the passage moves in the opposite direction, from "half utterance" to silent underground combustion where no utterance is yet possible.

Poetic self-consumption signifies a way of reconstituting virginity through trauma, Oakes Smith's particular version of the romantic quest for innocence through experience. She proposes the self-consuming woman as a counterpart to Emerson's self-reliant man. In contrast to his Poet's capacious "reception," Oakes Smith's later speakers decline to "receive and impart," promoting circulation within their bodies' limits rather than serving as a social conduit. They contradict their own declarations, however, by publicizing them, openly advocating the proliferation of secret spaces of private circulation. In a newspaper poem entitled "On Burning Letters," for example, the speaker celebrates the self-sustaining effects of inhaling the smoke of the words she burns. Whether the words come from her own unsent letter, or from an adulterous lover's forbidden epistle, the exercise of circumspection is the same:

> Into heart, and into brain,
> I their spirit deeply drink.
> Like Bacchante o'er again
> Draining goblets to the brink –
> Thus repeating sweetest pain,
> Soft in ecstasy I sink.
>
> Thus my life new life has found.
> All through her secret cells,
> As the green upon the ground

Where the hidden fountain wells,
And the blooms that cluster round
Of the blessed presence tells.

Now I see the flames enfolding
Words might win a poet's bays,
But my heart, their spirit holding,
Glows like martyr in a blaze,
Who, the heavens themselves beholding,
Folds his hands and inly prays.
The Willows, Patchogue, L. I.[70]

Drinking the spirit of the letter generates "new life" in "secret cells," both
a myriad of tiny prisons, and a biological building block of "Human Life."
The new life is a suicide; uniting with the flaming words, her heart "glows
like martyr in a blaze." The conflagration offers a spectacle of self-violence
that displays the completeness of dissolution and the expressiveness of
mute suffering. Self-consumption replaces confession, as the speaker makes
the reader witness to a secret that she will not reveal; or as fantasizing
about the reader's mystification generates the author's impression of holding something in reserve. The speaker nourishes herself at the expense of
the message's transmission; at the same time, she transmits her refusal to
circulate via the social conduit of print.

Even this compromised version of artistic optimism gives way to a more
cynical appraisal by the end of her autobiography, however, when Oakes
Smith laments the fragments she composed in search of "a perfect whole."
Sacrificial burning has ceased to offer a promise of return:

As I look back upon my life it shames me that I have so little concentrated my self
upon pure Art. I have heaps of poetry now suffering in flames, which, fragmentary
as they are, were designed for a perfect whole. I feel a sort of self-pity at these
fragmentary proofs of a something within me not to be utterly repressed and yet
so unsatisfactory to an artistic or constructive mind. (*HL* 324)

Like Emerson, she casts her poems as organic offspring – they suffer in the
fire because they embody her sensitivity – but in place of his buoyant proliferation stands painful self-destruction. Rather than "adorn[ing] nature with
a new thing," she enacts a ritual murder of the animated fragments, effigies
of self-consuming martyrdom.[71] The problem of "self-pity" emerges from
doubts over whether her words will be read: self-pity must make do where
sympathy should be. Oakes Smith's later writings mark their persistent
tonal difficulty – melodrama that begs to be taken seriously, self-parody
that shifts suddenly to a claim of sincere self-expression – as a problem

of reception. Her dramas of self-consumption display a passion for inner reserves that the poems cannot possess. Reiterating a problem they cannot solve, they also profess a failure to evoke the sympathy they seek for their dilemma.

Unable to procure sympathy for her own poetic demise in any way that would be productive of recognition, Oakes Smith assumes the place of sympathetic reader for another dead figure of female genius, Margaret Fuller. Drowned in a shipwreck with her husband and baby, her last book manuscript lost at sea, Fuller epitomizes failed aspirations for Oakes Smith:[72]

I have no doubt that the internal parliament of Margaret Fuller echoed and re-echoed with unspeakable eloquence, and with aspirations akin to those of a Hampden, a Milton, or a Cromwell. What if these never found a voicing? Shall the scroll, shriveled, scorched, lost on the whirlwinds, be accounted as non-existent, because the sibyl found no comprehending brain to save the precious utterance from destruction? Margaret had no fair chance, no blessed opportunity to be what she might have been, such as the poorest masculine dullard finds ready at hand, and crowds of approving onlookers waiting to give him a godspeed.[73]

Oakes Smith observes that the social network nurturing masculine ambition belies the myth of isolated genius, and that the woman writer who renounces popular forms of expression cleaves closer to the romantic rhetoric. The responsibility for Fuller's incapacity lies not with her, but with the lack of a "comprehending brain" outside her own that would provide a communicative outlet. Since genius is transactional, and since Fuller could not find a reader who would enable her to write, then she could only achieve "unspeakable eloquence" for which Oakes Smith provides a belated audience. She again encounters difficulties, however, because she speaks for Fuller just as she would speak for herself. She complains that Fuller "was always boasting that she stood alone, and she was well aware of the volcano passions that burned within herself; so much deeper than those of other women she felt them to be." Oakes Smith might as well be speaking about herself in the third person, for the same tonal difficulties emerge from the same causes: "Fuller" compensates for a lack of public recognition with boastful self-pity, all the while witnessing her own self-consumption.

In the last pages of her unfinished autobiography, Oakes Smith again professes her poetic failure:

The great poem floating in my brain – spiritual – Miltonic – worthy to be preserved – to become a part of human thought – and admiration had no shadow of coming. It will never be – it is part of the eternal unuttered melody. (*HL* 301)

Though her great poem lies unarticulated, its negative form commands attention just like any ghost, and Oakes Smith still cannot refrain from framing its absence with words. Her strange placement of the penultimate dash elides unforthcoming admiration with mental inertia, underscoring how closely she associates the need for a sympathetic reader with the possibility of bringing a poem into being. In compensation, she fantasizes that the poem's non-existence itself achieves immortality: unauthored, unwritten, and unredeemed in this world, perhaps this ghostly melody holds the place in heaven that it cannot occupy here.

Coda: the Raven's Return

The figure of Poe, icon of alienated genius, stands in for a lost circle of nineteenth-century poetesses; he is the sign of the company he kept. The pathos of his solitary mourning over the death of a beautiful woman gains mythic proportions in part because it alludes to erasures of multiple poetesses and their generic traditions. Oakes Smith's autobiography reminds an improbable future reader that forgotten celebrities once traded ideas with the representative men who came to be the signs of the times. She juxtaposes the ways that published reminiscences establish literary men like Emerson and Poe as cultural icons, while she is left to reminisce about herself to herself. Oakes Smith centers her sense of injustice as well as her hopes for futurity on Poe, figuring him as both the usurper and representative of the antebellum poetess, as the one who will be remembered in her stead. In an essay first published in *Beadle's Monthly* in February of 1867, republished more than once, and then clipped and pasted into her autobiography, Oakes Smith casts Poe as Hamlet, noting that the memorability of both figures is predicated on the death of a beautiful woman.[1] Watching actor Edwin Booth perform "in the midnight scene of the burial of Ophelia," she told herself that "he, to my mind, is neither Edwin Booth nor Hamlet, but Edgar Poe." Like Hamlet, Poe "exercises such a fascination over the human mind; it was so in his lifetime, and it will continue to be so, as long as his solemn 'nevermore' finds its echo in the common heart" (*HL* 316). Poe's nevermore confirms and extends his renown; at the same time his lament both honors the loss of woman and seals her tomb.

Oakes Smith's explanation of Poe's death allegorizes this appropriation. She claims that he was murdered because he refused to return a woman's love letters. The woman she will not name is Frances Sargent Osgood, as most nineteenth-century readers would know:

The whole sad story will probably never be known, but he had corresponded freely with a woman whose name I withhold, and they having subsequently quarreled, he refused to return her letters, nor did she receive them until Dr. Griswold gave them back after Poe's death. This retention not only alarmed but exasperated the woman, and she sent an emissary of her own to force the delivery, and who, failing of success, beat the unhappy man in a most ruffianly manner. A brain fever supervened, and a few friends went with him to Baltimore, his native city, which he barely reached when he died. (*HL* 318)

More than one Poe scholar has indignantly disproved this story, and certainly Oakes Smith herself could not have fully believed it. The letter scandal had played out years before his death, to no one's great satisfaction. Nevertheless, fantasizing that a woman could be the death of Poe, who even posthumously profited from the poetic death of beautiful women, must have provided some perverse satisfaction. Beaten senseless, Poe finally had to stop calling women's words his own.

Chapter 1 suggested that Poe's lyric expressions of emotional distress validate him as the sign of the woman poet. Oakes Smith notes with frustration that his performance secures his memorability at the expense of the women he commemorates. She admires "the element of pain, so much a thread in the organization of Poe" because it is the only way she can articulate legitimate sorrow for the poetess' plight (*HL* 321):

His poems awaken no hopefulness, no sympathy, no noble aspiration, only a lone, painful reminiscence, more distressing than beautiful. We listen as to a dirge, but it is not of noble sounding; it is as if a lost spirit stood beside some awe-engirdled shore where funeral *manes* walk slowly to and fro, and the silence is unbroken by the dead waves that kiss silently the gray pebbles, and then we hear coming out of the deep silence the solemn chant *nevermore.* (*HL* 322)

At home in Poe's scene of suffering (as Whitman was before her, wandering on "Night's Plutonian shores"), Oakes Smith's description of his silent pain echoes her own elegies to an unfulfilled poetic vocation. His "lost spirit" walking in a silent world of "dead waves" that kiss "gray pebbles" resembles her evocation of the "pulseless anguish of a shore / Where Silence is a God; a God's relief" (NYPL). While her attempt to speak the unspeakable on her own behalf is a self-canceling proposition, explicating his nevermore extends its echoing effect. If she could not convincingly testify to her own suffering, she could attest to a pain that resembled her own, promoting Poe's posthumous reputation in the process.

In a roundabout attempt to remind readers of forgotten women, herself in particular, Oakes Smith interprets Poe's "dirge" as an elegy for the woman poet whose voice is lost to posterity. She recreates a conversation in which

Poe confirms her sense that she and Sarah Helen Whitman are undeserving victims of future oblivion:

Then he referred to Mrs. Sarah Helen Whitman, remarking: "Such women as you, and Helena, and a few others ought to be installed as queens, and artists of all kinds should be privileged to pay you court. They would grow wise and holy under such companionship."

"Will not women hereafter be installed as teachers, counsellors, and friends, even as protectors in a high sense?" I replied.

"Ah! well, I shall see it only as Hamlet saw, in the mind's eye."

As I have said, to me Poe was more spectral than human.[2] (*HL* 322)

Poe's remarks might sound like a dismissal of women's accomplishments, but Oakes Smith offers them as proof that his "spectral" nature allows him to foresee the disappearance of herself and Helena. She casts her posthumous ventriloquy as Poe's positive reception, one that parallels Baudelaire's testimony to Poe's poetic genius. She moreover proposes that since Poe impersonates women's pain, a woman author would make a superior Poe. She records Poe saying precisely that: "Mr. Poe in conversation warmly commended the Sinless Child, and when his Eureka appeared he called upon me and said, 'In Eureka I am in the spirit what you are in the Sinless Child'" (*HL* 303). Claiming to be his prototype, Oakes Smith offers Poe's words as validation; but Sarah Helen Whitman warned John Ingram against Oakes Smith's reportage of "Apocryphal conversations," Ingram didn't trust her accounts, and her attempts to inscribe a validating reader were again frustrated (*PHR* 234).

Unable to shift the terms of reception, Oakes Smith protested them nevertheless. She dramatizes the competition between Poe and herself, and the poet and the poetess, by imagining aloud how his poem would change if a woman's bird took the raven's place:

Mr. Poe was pleased with the impression which "The Raven" produced upon me. In a morning call my canary alighted upon the head of an Apollo in my room.

"See, Mr. Poe," I said; "I do not keep a raven, but there is song to song. Why did you not put an owl on the head of Pallas? However there would have been no poem then."

"No, there is mystery about the raven."[3] (*HL* 322)

Oakes Smith suggests that Poe's scavenger mimic alights on the goddess of wisdom in order to confess the poet's parasitic relation to female poetic accomplishment when she goes "song to song," offering him the analogous spectacle of a canary, emblem of woman's song, finding its feet upon the male god of music. The somewhat silly scenario offers little competition, however, because the canary recalls the entrapped light-heartedness of the poetess, or "The Wife" of one of Oakes Smith's sonnets: "some sweet bird, content to sing / In its small cage."[4] She then substitutes for the canary the owl, the pet bird of both Pallas Athena, the Goddess of Wisdom, and of Oakes Smith herself (a "tame owl" flew around her library as she wrote) (*HL* 72). In the language of birds, Oakes Smith encourages Poe to embrace female wisdom by matching the bird to the bust. At the same time, her proclamation that "there would have been no poem then" suggests that Poe would have found no footing in the poetic world if he could not prey upon female accomplishment. Oakes Smith reminds the reader of the raven's foreign occupation by summoning the supplanted owl; at the same time she implicitly concurs with Poe that only such gendered appropriations and displacements can make poetry, a formula that disqualifies her lyric attempts at speaking for herself in feminine terms.

Oakes Smith was not the only woman to note a substitution. In *The Home Life of Edgar Poe*, Susan Archer Talley Weiss recalled that the raven was originally an owl:

His first intention, he said, had been to write a short poem only, based upon the incident of an Owl – a night bird, the bird of wisdom – with its ghostly presence and inscrutable gaze entering the window of a vault or chamber where he sat beside the bier of the lost Lenore. Then he had exchanged the Owl for the Raven, for the sake of the latter's "Nevermore"; and the poem, despite himself, had grown beyond the length originally intended.[5]

Once again the nevermore makes the difference between Poe's evacuated feminine aesthetic and the fulfilled sign of feminine force; the Raven's mimic speech overwrites the Owl's silence, its nevermore negating the possibility of female expression. In "adopting" the raven, however, Poe "evidently did not obliterate all traces of the Owl": why else would the bird be sitting on top of the bust of Pallas Athena? Encouraged by Poe, Weiss and Oakes Smith identify the shadow presence of an earlier version more fully aligned with female power and work to reveal Poe's debt. While reminding the reader of the raven's foreign occupation, however, they also confirm that only such gendered appropriations make memorable poetry.

Oakes Smith returned to confront her own oblivion and Poe's renown late in life, when she penned a parody of "The Raven" that attacks a Poe-identified bird. The unpublished "Lines, *Not* After the Mourner of Poe" is bereft of all collegial amicability, as the title's double-entendre implies: the lines do not take after the melancholic utterances of Poe's mourner in "The Raven," and Oakes Smith does not take after those who mourn

Poe. The speaker immediately contradicts the title's implications, however, by dwelling upon her inability to exorcise the critical gaze of an intrusive version of Poe's poetic bird. Sensing that "a sinister charm was there," the speaker opens a window and utters a paraphrase of a line from Poe's poem: "Art Devil-Angel there?" At an hour when "all decent birds are home in bed," an Owl with "huge eyeballs" set in a "big head" steps through the poet's window and plagues her attempts at writing with his prying stare. That Poe now grotesquely occupies the figure that Oakes Smith had previously coded as the sign of female wisdom suggests that his "sinister charm" has increased over time. No matter that Poe had been dead all those years: Oakes Smith stages a losing battle with a ghostly judge who denies her opportunity for poetic accomplishment.

In a perverse reversal of a nineteenth-century ideal of lyric process in which the poem emerges from sanctified solitude to purify the public world of print, the public eye invades the privacy of the speaker's study and peruses her manuscripts in their most intimate draft state. Sanctioned by the platitude that a woman's poems are unmediated revelations of self, the malevolent bird, specter of a magazine critic gone haywire, looks through the speaker's papers before she has submitted them for publication:

> He sidled near with eye askance –
> Shook all his feathers out –
> And cocked his bill with wicked glance
> Where my papers lay about –
> But I cried "Now stay thy speech –
> Thou ominous bird –
> For thou mayst look and loudly screech,
> I'll mind thee never a word.
> Oh what to thee? is there no spot
> Where one may ease the heart?
> Where one may write, and one may blot –
> And such as thou art not?
> Oh take thy great round eyes away –
> Thy somber voice hold back –
> Poets will sing till blind and grey
> And voices all acrack."
> . . . .
> Oh! Very loud, and savage stern
> Broke forth that Owl's great throat –
> 'Twas plain he did not grammar learn
> As he in youth had ought.
> "To who? To who?" he savage cried,
> And on my shoulder came –

> And kicked my odes from side to side
> To quench all hope of fame.
> "What matter to thee, malignant fiend,
> To whom I may have written
> A sonnet here – A lyric there
> When by the Muses smitten?
> Must such as thee all noiseless fly
> And smite us evermore?
> Ignore or damn, no reason why? –
> Kick from the Poet's door."[6]

The speaker suggests that voyeuristic perversion underpins the aesthetic of female transparency: the Owl craves to read premature writing at a developmental stage when the personal and the literary are undifferentiated, and secrets of private life can be deciphered. His critical intervention not only brutalizes her poems ("He kicked my odes from side to side"), but also injures her writing process; beneath the Owl's "glare," the speaker cannot transform therapeutic writing, "eas[ing] the heart," into poetry. The Poe-bird's "To who? To who?" melds two seemingly disparate fears into one: that the Owl will expose the identity of the speaker's illegitimate correspondent, or that there will never be an appreciative reader for her poetry. Despairing at the prospect of a fame denied by an idiot bird that cares more about illicit love affairs than the words on the page, the speaker consumes her own words in a fit of rage at the absurdity of her fate. Lacking subject or object, "Kick from the Poet's door" suggests that, while the speaker might be the one kicked away from the inner sanctum, she would like to kick others in turn, in a futile attempt to assuage her anger.

Oakes Smith never published the "Lines, *Not* After the Mourner of Poe," and indeed the poet's scrawl renders some words in the full poem indecipherable. The scrap of paper upon which it is written has been crumpled up and then re-smoothed, as if even the manuscript had an uncertain fate. Oakes Smith's repeated and increasingly pessimistic predictions that there is no exit for the woman poet did not prevent her from staging an ingenious lifelong battle against recalcitrant poetic constraints that illuminates the gender dynamics of cultural transmission in this period of literary history and its legacies in contemporary critical practice. Though she acknowledges her own demise in cultural memory, she explores the process by which lyric's interpersonal and trans-gendered dynamics become absorbed into a singular, static, masculine figure – in this case, the figure of Poe. Just as Poe performs his indebtedness to the poetess' reception, this poetess performs her inability to extract herself from her role as Poe's medium in order to command a readership of her own. While Poe gains the adoring attention of poetesses to the extent that they serve as his conduits, Oakes Smith, not through lack of trying, cannot find a way to frame her complaint that will make readers respond by cherishing her name.

That the problem is not hers alone should be clear to anyone interested in scholarship on nineteenth-century American women's poetry, which has encountered more than usual difficulties in establishing itself as an influential area of inquiry. As Jackson and Prins have observed, a persistent rhetoric of recovery has had the paradoxical effect of burying the poetesses whom critics seek to revive.[7] Attempts to recover poetesses encounter the same pitfalls that Oakes Smith, Whitman, and Osgood diagnose with such wit and poignancy. Even those critics most deeply committed to the study of women's poetry are quick to identify a range of formal failings: extreme generic constraint; conflicts between personality and publicity that rupture authenticity; an inability to assume a persuasive lyric subject position; a tendency towards tonal disjunctions, exaggerations, and excesses; unmoored aestheticism and political disengagement. We fail to note, however, that the poetess herself diagnosed her lyrical problems, not as a sign of individual weakness, but as the result of her cultural identity as the personification of lyric mediumship. Just as Poe and his critics have appropriated women's work while dismissing its importance, we level formal charges against the poetesses that they themselves eloquently addressed, without registering our debt. By failing to read women's poetry in terms of their circulation, we have overlooked their incisive critique of the social limits on women's poetic expression; we have minimized the formative influence of poetic reception on poetic production; and we have overlooked the ways we continue to operate within the nineteenth-century terms of evaluation that we have inherited. By privileging genius over mimicry and dismissing poetesses on this basis, we mimic an Emersonian perspective while denying, as he did, what we repeat. In other words, we have inherited the poetess' terms of reception and reiterate them in our attempts to leave them behind. If instead we followed the poetesses and acknowledged our mimic practices, we could explore the consequences of that recognition and better understand inherited terms of cultural transmission.

Believing that attempts to revive the poetesses have obscured their legacy, I have chosen instead to foreground the terms of their ephemeral celebrity, cultural demise, and nameless haunting of American literary forms and history. I have suggested that interpreting these self-dissolving, ephemeral, and dispossessed poems affords a way to understand the social forces that both enable and disable lyric forms of literary authority and social communication. I have sought to demonstrate that one can critique what one cannot necessarily transform, that one can study what one cannot necessarily resurrect, and that one can analyze and interpret the terms of forgetting as productively as one can recover and memorialize. Rather than reviving Osgood, Whitman, Oakes Smith, or even Poe, I have wished to demonstrate the ways in which forgetting their collaborative practices continues to shape a range of discursive practices. The influence of poetesses extends far beyond their immediate effects in ephemeral publications, into the dynamic structures of circulation and transmission in the print public sphere of their own time and in today's scholarship.

Studies of nineteenth-century American women's poetry have equated the lyric speaker with the woman writer, and then evaluated the extent to which sentimental convention constrains the true voice of the woman; or they have argued that the pathos of the woman's poem derives from the inability of any particular woman to speak through the figure of the Poetess. But if we have come to question the idea that great writers transcend their age, and have come to think that the idea of transcendence is of an age, then it is worth asking why we dismiss women poets whose work registers their terms of reception, rather than analyzing the nature of that constriction, the transformative functions of poetic convention, and the idiosyncratic deployment of generic structures by particular poetesses. In this respect we can learn from Frances Sargent Osgood, Sarah Helen Whitman, Elizabeth Oakes Smith, and even Edgar Allan Poe, the honorary Poetess, who accept generic and cultural constraint as the prerequisite for poetic practice. Reading their poetry in circulation shows us much about a cultural field and a literary history in which genius is a product of mimicry and poetesses continue to influence the structures that repudiate their importance. They show us the range of ways that persons become personifications of poetic media, as well as the ways that the unremembered, along with those remembered by name, transmit their legacy via genius and mimicry.

Notes

INTRODUCTION

1. According to Meredith McGill, "the critical investment in Poe as a figure who could remain detached from the conditions of production finds its origin in the intersection of Poe's career with the very coteries from which critics have tried to distance him." "Poe, Literary Nationalism, and Authorial Identity," *The American Face of Edgar Allan Poe*, ed. Shawn Rosenheim and Stephen Rachman (Baltimore: Johns Hopkins University Press, 1995), 271. I build on her insight here. Arguing that writing is "a public gesture, not a private act," Stephen Railton defines "literary performance" as "how writers conceive of and address themselves to an audience." *Authorship and Audience: Literary Performance in the American Renaissance* (Princeton: Princeton University Press, 1991), 4, 12. I suggest that categories of production and reception overlap, especially because antebellum authors read and wrote for each other. Rather than a one-man show, the "drama of literary creation" is a collaboration (4).

2. Frank Luther Mott estimates from 1825–1850 periodicals (other than newspapers) increased from less than 100 to about 600. *A History of American Magazines 1741–1850* (Cambridge: Belknap Press of Harvard University Press, 1930), 341–342.

3. On expansion of print networks see Ronald Zboray, *A Fictive People: Antebellum Economic Development and the American Reading Public* (New York: Oxford University Press, 1993).

4. Timothy Morris argues that the "poetics of presence" underpins the canonical tradition of American poetry. *Becoming Canonical in American Poetry* (Urbana: University of Illinois Press, 1995), xi.

5. Virginia Jackson and Yopie Prins diagnose the interpretive problems generated by assuming that the poetess speaks for herself in "Lyrical Studies," *Victorian Literature and Culture* 7: 2 (2000), 521–529. Mary Loeffelholz advances a way to interpret the Davidson sisters as cultural types rather than persons in "Who Killed Lucretia Davidson? Or, Poetry in the Domestic-Tutelary Complex," *The Yale Journal of Criticism* 10: 2 (1997), 271–293.

6. Stephen Cushman argues that poets develop "fictions" about the way poetic language operates that reflect and respond to national conditions. *Fictions of Form in American Poetry* (Princeton: Princeton University Press, 1993). In *Romantic*

Poets and the Culture of Posterity (Cambridge: Cambridge University Press, 1999), Andrew Bennett contrasts a masculine preoccupation with posterity and women poets' "alternative trajectories," including their "active rejection of fame both contemporary and posthumous and her expression of a desire for oblivion" (66). Countering Bennett, Lucy Newlyn argues that "women poets did not so much relinquish the quest for posterity as seek to maintain identity in a culture where they were constructed as temporary rather than permanent, sympathetically receptive rather than creative." *Reading, Writing, and Romanticism: The Anxiety of Reception* (Oxford: Oxford University Press, 2000), 252.

7. On the identification of nineteenth-century – primarily British – women poets with generic types, see Tricia Lootens, *Lost Saints: Silence, Gender, and Victorian Literary Canonization* (Charlottesville: University Press of Virginia, 1996); and Yopie Prins, *Victorian Sappho* (Princeton: Princeton University Press, 1999). I build on their work in this study.

8. Andrew Bennett offers a related formulation: "Masculinity . . . is always already determined by . . . the other it attempts to exclude" (*Romantic Poets*, 66).

9. I address this issue in "Women's Place in Poe Studies," *Poe Studies / Dark Romanticism* 33: 1 and 2 (2000), 10–14. For treatments of the figure of the dead woman in Poe, see Marie Bonaparte, *The Life and Works of Edgar Poe*, trans. John Rodker (London: Hogarth Press, 1949); Mutlu Blasing, *American Poetry: The Rhetoric of its Forms* (New Haven: Yale University Press, 1987), 17–35; J. Gerald Kennedy, *Poe, Death, and the Life of Writing* (New Haven: Yale University Press, 1987), 76; Joan Dayan, *Fables of Mind: An Inquiry into Poe's Fiction* (New York: Oxford University Press, 1987); Leland Person, *Aesthetic Headaches: Women and a Masculine Poetics in Poe, Melville, and Hawthorne* (Athens: University of Georgia Press, 1988), 23; Elisabeth Bronfen, *Over Her Dead Body: Death, Femininity and the Aesthetic* (New York: Routledge, 1992), 71; J. Gerald Kennedy, "Poe, 'Ligeia,' and the Problem of Dying Women," *New Essays on Poe's Major Tales*, ed. Kenneth Silverman (New York: Cambridge University Press, 1993), 127.

10. In *The Gendered Lyric: Subjectivity and Difference in Nineteenth-Century French Poetry* (West Lafayette: Purdue University Press, 1999), Gretchen Schultz argues that "nineteenth-century critics and poets rebuffed women poets' attempts to become writing subjects" because "sexual difference," and particularly "the objectification of women" "functioned symbolically to define lyricism itself" (ix).

11. Myra Jehlen, "Archimedes and the Paradox of Feminist Criticism," *Feminisms: An Anthology of Literary Theory and Criticism*, ed. Robyn R. Warhol and Diane Price Herndl (New Brunswick: Rutgers University Press, 1996), 76.

12. Jonathan Elmer, *Reading at the Social Limit: Affect, Mass Culture, and Edgar Allan Poe* (Stanford: Stanford University Press, 1995).

13. Meredith McGill, *American Literature and the Culture of Reprinting* (Philadelphia: University of Pennsylvania Press, 2003), 145.

14. On poetry as a mode of social communication see Mary Louise Kete, *Sentimental Collaborations: Mourning and Middle-Class Identity in Nineteenth-Century*

America (Durham: Duke University Press, 2000); and Paula Bennett, *Poets in the Public Sphere: The Emancipatory Project of American Women's Poetry, 1800–1900* (Princeton: Princeton University Press, 2003), 5.

15. Groundbreaking studies such as Nancy F. Cott's *The Bonds of Womanhood: "Woman's Sphere" in New England, 1780–1835* (New Haven: Yale University Press, 1977) and Mary Kelley's *Private Woman, Public* Stage: *Literary Domesticity in Nineteenth-Century America* (New York: Oxford University Press, 1984) identified ways in which the rhetoric of separate spheres underwrote the restriction of women's activities to the home and left to men the privileges and risks of business and politics. More recent studies have identified overlays, discontinuities, and doublings that blur, dissolve, and conflate distinctions between the gendered values previously allocated to distinct spheres. See, for example, Julie Ellison, *Cato's Tears: The Making of Anglo-American Emotion* (Chicago: University of Chicago Press, 1999); Glenn Hendler, *Public Sentiments: Structures of Feeling in Nineteenth-Century American Literature* (Chapel Hill: University of North Carolina Press, 2001); and Caroline Levander, *Voices of the Nation: Women and Public Speech in Nineteenth-Century American Literature and Culture* (New York: Cambridge University Press, 1998). Two recent collections renounce the distinction entirely: *Separate Spheres No More: Gender Convergence in American Literature, 1830–1930*, ed. Monika Elbert (Tusacloosa: University of Alabama Press, 2000); and *No More Separate Spheres! A Next Wave American Studies Reader*, ed. Cathy Davidson (Durham: Duke University Press, 2002).

16. Lauren Berlant, "The Female Woman: Fanny Fern and the Form of Sentiment," *American Literary History* 3 (Fall 1991), 434. See also Lauren Berlant, "The Female Complaint," *Social Text* 19: 20 (Fall 1988), 237–259.

17. Joan Hedrick discusses the importance of literary production for 1830s, parlor culture in *Harriet Beecher Stowe: A Life* (New York: Oxford University Press, 1994), 77–88. She notes that the literary club, a close cousin of the salon, helped "letters produced for domestic consumption make their way from the parlor to the press" (82).

18. Julia Ward Howe, "The Salon in America," *Is Polite Society Polite? and Other Essays* (New York: Lamson, Wolfe, and Co. 1895), 114.

19. John Kasson, *Rudeness and Civility: Manners in Nineteenth-Century Urban America* (New York: Hill and Wang, 1990), 3.

20. Ann Marie Dolan, *The Literary Salon in New York: 1830–1860* (Ph.D. Diss. Columbia University, 1957), 103–107. Also *AWP* xxii–xxiii.

21. *Memoirs of Ann C. L. Botta*, ed. Vincenzo Botta (New York: J. S. Tait & Sons, 1894), 186. Kirsten Silva Gruesz compares Lynch's and Longfellow's cosmopolitanism in "Feeling for the Fireside: Longfellow, Lynch, and the Topography of Poetic Power," *Sentimental Men: Masculinity and the Politics of Affect in American Culture*, ed. Mary Chapman and Glenn Hendler (Berkeley: University of California Press, 1999), 43–63.

22. Quoted in Dolan, *Literary Salon*, 96.

23. Dolan, *Literary Salon*, 82–100.

24. Both quotes in Dolan, *Literary Salon* 90.

25. Elizabeth Oakes Smith, "Margaret Fuller," clipping (Virginia).
26. Terry Mulcaire explores the paradox of Walt Whitman's public privacy in "Publishing Intimacy in *Leaves of Grass*," *ELH* 60: 2 (1993), 471–501. Glenn Hendler argues that the social formation of publicity in the nineteenth century gave rise to subjects who "performed their public identities through the very categories that seem to distance and differentiate them from the public sphere: particularities like race and gender, categories like personality and intimacy, forms of affect like sympathy" (*Public Sentiments*, 26). Building on this formulation, I claim that public identities are crafted in transaction among individuals, and that there is both a difference and a complex relation between the public circulation of identic types and the identities of embodied individuals.
27. James David Hart, *The Popular Book; A History of America's Literary Taste* (Berkeley: University of California Press, 1950), 138.
28. William Charvat, *The Profession of Authorship in America, 1800–1870* (New York: Columbia University Press, 1992), 102.
29. Mott, *History*, 344, 351.
30. Mott, *History*, 495–525.
31. Fred Lewis Pattee, *The Feminine Fifties* (New York: Appleton-Century, 1940), 50.
32. Nina Baym, "The Rise of the Woman Author," *Columbia Literary History of the United States* (New York: Columbia University Press, 1988), 297.
33. On women's periodical poetry see *Nineteenth-Century American Women Poets*, ed. Paula Bennett (Oxford: Blackwell, 1998), xli–xlii. The three anthologies were *The American Female Poets*, ed. Caroline May (Philadelphia: Lindsay and Blakiston, 1848); *Female Poets of America*, ed. Rufus Griswold (Philadelphia: Carey and Hart, 1848); and *The Female Poets of America*, ed. Thomas Buchanan Read (Philadelphia: E. H. Butler and Co., 1849).
34. Poe was assistant editor by the end of February, 1845 and sole editor by October 25, 1845 (*EAP* 244, 274). A woman's poem occupies the lead position on August 30, September 6, October 4, November 1, November 8, November 15, and November 29.
35. Quoted in *AWP* xxi.
36. Alexis de Tocqueville, *Democracy in America* (New York: Knopf, 1972), 71.
37. "Poetry and Imagination," *RWE* 471.
38. G. G. Foster, "The Fountain – A Night Rhapsody," *Graham's* 23: 2 (August 1843), 104.
39. Laura Wendorff, *Race, Ethnicity, and the Voice of the "Poetess" in the Lives and Works of Four Late-Nineteenth-Century American Women Poets: Frances E. W. Harper, Emma Lazarus, Louise Guiney, and Ella Wheeler Wilcox* (Ph.D. Diss. University of Michigan, 1992). Wendorff argues that later in the century women poets adapted the convention to their expressive needs. See also Cheryl Walker, *The Nightingale's Burden: Women Poets and American Culture Before 1900* (Bloomington: Indiana University Press, 1982), 27.
40. Nathaniel Hawthorne. *Hawthorne's Poems*, ed. Peck and Peck (Charlottesville: University of Virginia Bibliographical Society, 1967), v.

41. Griswold, *Female Poets*, 8.
42. Alicia Ostriker, *Stealing the Language: The Emergence of Women's Poetry in America* (Boston: Beacon Press, 1986), 30.
43. Charvat, *Profession of Authorship*, 155–167.
44. Gordon Haight, *Mrs. Sigourney: The Sweet Singer of Hartford* (New Haven: Yale University Press, 1930), 34–37; *AWP* xxi; Walker, *Nightingale's Burden*, 79.
45. Graham offered Osgood "twenty-five dollars a story and ten dollars a poem, 'one or the other monthly,' in 1843" (Mott, *History*, 508). Robert Conrad, editor of *Graham's*, agreed to pay Osgood five dollars per page of prose and ten dollars per poem on April 17, 1848 (Houghton bMS Am 1355 [8]). She asked James Fields to find a publisher for a children's book "who would be likely to publish it at twenty or twenty-five dollars" (Houghton bMS Am 2016 [61]).
46. Theodore Adorno, "Lyric Poetry and Society," *The Adorno Reader*, ed. Brian O'Connor (Oxford: Blackwell, 2000), 213.
47. Noah Webster, *An American Dictionary of the English Language*, 1828 (reprint, San Francisco: Foundation for an American Christian Education, 1985).
48. Mark Maslan, *Whitman Possessed* (Baltimore: Johns Hopkins University Press, 2001), 1–2.
49. Elin Diamond, "Mimesis, Mimicry, and the 'True-Real,'" *Acting Out: Feminist Performances*, ed. Lynda Hart and Peggy Phelan (Ann Arbor: University of Michigan Press, 1993), 363.
50. Homi Bhabha, "Of Mimicry and Man," *The Location of Culture* (New York: Routledge, 1994), 87.
51. Judith Butler, *Gender Trouble: Feminism and the Subversion of Identity* (New York: Routledge, 1990), 141, 137.
52. I follow Diamond's reading (370). She calls Irigaray's revisionary reading of Plato "mimesis-mimicry, in which the production of objects, shadows, and voices is excessive to the truth/illusion structure of mimesis" (371).
53. Luce Irigaray, *Speculum of the Other Woman*, trans. Gillian C. Gill (Ithaca: Cornell University Press, 1985), 292.
54. I paraphrase Rei Terada: "mimicry tips the hand of its nonoriginality and implies the nonoriginality of that which it mimics." *Derek Walcott's Poetry: American Mimicry* (Boston: Northeastern University Press, 1992), 1.
55. Harold Bloom, *Anxiety of Influence: A Theory of Poetry* (New York: Oxford University Press, 1987).
56. *RWE* 432. This essay first appeared in the *North American Review* in 1868.
57. One of the essays in Emerson's *Representative Men* (1850) is entitled "Swedenborg; or, the Mystic."
58. Julie Ellison, *Emerson's Romantic Style* (Princeton: Princeton University Press, 1984), 152–153.
59. Susan Rosenbaum takes this double-edged response as her subject in her book manuscript entitled *Lyric Professions: Sincerity, Authorship, and Romantic Tradition*.
60. Ostriker, *Stealing the Language*, 28.
61. Walker, *Nightingale's Burden*, 22.

62. Bennett, *Nineteenth-Century*, xxxvi.

63. Janet Todd, *Sensibility: An Introduction* (New York: Methuen, 1986), 6–8; Elizabeth Barnes, *States of Sympathy: Seduction and Democracy in the American Novel* (New York: Columbia University Press, 1997); Bruce Burgett, *Sentimental Bodies: Sex, Gender, and Citizenship in the Early Republic* (Princeton: Princeton University Press, 1998); Ellison, *Cato's Tears*; Hendler, *Public Sentiments*; Joycelyn Moody, *Sentimental Confessions: Spiritual Narratives of Nineteenth-Century African American Women* (Athens: University of Georgia Press, 2001); Marianne Noble, *The Masochistic Pleasures of Sentimental Literature* (Princeton: Princeton University Press, 2000); *The Culture of Sentiment: Race, Gender, and Sentimentality in Nineteenth-Century America*, ed. Shirley Samuels (New York: Oxford University Press, 1992); Julia Stern, *The Plight of Feeling: Sympathy and Dissent in the Early American Novel* (Chicago: University of Chicago Press, 1997).

64. Ann Douglas, *The Feminization of American Culture* (New York: Knopf, 1977); Jane Tompkins, "Sentimental Power: Uncle Tom's Cabin and the Politics of Literary History," *Ideology and Classic American Literature*, ed. Sacvan Bercovitch and Myra Jehlen (New York: Cambridge University Press, 1986), 267–292.

65. Nina Baym, "Re-inventing Lydia Sigourney," *The (Other) American Traditions: Nineteenth-Century Women Writers*, ed. Joyce Warren (New Brunswick: Rutgers University Press, 1993), 54–72; Sandra Zagarell, "Expanding 'America': Lydia Sigourney's Sketch of Connecticut, Catharine Sedgwick's Hope Leslie," *Redefining the Political Novel: American Women Writers, 1797–1901*, ed. Sharon Harris (Knoxville: University of Tennessee Press, 1995), 43–65.

66. In addition to the studies already cited, see Joanne Dobson, *Dickinson and the Strategies of Reticence: The Woman Writer in Nineteenth-Century America* (Bloomington: Indiana University Press, 1989); Virginia Jackson, "Longfellow's Tradition: Or, Picture-Writing a Nation," *Modern Language Quarterly* 59 (1998), 471–496; Mary Loeffelholz, "Religion of Art in the City at War: Boston's Public Poetry and the Great Organ, 1863," *American Literary History* 13: 2 (2001), 212–241; Mary Loeffelholz, *From School to Salon: Reading Nineteenth-Century American Women's Poetry* (Princeton: Princeton University Press, 2004); Kirsten Silva Gruesz, *Ambassadors of Culture: The Transamerican Origins of Latino Writing* (Princeton: Princeton University Press, 2002); Elizabeth Petrino, *Emily Dickinson and Her Contemporaries: Women's Verse in America, 1820–1885* (Hanover: University of New England Press, 1995).

67. Emily Stipes Watts, *The Poetry of American Women from 1632 to 1945* (Austin: University of Texas Press, 1977), 71.

CHAPTER 1

1. "Echo Song," *Broadway Journal* (September 6, 1845), 129. "To One Who Swept the Sounding Lyre" (*FSOP* 465–466). Hervey Allen, *Israfel: The Life and Times of Edgar Allan Poe* (New York: Farrar and Rinehart, 1934). Mabbott attributes Allen's title to Osgood's influence (*CWP* 173).

2. "Israfel" appeared in Poe's *Poems* (1831); in the *Southern Literary Messenger* for August 1836, while he was editor; in *Graham's* for October 1841, while he was the reviewer; in the *Broadway Journal* on July 26, 1845, while he was editor, and in *The Raven and Other Poems* (1845) (*CWP* 173; *PL* 221, 555).

3. Richards, "Women's Place," 10.

4. Examples include Bonaparte, *Life and Works*; Daniel Hoffman, *Poe Poe Poe Poe Poe Poe Poe* (Garden City: Doubleday, 1972); Blasing, *American Poetry*, 17–35; Person, *Aesthetic Headaches*; Kennedy, "'Ligeia' and the Problem of Dying Women"; Bronfen, *Over Her Dead Body*.

5. Edwin Fussell, *Lucifer in Harness: American Meter, Metaphor and Diction* (Princeton: Princeton University Press 1973), 27.

6. Blasing, *American Poetry*, 20.

7. Charles Baudelaire, *The Painter of Modern Life and Other Essays*, trans. and ed. Jonathan Mayne (London: Phaidon, 1964), 96.

8. Eugene Didier, *The Poe Cult and Other Poe Papers* (New York: Broadway Publishing Co., 1909). Much Poe criticism is extraordinarily partisan, pleading the maligned writer's case, making extravagant claims for his talent (that he anticipated the theory of the expanding universe, that he invented the science fiction and detective genres, etc.). There is also a longstanding counter-tradition of Poe-debunking. On the nascence of this tension, see J. Gerald Kennedy, "Elegy For a Rebel Soul," *Poe and His Times: The Artist and His Milieu*, ed. Benjamin Franklin Fisher (Baltimore: Edgar Allan Poe Society, 1990), 226–234; and Kevin Ljundquist and Cameron Nickels, "Elizabeth Oakes Smith on Poe: A Chapter in the Recovery of His Nineteenth-Century Reputation," Fisher, ed. *Poe and His Times*, 235–246.

9. On the history of mesmerism and related movements, see Alan Gauld, *A History of Hypnotism* (Cambridge: Cambridge University Press, 1992); and Taylor Stoehr, "Hawthorne and Mesmerism," *Huntington Library Quarterly* 32: 1 (Nov. 1969), 33–60.

10. Quoted in *EAP* 279; also 237–238.

11. Quoted in *EAP* 284.

12. Rufus Griswold, "Death of Edgar Allan Poe," 1849. Reprinted in *Edgar Allan Poe: The Critical Heritage*, ed. I. M. Walker (New York: Routledge, 1986), 298.

13. Stoehr, "Hawthorne and Mesmerism," 53. Shoshana Felman claims that Poe's poetry generates "what might be called a genius effect: the impression of some undefinable but compelling force to which the reader is subjected." "On Reading Poetry: Reflections on the Limits and Possibilities of Psychoanalytic Approaches," *The Purloined Poe: Lacan, Derrida, and Psychoanalytic Reading*, ed. John P. Muller and William J. Richardson (Baltimore: Johns Hopkins University Press, 1988), 134.

14. Elizabeth Oakes Smith, *Selections from the Autobiography of Elizabeth Oakes Smith*, ed. Mary Alice Wyman (Lewiston, ME: Lewiston Journal, 1924), 88.

15. Quoted in Ljungquist and Nickels, 243.

16. Oakes Smith, *Selections*, 119.

17. Osgood, "Echo Song."

18. George William Curtis, quoted in "Introduction," *SHWP*.
19. For example see Hoffman, *Poe Poe Poe*, 93–94. Joan Dayan notes "Poe's serious attention to women writers," yet dismisses his reviews of Osgood and Sigourney as "cloying and sentimental" without explaining why we should pay attention to some reviews and ignore others. "Amorous Bondage: Poe, Ladies, and Slaves," Rosenheim and Rachman, eds. *American Face*, 199.
20. Poe, *Marginalia*, ed. John Carl Miller (Charlottesville: University Press of Virginia, 1981), 58–59.
21. *The Collected Writings of Edgar Allan Poe*, ed. Burton Pollin, Vol. 3, pt. I. *Broadway Journal Prose* (New York: Gordian Press, 1986), 358.
22. Julie Ellison explores male romanticism's feminine identifications and Margaret Fuller's attempts to reconfigure the gendered paradigms in *Delicate Subjects: Romanticism, Gender, and the Ethics of Understanding* (Ithaca: Cornell University Press, 1990).
23. Griswold, *Female Poets*, 7.
24. On Poe's associations of "convertibility" with female figures see Dayan, *Fables of Mind*, 133–192.
25. Kennedy, *Poe, Death, and the Life of Writing*, 75.
26. Poe, *Marginalia*, 150.
27. Dayan argues that Poe "repeats, exaggerates, and transforms the immutable, romanticized attributes white women are granted by men. He dramatizes the fact of appropriation, and thereby undefines the definitions that mattered to civilized society" ("Amorous Bondage," 190). I claim instead that Poe dramatizes the fact of his own appropriation of female achievement. Dayan claims that Poe's inhabitance of women's place is "no mere appropriation: the 'possession' is reciprocal." "Poe's Women: A Feminist Poe?," *Poe Studies* 26: 1 and 2 (June/December 1993), 9. While I agree on this point, I disagree that "Poe is after nothing less than an exhumation of the lived, but disavowed or suppressed experiences of women in his society" (10). It is not women's place in patriarchy, but the intimacy with lyric enabled by that place that concerns Poe.
28. On the language of flowers in Dickinson and Osgood see Petrino (129–160).
29. On the relation between "Irenë" and "The Sleeper" see *CWP* 179–185.
30. Mabbott says that Poe's dedication "seems to be a tacit recognition of his own . . . debt to her" (*CWP* 357). Poe's review appeared in the *Broadway Journal* (January 11, 1845). "The Raven" first appeared in the *Evening Mirror* (January 29, 1845). On the relation between "Lady Geraldine's Courtship" and "The Raven" see Mabbott's comments (*CWP* 356–357).
31. *Elizabeth Barrett Browning: Selected Poems*, ed. Margaret Forster (Baltimore: Johns Hopkins University Press, 1988), 105. I follow the octameter lineation of Barrett's American edition (1844) because Poe quotes her lines in this form in his review (*ER* 128–129). Mabbott says: "unquestionably the cardinal source of the final stanzaic form of Poe's poem was Elizabeth Barrett's 'Lady Geraldine's Courtship'" (*CWP* 356).
32. McGill offers a related assessment of Poe's poetics: "Authorial possession appears as its Gothic opposite – the haunting by another – yet these states

are curiously reciprocal. Dispossession is experienced by the author as propri-etorship" ("Literary Nationalism," 297).

33. Kennedy attributes the speaker's wish "both to forget and to remember" to "a conflict between memory and denial" central to the logic of bereavement and writing (*Poe, Death, and the Life of Writing*, 68).

34. Whitman, *EPC* 42–43. In "The Poetics of Extinction," Gillian Brown argues that Poe's fiction relies upon a "single-minded prohibition of female gener-ativity in order to produce evidence of a particular instance" of "individual consciousness" (Rosenheim and Rachman, eds. *American Face*, 341–342). I argue, to the contrary, that Poe's poetry enacts a male indebtedness to a female intellectual productivity imagined to be superior.

35. Burton Pollin, "Poe and Frances Osgood, as Linked Through 'Lenore,'" *Missis-sippi Quarterly* 46: 2 (1993), 185–197. Buford Jones and Kent Ljungquist, "Poe, Mrs. Osgood, and 'Annabel Lee,'" *Studies in the American Renaissance*, ed. Joel Myerson (Charlottesville: University Press of Virginia, 1983), 75–280. See also John Reilly's rebuttal, "Mrs. Osgood's 'Life Voyage' and 'Annabel Lee,'" *Poe Studies/Dark Romanticism* 17: 1 (1984): 23. Dayan suggests: "Think about what it would mean to reread Poe from the ground of those women he read, wrote about, and wrote to" ("Poe's Women," 12 n. 24).

36. Sharon Cameron argues that Emerson represents profound mourning as reti-cence; this model is comprehensible as a reaction to elegiac modes that identify mourning with an outpouring of grief. "Representing Grief: Emerson's 'Expe-rience,'" *Representations* 15 (Summer 1986), 15–41.

37. Several critics have noted that "The Philosophy of Composition" serves as an extension of "The Raven." See, for example, Donald Pease, *Visionary Compacts: American Renaissance Writings in Cultural Context* (Madison: University of Wisconsin Press), 184; and Elmer, *Reading at the Social Limit*, 210–213.

38. Sarah Helen Whitman, Sarah Anna Lewis, and Elmira Shelton; Frances Osgood, Virginia Poe, or Nancy Richmond have also been suggested as can-didates (*CWP* 468–477).

39. Hoffman, *Poe Poe Poe*, 91.

40. *Baudelaire on Poe: Critical Papers*, trans. and ed. Lois and Francis Hyslop (State College: Bald Eagle Press, 1952), 122.

41. Karen Halttunen, *Confidence Men and Painted Women: A Study of Middle-Class Culture in America, 1830–1870* (New Haven: Yale University Press, 1982).

42. Baudelaire's figuration of Poe goes against Butler's claims for drag's subversive powers. Here drag reinforces male privilege.

43. Hoffman, *Poe Poe Poe*, 94.

44. Roy Harvey Pearce echoes Emerson's characterization approvingly in *The Con-tinuity of American Poetry* (Princeton: Princeton University Press, 1961), 139.

45. Douglas, *Feminization*, 84.

46. "American Renaissance" studies commonly assert that the antebellum demo-cratic market economy was hostile to literary excellence, and that "great" writers' resistance to the marketplace is the generative force behind their art. Michael Gilmore claims that "while the romantics were still producing the masterpieces still read today, domestic novels written by women commanded

the enthusiasm of the antebellum public." *American Romanticism and the Marketplace* (Chicago: University of Chicago Press, 1985), 7; also David Reynolds, *Beneath the American Renaissance: The Subversive Imagination in the Age of Emerson and Melville* (New York: Knopf, 1988); and Douglas, *Feminization*. Roy Harvey Pearce advances this argument in terms of an American poetic tradition in *The Continuity of American Poetry*. Terence Whalen makes this argument in relation to Poe in *Edgar Allan Poe and the Masses: The Political Economy of Literature in Antebellum America* (Princeton: Princeton University Press, 1999); In *Reading at the Social Limit*, Elmer complicates this distinction by defining it as a dynamic of ambivalence that goes on within the individual artist (and also within the social body); still, the dichotomy remains.

CHAPTER 2

1. First two quotes from a newspaper clipping (Houghton: bMS Am 1355 [52]). Third quote from a letter by Grace Greenwood in *Home Journal* (quoted in *LL*18). Fourth quote from a review of Osgood's work in *Graham's* 28: 2 (February 1846), 93. Osgood's performances contradict assertions that the period only supported public performances of "passionlessness" on the part of middle-class women. Nancy Cott, "Passionlessness: An Interpretation of Victorian Sexual Ideology, 1790–1850," *A Heritage of Her Own*, ed. Nancy Cott and Elizabeth Pleck (New York: Simon and Schuster, 1979), 162–181. Treatments of restrictive public expectations for women authors include Susan Coultrap-Mcquin, *Doing Literary Business: American Women Writers in the Nineteenth Century* (Chapel Hill: University of North Carolina Press, 1979), 162–181; Berlant's articles; and Kelley, *Private Women, Public Stage*.
2. The phrase is Tompkins' in "Sentimental Power" (269). Cheryl Walker says that "the realm in which women's poetry flourished was for most of the century considered a distinctly separate sphere" (*AWP* xv–xvi).
3. "Literary Women of America," *The Ladies Repository* 20: 3 (March 1860), 170.
4. For a recent treatment of women's strategies of disembodied expressions of sexuality in public, see Levander, *Voices of the Nation*. My formulation is influenced by Michael Warner's discussion of "being-in-print" in *Letters of the Republic: Publication and the Public Sphere in Eighteenth-Century America* (Cambridge: Harvard University Press, 1990), 95. Warner argues that Benjamin Franklin "authoriz[es] as his own the voice of the document, as publication comes literally to constitute the public" (96). Osgood's case is reversed; the print public sphere authorizes her as its printed voice.
5. At least three of her poems of her poems were set to music in the 1840s: "Echo Song," "Lulu," and "Call Me Pet Names Dearest." *Bibliography of American Literature*, Vol. 6, ed. Jacob Blanck (New Haven: Yale University Press, 1973), 508–510.
6. Levander, *Voices of the Nation*, 7.
7. Quoted in Ann Douglas Wood, "Mrs. Sigourney and the Sensibility of Inner Space," *The New England Quarterly* (June 1972), 166.

8. Haight, *Mrs. Sigourney*, 34.
9. Lydia Sigourney, *Select Poems* (Philadelphia: Parry and McMillan, 1857), 30.
10. On death and the Victorian memento, see Barton Levi St. Armand, *Emily Dickinson and Her Culture: The Soul's Society* (New York: Cambridge University Press, 1984), 60–65. Also Karen Sanchez-Eppler, "Then When We Clutch Hardest: On the Death of a Child and the Replication of an Image," Chapman and Hendler, eds. *Sentimental Men*, 64–87.
11. Quoted in Douglas, *Feminization*, 206.
12. Quoted in Wood, "Mrs. Sigourney," 177; see also Haight, *Mrs. Sigourney*, 45.
13. Elmer discusses Sigourney's sentimental liquidity in *Reading at the Social Limit* (97–98).
14. Nina Baym, "Re-inventing Lydia Sigourney," 55. Dismissals include Haight, *Mrs. Sigourney*; and Douglas, *Feminization*.
15. *The Weeping Willow* (Hartford: H. S. Parsons, 1847), 56; *The Faded Hope* (New York: R. Carter & Bros., 1853); *Letters to My Pupils* (New York: R. Carter and Bros., 1853).
16. Mary Loeffelholz forges a related line of argument in "The School of Lydia Sigourney," chapter 2 in *From School to Salon*. Loeffelholz proposes that "we consider the school as the common social location of Sigourney's characteristic literary genres, history and elegy – as the matrix of the social relations of Sigourney's poetic and prose genres, inseparable from their matrix of republican ideas."
17. Mary Louise Kete argues that Sigourney and Longfellow develop competing "sentimental nationalisms" that rely on the trope of the "lost family" (*Sentimental Collaborations*, 117).
18. Sigourney, *Select Poems*, 59.
19. Haight, *Mrs. Sigourney*, 45.
20. Quoted in Haight, *Mrs. Sigourney*, 53.
21. May 1, 1848. Virginia (box 1[1–6]).
22. Frances Sargent Osgood, *The Cries of New York* (New York: John Doggett, Jr., 1846), 3.
23. Thomas Gray, *Progress of Poesie* (III. 3). *The Poems of Thomas Gray, William Collins, Oliver Goldsmith*, ed. Roger Lonsdale (London: Harlow, Longman, 1969), 175. Patricia Crain discusses the erotics of literacy in *The Story of A: The Alphabetization of America From The New England Primer to The Scarlet Letter* (Stanford: Stanford University Press, 2000), 103–131. Osgood's emphasis on male seduction deviates from the category of maternal eroticism that Crain delineates.
24. Griswold, *Female Poets*, 93.
25. Osgood's work is representative of a larger trend in women's erotic poetry traceable from L. E. L., Maria Brooks, Fanny Kemble through twentieth-century figures like Edna St. Vincent Millay and beyond.
26. Frances Sargent Osgood, "Kate Carol to Mary S.," *The Columbian Magazine* 7: 5 (May 1847), 207. "Kate Carol" is one of Osgood's pseudonyms.

27. Michael Moon has worked out this reading of Whitman with acuity in *Disseminating Whitman: Revision and Corporeality in Leaves of Grass* (Cambridge: Harvard University Press, 1991); see also Maslan, *Whitman Possessed.*
28. Joanne Dobson, "Sex, Wit, and Sentiment: Frances Osgood and the Poetry of Love," *American Literature* 65: 4 (1993), 634.
29. See n. 46, chapter 1.
30. Bennett notes that Dobson later discovered that one of the manuscript poems was published in the *Ladies Companion* in November 1839 (*Poets in the Public Sphere* 37; 225, n. 49).
31. Quoted in Dobson, "Sex, Wit, and Sentiment," 634.
32. Frances Sargent Osgood, "Life in New York: A Sketch of a Literary Soirée," *Graham's* 30: 3 (March 1847), 177–179.
33. Edgar Allan Poe, Review of *Poems*, by Frances S. Osgood (New York: Clark and Austin), *Broadway Journal* (December 13, 1845) (*PL* 603).
34. Osgood, "Kate Carol to Mary S." (206).
35. Included under the title of "Caprice" in *FSOP* 212; italics are eliminated in that version.
36. Frances Sargent Osgood, *A Letter About the Lions, A Letter to Mabel in the Country* (New York: G. P. Putnam, 1849).
37. Fannie Hunnewell, *The Life and Writings of Frances Sargent Osgood* (Ph.D. Diss. University of Texas, 1924), 51–52, n. 5.
38. Richard Brodhead characterizes a "spectatorially consumable form of other or represented life" in *Cultures of Letters: Scenes of Reading and Writing in Nineteenth-Century America* (Chicago: University of Chicago Press, 1993), 66.
39. "And all the souls he did not draw – / And he drew out his share" (9).
40. Gray, *Progress of Poesie*, III. 3.
41. Julie Ellison, "The Politics of Fancy in the Age of Sensibility," *Re-visioning Romanticism: British Women Writers, 1776–1837* (Philadelphia: University of Pennsylvania Press, 1994), 228.
42. Ellison, *Cato's Tears*, 101.
43. *The Complete Poetical Works of John Keats* (Boston: Houghton Mifflin 1899), 124; lines 1, 5, 9.
44. Published in *The Columbian Magazine* 3: 4 (April 1845), 185.
45. Maslan neglects to account for this prevalent heterosexual tradition when placing homoerotic scenarios of inspiration at the center of literary tradition in his study of Walt Whitman's homosexual politics of union (6–7). Osgood shares in a broader "celebration of fancy as an allegory of women's literary ambition" that Ellison explores in the work of Barbauld and Wheatley: "the fanciful subject is powerful, mobile, and self-pleasing, if only briefly so" (*Cato's Tears*, 122). This whimsicality has a political dimension because "sensibility, the language that turns politics into psychodrama . . . makes fancy a legitimate vehicle of cultural criticism" (122).
46. William Wordsworth, *Wordsworth: Poetical Works* (New York: Oxford University Press, 1969), 148; lines 9–10. Mrs. Mary Sumner, "Fanny," *Graham's* 30: 3 (March 1847), 179.

47. Frances Sargent Osgood, "The Coquette's Vow," *Graham's* 36: 1 (January 1850), 68. First five and last four stanzas quoted; seven middle stanzas omitted.
48. *FSOP* 97. Published in *Graham's* 26: 4 (April 1845), 166–167.
49. On Longfellow's experiments with visual speech in *Hiawatha*, see Jackson, "Picture-Writing a Nation."
50. The definition of "fan" as passionate follower of a hobby or celebrity arose in the nineteenth century, according to the *Oxford English Dictionary*; the earliest citation is from 1889; the poem was written earlier.
51. Published in *The Columbian Magazine* 7: 2 (February 1847), 62. Reprinted without italics in *FSOP* 169.
52. McGill analyzes the writing hand as a figure of Poe's subjection to market forces, concluding that "the hand caught in the act of inscription seems to have stopped for direction, waiting on the dictates of its audience to manipulate the truth" (*American Literature*, 184).
53. Paraphrase of Lydia Sigourney's book title *Letters to Mothers* (Hartford: Hudson and Skinner, 1838).
54. Griswold, quoted in *LL* 19.
55. Billet doux (Houghton bMS Am 1355 [53]); *LL* 17.
56. Quoted in John Evangelist Walsh, *Plumes in the Dust: The Love Affair of Edgar Allan Poe and Fanny Osgood* (Chicago: Nelson Hall, 1980), 11. From Oakes Smith, "Autobiographic Notes. Men and Women Greater Than Books," *Beadle's Monthly* 3: 6 (January 1867), 33.
57. Quoted in Mary Alice Wyman, *Two American Pioneers: Seba Smith and Elizabeth Oakes Smith* (New York: Columbia University Press, 1927), 123.
58. Letter, November 21, 1848 (Houghton bMS Am 1355 [15]).
59. Quoted in May, *American Female Poets*, 382.
60. December 11, 1842 (Houghton bMS Am 1355 [15]).
61. Houghton, bMS Am 1355 [16].
62. May 14, 1845 (Houghton, bMS Am 1355 [16]).
63. *EAP* 278–293; Sidney Moss attributes responsibility for "Poe's downfall as a critic" to the scandal. *Poe's Literary Battles: The Critic in the Context of His Literary Milieu* (Carbondale: Southern Illinois University Press, 1963), 190. Moss treats the *Broadway Journal* exchange as a flirtation which Osgood initiated, Poe "gallantly" acquiesced to, and Ellet vindictively intervened in (207–221).
64. Also Allen, *Israfel*, 510.
65. For a version of this narrative, see *EAP* 286.
66. Mary De Jong, "Lines From a Partly Published Drama: The Romance of Frances Sargent Osgood and Edgar Allan Poe," *Patrons and Protégées: Gender, Friendship, and Writing in Nineteenth-Century America* (New Brunswick: Rutgers University Press, 1988), 31–58. On Osgood's reputation see Mary De Jong, "Her Fair Fame: The Reputation of Frances Sargent Osgood, Woman Poet," *Studies in the American Renaissance*, ed. Joel Myerson (Charlottesville: University Press of Virginia, 1987), 269.
67. In one suggestive sketch, for example, published during the Osgood–Poe flirtation, a coquettish widow falls in love with a sensitive man trapped in a loveless

marriage and writes in her journal about her feelings. "Ida Grey," *Graham's* 27: 2 (August 1845), 82–84. See De Jong, "Lines," 38–39.

68. Whitman, *EPC* 37.

69. Edgar Allan Poe, Review of *Poems*, by Frances S. Osgood, *Broadway Journal* (December 13, 1845).

70. Shawn Rosenheim suggests that Poe cultivates this style of paranoid reading in *The Cryptographic Imagination: Secret Writing from Poe to the Internet* (Baltimore: Johns Hopkins University Press, 1995), chapters 1–3.

71. "A Presentation at a Literary Soirée," *Broadway Journal* (April 12, 1845), 232.

72. Frances S. Osgood, "Love's Reply"; Violet Vane, "Spring," *Broadway Journal* (April 12, 1845), 231.

73. Kate Carol, "The Rivulet's Dream"; Violet Vane, "So Let it Be," *Broadway Journal* (April 5, 1845), 215, 217.

74. Edgar Allan Poe, "To F——" (signed E); "Impromptu: To Kate Carol," *Broadway Journal* (April 26, 1845), 260, 271. Attributions in *PL* 529.

75. Poe was assistant editor by the end of February, 1845 and sole editor by October 25, 1845 (*EAP* 244, 274).

76. De Jong says that Osgood's "poems were not just printed in the *Journal*, they were placed" ("Lines," 42).

77. Frances Sargent Osgood, "Slander," *Broadway Journal* (August 30, 1845), 113.

78. Edgar Allan Poe, "William Wilson," *Broadway Journal* (August 30, 1845), 113.

79. Osgood, "Echo-Song."

80. On Poe's "poems of intimate, empty address," see McGill, *American Literature*, 158–160.

81. Frances Sargent Osgood, "To——," *Broadway Journal* (November 22, 1845), 307.

82. Frances Sargent Osgood, "To——," *Broadway Journal* (November 29, 1845), 318. The two-page spread underscores the theme of poetic (rather than corporeal) desire. Beneath Osgood's poem is Walter Whitman's "Art-Singing and Heart-Singing" (hinting at young Whitman's apprenticeship to women's "song"), which calls for "national lyrics" to appeal "to the throbbings of the great heart of humanity." On the next page, "Lines to Her Who Can Understand Them" by Fitz Greene Halleck depicts an erotic encounter with a woman's poem: "Blest be the lips that breathe it! / As mine have been – As mine have been / When pressed, in dreams, beneath it."

83. Frances Sargent Osgood, "Lines to An Idea That Wouldn't 'Come'" *Graham's* 34: 5 (May 1849), 245 (reprinted in *FSOP* 177); Frances Sargent Osgood, "The Coquette's Vow," *Graham's* 36: 1 (January 1850), 68.

84. Henry James, *A Small Boy and Others* (New York: Charles Scribner's and Sons, 1913), 60–61. Thanks to Meredith McGill for pointing out this passage.

85. A note in the Osgood manuscript file at the American Antiquarian Society corrects James. The portrait is held by the Massachusetts Historical Society.

CHAPTER 3

1. "The Phantom Voice" is the title of one of Sarah Helen Whitman's tributes to Poe published in *Graham's* 36: 1 (January 1850), 91. The phrase is from Poe's

"Scenes From 'Politian'"; Whitman quotes his lines in her epigraph: "It is *a phantom voice*: / Again! – again! How solemnly it falls / Into my heart of hearts!" Included without epigraph in *SHWP* 83.

2. Letter, Lilly.
3. Helen Sword makes this connection in *Ghostwriting Modernism* (Ithaca: Cornell University Press, 2002), 33.
4. Walt Whitman, "Preface," *Leaves of Grass* (New York: Library of America, 1992), 7. "I am large, I contain multitudes" from the poem proper (246).
5. Maslan, *Whitman Possessed*, 143.
6. Whitman, "Preface," 11.
7. E. W. Capron, *Modern Spiritualism* (New York: Partridge and Brittan, 1855), 235–237.
8. Oral Sumner Coad says that "Mrs. Whitman wrote the first sound and informed appraisal" of Poe ("Introduction," Whitman, *EPC* 19). Arthur Hobson Quinn calls it "the first book in [Poe's] defence – which still remains . . . one of the most sympathetic and brilliant interpretations of his poetry and fiction." *Edgar Allan Poe: A Critical Biography* (1941, reprint, introduction by Shawn Rosenheim. Baltimore: Johns Hopkins University Press, 1998), 572. Claiming that Whitman's evaluation of Poe anticipates twentieth-century recognition of his "profound pessimism," John E. Reilly says that she is "at least a candidate for the most underrated critic of Poe in the nineteenth century." "Sarah Helen Whitman as a Critic of Poe," *University of Mississippi Studies in English* 3 (1982), 122, 120.
9. *PHR* 202; *SP* 252, 462.
10. *SP* 390–393, 462–463.
11. William Whitman Bailey, "Recollections of Sarah Helen Whitman" (Brown University, John Hay Library, MS 30.8, 4).
12. Capron, *Modern Spiritualism*, 226; *SP* 245.
13. Quoted in R. Laurence Moore, *In Search of White Crows: Spiritualism, Parapsychology and American Culture* (New York: Oxford University Press, 1977), 11.
14. *PL* 728–729; *PH* 44–45; *EAP* 349; *SP* 284.
15. See *EAP*, Blasing, *American Poetry*, 17–35, and Elisabeth Bronfen, "Risky Resemblances: On Repetition, Mourning and Representation," *Death and Representation*, ed. Elisabeth Bronfen (Baltimore: Johns Hopkins University Press, 1993), 103–129.
16. Filling in the blanks and materializing the spiritual code, Mabbott titled this poem "To Helen [Whitman]" (*CWP* 445–447). I discuss this poem in chapter 1.
17. *CWP* 445; 11; "A Hollow in the Hills," *SHWP* 61.
18. On woman as medium in Poe see Dayan, *Fables of the Mind*, 133–192; and Dayan, "Amorous Bondage," 185.
19. The introduction identifies their relationship as a formative element in her poetic career (*SHWP* viii). The autobiographic form and coded allusions encourage readers to identify Whitman and Poe as the lovers to whom she refers.
20. *PH* 52–55; *EAP* 360.

21. Moore, *White Crows,* 10; see also Ruth Brandon, *The Spiritualists: The Passion for the Occult in the Nineteenth and Twentieth Centuries* (New York: Knopf, 1983), 13.
22. On the relation of spiritualism to telegraphy, see Jeffrey Sconce, *Haunted Media: Electronic Presence From Telegraphy to Television* (Durham: Duke University Press, 2000), esp. chapter 1; Ann Braude, *Radical Spirits: Spiritualism and Women's Rights in Nineteenth-Century America* (Boston: Beacon Press, 1989), 4–5, 15; Rosenheim, *Cryptographic Imagination,* chapters 4 and 5.
23. Brandon, *Spiritualists,* 6.
24. Moore, *White Crows,* 4.
25. Braude, *Radical Spirits,* 27.
26. Moore, *White Crows,* 3; Brandon, *Spiritualists,* 41.
27. Quoted in Howard Kerr, *Mediums, and Spirit-Rappers, and Roaring Radicals: Spiritualism in American Literature 1850–1900* (Urbana: University of Illinois Press, 1972).
28. Moore, *White Crows,* 26.
29. Quoted in Brandon, *Spiritualists,* 39.
30. Sconce, *Haunted Mediums,* 25.
31. Braude, *Radical Spirits,* 50.
32. Braude, *Radical Spirits,* 36–37.
33. Capron, *Modern Spiritualism,* 232–234.
34. Achsa Sprague, *The Poet and Other Poems* (Boston: William White and Co., 1864), xi–xxiii.
35. *PIL* 152; see also Moore, *White Crows,* 24.
36. Thomas Lake Harris, "Appendix," *A Lyric of the Morning Land* (New York: Partridge and Brittan, 1854); Thomas Lake Harris, "Preface," *Hymns of Spiritual Devotion* (New York: New Church Publishing Associates, 1857).
37. John Hollander claims that "poems trope their own schemes, allegorize their own arrangements." *Melodious Guile: Fictive Pattern in Poetic Language* (New Haven: Yale University Press, 1988), ix.
38. Harris, "Preface," *Hymns.*
39. Thomas Lake Harris, "Preface," *An Epic of the Starry Heaven* (New York: Partridge and Brittan, 1854). Sharon Cameron explores the poetic rehearsal of death, a concept she terms the *figura,* in *Lyric Time: Dickinson and the Limits of Genre* (Baltimore: Johns Hopkins University Press, 1979). Not restricted to Dickinson, the practice is widespread. Cameron underestimates the mystical belief in poetic form as receptacle rather than forum for dramatic rehearsal.
40. According to Sword, spirit communication "becomes a metaphor for poetry ... for the inscrutability of poetic inspiration, the frustrations of poetic production, and the death-defying power of words" only in the twentieth century (*Ghostwriting Modernism,* 35). I see little difference in the nineteenth-century logic.
41. Braude, *Radical Spirits,* 25; Brandon, *Spiritualists,* 40.
42. Quoted in Braude, *Radical Spirits,* 23.
43. May, *American Female Poets,* v; Braude, *Radical Spirits,* 23.

44. Quoted in Braude, *Radical Spirits*, 23.
45. Braude, *Radical Spirits*, 83.
46. Sarah Gould, *Asphodels* (New York: Proof Sheets, 1856).
47. Rosenheim, *Cryptographic Imagination*, 136. I take issue here with Rosenheim's reading of Doten's spirit poems as the vacuous inversion of Poe's brilliant originals (118–134).
48. Yopie Prins, "Sappho Doubled: Michael Field," *Yale Journal of Criticism* 8 (1995), 179. See also Prins, *Victorian Sappho*. On "voice" as textual figure, see Jonathan Culler, "Changes in the Study of Lyric," *Lyric Poetry: Beyond New Criticism*, ed. Chaviva Hosek and Patricia Parker (Ithaca: Cornell University Press, 1985), 50.
49. Gould, *Asphodels*, iii.
50. "Lyric Possession," *Critical Inquiry* 22 (1995), 37. See also Susan Stewart, *Poetry and the Fate of the Senses* (Chicago: University of Chicago Press, 2002), chapter 3.
51. Sword relates the Bloomian model of authorial inspiration to mediumship: "these writers affirm and imitate the mechanics of mediumship, with all its Oedipal posturings and gendered power plays, even while spiritualist ghost-writers attempt to imitate the mechanics of authorship" (*Ghostwriting Modernism*, 33).
52. Quoted in Barton St. Armand, "Veiled Ladies: Dickinson, Bettine, and Transcendental Mediumship," *Studies in the American Renaissance*, ed. Myerson (1987), 5.
53. Whitman, *EPC* 81.
54. Quoted in Kerr, *Mediums*, 18.
55. Quoted in *PH* 128.
56. Poem is retitled "To Him 'Whose Heart-Strings Were a Lute'" (*LL* 163–164).
57. Of her association of the word "power" with Poe, Silverman argues that she "evidently sought to stamp the incongruous lineaments of her father" on Poe (*EAP* 357).
58. "Arcturus, Written in October," and "Arcturus, Written in April" (*SHWP* 86, 96).
59. *SP* 390; 468–469.
60. Gould, *Asphodels*, 157.
61. *SP* 383, 601.
62. See *PHR* xxvii–xxviii.
63. Eveleth to Whitman, April 15, 1854 (Lilly).
64. Eveleth to Whitman, December 19, 1853 and November 9, 1854 (Lilly).
65. November 8, 1865 (Lilly).
66. February 3, 1867 (Lilly).
67. April 19, 1865 (Lilly).
68. September 1867 (Lilly).
69. October 25, 1864 (Lilly).
70. April 26, 1874 (Lilly).
71. September 18, 1867 (Lilly).

72. McGill traces this shift through nineteenth-century American copyright laws in "The Matter of the Text: Commerce, Print Culture, and the Authority of the State in American Copyright Law," *American Literary History* 9: 1 (1997), 21–59; 52. See also McGill, *American Literature*, 1–44.
73. September 8, 1853 (Brown, folder 122).
74. Quoted in John Carl Miller, "Introduction," Ingram–Poe Collection Website, Special Collections, University of Virginia: (http://www.lib.virginia.edu/speccol/colls/poemill.html).
75. Letter, Ingram to Whitman (*PHR* 1).
76. Rosenheim notes this scene of inspiration when discussing Ingram's "overwhelming identification with Poe's writing," and states that Ingram "us[ed] his textual reconstruction as the basis of a new joint identity with Poe" (*Cryptographic Imagination*, 123).
77. Ingram's major work on Poe was entitled *Edgar Allan Poe; His Life, Letters and Opinions; With Portraits of Poe and His Mother*, 2 vols. (London: Hogg, 1880).
78. See Miller's introduction, "The Ingram–Poe Collection" for a discussion of the battles over Poe memorabilia and national identity.
79. Rosenheim and Rachman, eds. *American Face*, x–xi.
80. Whalen, *Poe and the Masses*, 3–4. On French traditions of Poe criticism, see Patrick Quinn, *The French Face of Edgar Poe* (Carbondale: Southern Illinois University Press, 1957); and Muller and Richardson eds. *The Purloined Poe*.
81. Virginia Woolf, "Poe's Helen," *Granite and Rainbow* (New York: Harcourt and Brace, 1958), 225.
82. Noelle Baker calls for an expanded study of Whitman in "'This Slender Foundation . . . Made me Immortal': Sarah Helen Whitman vs. Poe's Helen," *Poe Studies/Dark Romanticism* 32: 1– 2 (1999), 8–26. See also Noelle Baker, *Sarah Helen Whitman's Literary Criticism: A Critical Edition* (Ph.D. Diss. Georgia State University, 1999).
83. Rosenheim, *Cryptographic Imagination*, 90.

CHAPTER 4

1. McGill, *American Literature*, 183.
2. Vitruvius Pollio. *Vitruvius, the Ten Books on Architecture*, ed. and trans. Morris Hicky Morgan (Cambridge: Harvard University Press, 1914), 6–7.
3. Tricia Lootens observes: "More like papier mache than marble, the metaphoric figures of such canonized nineteenth-century women poets were shaped around vacancy: if their literary 'relics' were revered, it was not as embodiments but as representations of a transcendent and definitively absent feminine glory" (*Lost Saints*, 10).
4. *Poems of Alice and Phoebe Cary* (1850) was followed by *Clovernook; Or, Recollections of Our Neighborhood in the West* (1852). *AWP*168–69, 198–199; Bennett, *Nineteenth-Century*, 89–90, 95–96.
5. "The Acorn," *The Sinless Child and Other Poems*, ed. John Keese (NY: Wiley and Putnam, 1843), 141–157; 152.

6. Susan Conrad, *Perish the Thought: Intellectual Women in Romantic America, 1830–1860* (New York: Oxford University Press, 1976), 128–129; also *HL* 105. Respecting Oakes Smith's choice to modify her married name, I call her by both names even though they are not hyphenated.

7. Prins discusses this dilemma in relation to Caroline Norton's *English Laws for Women in the Nineteenth Century* (1854): "The 'I' is not an original self entitled to self-possession but appears as a negated subject already dispossessed of what it cannot properly own" (*Victorian Sappho*, 220).

8. This formulation revises the oppositional models of both Berlant ("Female Woman") and Bennett (*Poets in the Public Sphere*).

9. Jackson and Prins, "Lyrical Studies," 526.

10. M. H. Abrams, *The Mirror and the Lamp: Romantic Theory and the Critical Tradition* (New York: Oxford University Press, 1953). In "Dickinson's Figure of Address," Virginia Jackson discusses Dickinson's figuration as the type of the romantic artist. *Dickinson and Audience*, ed. Martin Orzeck and Robert Weisbuch (Ann Arbor: University of Michigan Press, 1996), 77–104. Catherine Gallagher argues that eighteenth-century British women prose writers do not belong to a separate tradition but rather are "special in their extreme typicality." She notes that "women, authorship, and marketplace had – literally – nothing in common." *Nobody's Story: The Vanishing Acts of Women Writers in the Marketplace, 1670–1820* (Berkeley: University of California Press, 1994), xv.

11. On Oakes Smith's publishing history, see Wynola Louise Richards, *A Review of the Life and Writings of Elizabeth Oakes Smith, Feminist, Author, and Lecturer: 1806–1893* (Ph.D. Diss. Ball State University, 1981), especially 27, 38, 119–133. Also Conrad, *Perish the Thought*, 222.

12. Richards, *Review*, 61–62. Elizabeth Oakes Smith, *Woman and Her Needs* (New York: Fowlers and Wells, 1851). *Liberating the Home*, ed. Leon Stein and Annette Baxter (New York: Arno Press), 1–120, 72.

13. Clipping labeled "Evening Leader, July 13, 1885" (NYPL).

14. Oakes Smith, *The Sinless Child, Southern Literary Messenger* (January 1842): 86–89 (February 1842), 121–129. A longer version was first published in *The Sinless Child and Other Poems*. I work from the revised longer version published in *The Poetical Writings of Elizabeth Oakes Smith* (NY: J. S. Redfield, 1845), 15–84.

15. John Keese, "To the Reader," Oakes Smith, *The Sinless Child and Other Poems*, x–xi.

16. Quoted in J. C. Derby, *Fifty Years Among Authors, Books and Publishers* (New York: G. W. Carleton and Co, 1884), 546.

17. Watts says that "except for 'The Sinless Child' and one short poem, her verse is undistinguished. It is highly derivative ('Love Dead' is a poor 'The Raven') and highly impersonal" (*Poetry of American Women*, 97). She gives this negative evaluation after naming Oakes Smith as one of "the three most important" "women poets writing in America at this time," along with Sigourney and Osgood (83). I claim that "Love Dead" deliberately thematizes the impoverishing effects of repetition later in this chapter. See also Ostriker, *Stealing the Language*, 214.

18. Tompkins, "Sentimental Power," 271.

19. Oakes Smith, *Woman and Her Needs*, 83.

20. Sigourney, *Select Poems*, 84.

21. In "Revelations," God sits on a throne surrounded by beasts that "were full of eyes within: and they rest not day and night, saying Holy, holy, holy, Lord God Almighty, which was, and is, and is to come" (ch. 4, v. 8).

22. H. T. Tuckerman, from a review that "appeared recently in *Graham's*," quoted in *SC* xvii–xviii.

23. "Intimations of Immortality," Wordsworth 460; 64–65.

24. For a classic formulation see Harold Bloom, "Internalization of the Quest Romance." *Romanticism and Consciousness*, ed. Harold Bloom (New York: Norton and Co., 1970), 3–24.

25. Eva's transformation into Edgar's tonality follows the gender dynamics of public rhetoric analyzed by Levander, in which women are praised for the way they sound and denied sense (*Voices of the Nation*, 1–11).

26. Jackson and Prins assert: "The 'pure virgin of the soul' becomes at the end of the poem what she always already was, 'the vestibule of Heaven,' the embodiment of an ideal that has no body in which to descend into history" ("Lyrical Studies," 527). They conclude that "in 'The Sinless Child,' it is the subjectivity attached to lyric that is unbearable" (528).

27. Oakes Smith writes in her diary that she adopted the pseudonym in order to make more money by doubling her submissions (Richards, *Review*, 45–46).

28. Elizabeth Oakes Smith, *The Salamander* (New York: George P. Putnam, 1848).

29. Review, Elizabeth Oakes Smith, *The Salamander. Southern Literary Messenger* 14: 12 (1848), 764.

30. Ernest Helfenstein, "Thoughts Before a Duel," *Graham's* 26: 3 (September 1844), 110–112. Ernest Helfenstein, "Stanzas To Julia," *United States Magazine* 3: 3 (September 1856), 248.

31. Ernest Helfenstein, "The Soul's Ideal," *Graham's* 25: 2 (February 1844), 52.

32. Elizabeth Oakes Smith, "Mental Solitude," *Graham's* 25: 5 (May 1844), 218.

33. Ernest Helfenstein, "To __," *Graham's* 23: 2 (August 1843), 67. "The Gift," *Home Journal*, clipping (Virginia); Kete argues that poems circulate in a gift economy that shapes collaborative individuals and communities (54). If this is so, Ernest stages a refusal to share the gift he wants to give, protesting that it would be lost in the exchange.

34. Quoted in Richards, *Review*, 106.

35. May, *American Female Poets*, 279.

36. See Christine Battersby on historical and etymological associations of genius with the phallus in *Gender and Genius: Towards a Feminist Aesthetics* (Bloomington: Indiana University Press, 1989).

37. May, *American Female Poets*, 279.

38. *Samuel Taylor Coleridge*, ed. H. J. Jackson (Oxford: Oxford University Press, 1985), 52.

39. Bennett, *Nineteenth-Century*, 45.

40. *Samuel Taylor Coleridge*, 103.

41. Richards, *Review*, 34–35; *HL* 2.
42. Quoted in Richards, *Review*, 38
43. Elizabeth Oakes Smith, "To the Editor of the *Evening Mirror*," around December 1854. Clipping (Virginia).
44. Oakes Smith's formulation recalls Berlant's in "The Female Complaint."
45. "The Poet," *RWE* 198.
46. *Biographia Literaria* (*Samuel Taylor Coleridge*, 41).
47. Oakes Smith, *Woman and Her Needs*, 72.
48. Oakes Smith, *Woman and Her Needs*, 56.
49. Originally published in "Autobiographic Notes. Men and Women," 31.
50. "Shakspeare; or, the Poet," *RWE* 329.
51. Oakes Smith, "Autobiographic Notes. Men and Women," 31.
52. "Carlyle and Poetry," "For the *Free Religious Index*." "Please preserve" written against the margin. Clipping (NYPL).
53. Quoted in Richards, *Review*, 29–30.
54. Oakes Smith, "Books and Bookmaking." Clipping (NYPL).
55. Oakes Smith, *Woman and Her Needs*, 20.
56. "Massachusetts Constitutional Convention," the UNA, June 1853. Quoted in Conrad, *Perish the Thought*, 132.
57. Oakes Smith, *Woman and Her Needs*, 21.
58. Mary Forrest (pseudonym for Julia Deane Freeman), "For the *Evening Mirror*." Clipping, around December 1854 (Virginia).
59. Mary Forrest, "To the Editor of the *Evening Mirror*." Clipping, around February 1855 (Virginia).
60. Mary Forrest, "To Mrs. E. Oakes Smith," *Evening Mirror*. Clipping, around February 1855 (Virginia).
61. Elizabeth Oakes Smith, "To Mary Forrest," *Evening Mirror* (March 1, 1855). Clipping (Virginia).
62. Mary Forrest, "Mrs. E. Oakes Smith," *Evening Mirror* (March 9, 1855). Clipping (Virginia).
63. Elizabeth Oakes Smith, "To Mary Forrest." *Evening Mirror*, around March 1855. Clipping (Virginia).
64. Pearce, *The Continuity of American Poetry*, 139.
65. Elizabeth Oakes Smith, *Evening Mirror*, around March 1855. Clipping (Virginia).
66. Elizabeth Oakes Smith, "Thoughts on Woman," "For the *Home Journal*." Clipping (Virginia). Editor's note identifies poem's original context and states that it was being published over forty years after it was delivered.
67. Leigh Kirkland, "Introduction," *HL* 9. Kirkland asserts that "much of the poignancy of this text lies in her implicit struggle against the possibility that she will be forgotten" (11). Kirkland's dissertation makes Oakes Smith's autobiography available in a carefully annotated form, accompanied by a helpful critical introduction.
68. *HL* 175; quote from "Song of Solomon": "A garden inclosed is my sister, my spouse; a spring shut up, a fountain sealed" (ch. 4, v. 12)

69. *HL* 174. Other versions in Oakes Smith's unpublished sonnet book (NYPL) and *Godey's Lady's Book*, 32 (1846), 12.

70. Elizabeth Oakes Smith, "On Burning Letters," newspaper clipping (NYPL). Handwritten in the margin: "Sent to Home Journal March 30th 80."

71. In "The Poet" Emerson asserts: "It is not metres, but a metre-making argument, that makes a poem, – a thought so alive, that, like the spirit of a plant or an animal, it has an architecture of its own, and adorns nature with a new thing" (*RWE* 200).

72. "Margaret Fuller," *Dictionary of Literary Biography*, vol. 239: *American Women Prose Writers, 1820–1870*, ed. Katherine Rodier and Amy E. Hudock (Berkeley: The Gale Group, 2001), 128.

73. Elizabeth Oakes Smith, "Margaret Fuller" ("1851" handwritten). Clipping (Virginia).

CODA

1. Elizabeth Oakes Smith, "Recollections of Poe," *Beadle's Monthly* (February 1867), 147; reprinted in the *Home Journal* (March 15, 1876). Kirkland provides citations (*HL* 371).

2. Oakes Smith recounts a slightly different version of this conversation in "Autobiographic Notes. Edgar Allan Poe." *Beadle's Monthly* 3: 7 (February 1867), 152.

3. A slightly different account published in Oakes Smith, "Autobiographic Notes. Edgar Allan Poe" (152).

4. Griswold, *Female Poets*, 167.

5. Susan Archer Weiss, *The Home Life of Poe* (New York: Broadway Publishing Company, 1907), 185.

6. The manuscript poem is marked "Hollywood, North Carolina," where Oakes Smith moved in 1874 (Virginia).

7. Jackson and Prins, "Lyrical Studies," 521.

Select Bibliography

Abrams, M. H. *The Mirror and the Lamp: Romantic Theory and the Critical Tradition*. New York: Oxford University Press, 1953.

Adorno, Theodore. "Lyric Poetry and Society." *The Adorno Reader*, ed. Brian O'Connor. Oxford: Blackwell, 2000, 211–229.

Allen, Hervey. *Israfel: The Life and Times of Edgar Allan Poe*. New York: Farrar and Rinehart, 1934.

Allen, Michael. *Poe and the British Magazine Tradition*. New York: Oxford University Press, 1969.

Baker, Noelle. "This Slender Foundation . . . Made me Immortal': Sarah Helen Whitman vs. Poe's Helen." *Poe Studies/Dark Romanticism* 32: 1–2 (1999), 8–26.

Battersby, Christine. *Gender and Genius: Towards a Feminist Aesthetics*. Bloomington: Indiana University Press, 1989.

Baudelaire, Charles. *Baudelaire on Poe: Critical Papers*, trans. and ed. Lois and Francis Hyslop. State College: Bald Eagle Press, 1952.

— *The Painter of Modern Life and Other Essays*, trans. and ed. Jonathan Mayne. London: Phaidon, 1964.

Baym, Nina. "Re-inventing Lydia Sigourney." *The (Other) American Traditions: Nineteenth-Century Women Writers*, ed. Joyce Warren. New Brunswick: Rutgers University Press, 1993, 54–72.

— "The Rise of the Woman Author." *Columbia Literary History of the United States*. New York: Columbia University Press, 1988, 289–305.

Bennett, Andrew. *Romantic Poets and the Culture of Posterity*. Cambridge: Cambridge University Press, 1999.

Bennett, Paula, ed. *Nineteenth-Century American Women Poets*. Oxford: Blackwell, 1998.

— *Poets in the Public Sphere: The Emancipatory Project of American Women's Poetry, 1800–1900*. Princeton: Princeton University Press, 2003.

Berlant, Lauren. "The Female Woman: Fanny Fern and the Form of Sentiment." *American Literary History* 3 (Fall 1991), 429–54.

— "The Female Complaint." *Social Text* 19: 20 (Fall 1988), 237–59.

Bhabha, Homi. "Of Mimicry and Man." *The Location of Culture*. New York: Routledge, 1994, 84–92.

Blanck, Jacob, ed. *Bibliography of American Literature*. Vol. 6 (New Haven: Yale University Press, 1973).

Blasing, Mutlu. *American Poetry: The Rhetoric of its Forms*. New Haven: Yale University Press, 1987.

Bloom, Harold. *Anxiety of Influence: A Theory of Poetry*. New York: Oxford University Press, 1987.

— "Internalization of the Quest Romance." *Romanticism and Consciousness*, ed. Harold Bloom. New York: Norton and Co., 1970, 3–24.

Bonaparte, Marie. *The Life and Works of Edgar Poe*, trans. John Rodker. London: Hogarth Press, 1949.

Botta, Vincenzo, ed. *Memoirs of Ann C. L. Botta*. New York: J. S. Tait & Sons, 1894.

Brandon, Ruth. *The Spiritualists: The Passion for the Occult in the Nineteenth and Twentieth Centuries*. New York: Knopf, 1983.

Braude, Ann. *Radical Spirits: Spiritualism and Women's Rights in Nineteenth-Century America*. Boston: Beacon Press, 1989.

Brodhead, Richard. *Cultures of Letters: Scenes of Reading and Writing in Nineteenth-Century America*. Chicago: University of Chicago Press, 1993.

Bronfen, Elisabeth. *Over Her Dead Body: Death, Femininity and the Aesthetic*. New York: Routledge, 1992.

— "Risky Resemblances: On Repetition, Mourning and Representation," *Death and Representation*, ed. Elisabeth Bronfen. Baltimore: Johns Hopkins University Press, 1993, 103–129.

Brown, Gillian. "The Poetics of Extinction." In Shawn Rosenheim and Stephen Rachman, eds. *The American Face of Edgar Allan Poe*. Baltimore: Johns Hopkins University Press, 1995, 341–342.

Browning, Elizabeth Barrett. *Elizabeth Barrett Browning: Selected Poems*, ed. Margaret Forster. Baltimore: Johns Hopkins University Press, 1988.

Butler, Judith. *Gender Trouble: Feminism and the Subversion of Identity*. New York: Routledge, 1990.

Cameron, Sharon. *Lyric Time: Dickinson and the Limits of Genre*. Baltimore: Johns Hopkins University Press, 1979.

— "Representing Grief: Emerson's 'Experience.'" *Representations* 15 (Summer 1986), 15–41.

Capron, E. W. *Modern Spiritualism*. New York: Partridge and Brittan, 1855.

Chapman, Mary and Hendler, Glenn, eds. *Sentimental Men: Masculinity and the Politics of Affect in American Culture*. Berkeley: University of California Press, 1999.

Charvat, William. *The Profession of Authorship in America, 1800–1870*. New York: Columbia University Press, 1992.

Coleridge, Samuel Taylor. *Samuel Taylor Coleridge*, ed. H. J. Jackson Oxford: Oxford University Press, 1985.

Conrad, Susan. *Perish the Thought: Intellectual Women in Romantic America, 1830–1860*. New York: Oxford University Press, 1976.

Cott, Nancy F. *The Bonds of Womanhood: "Woman's Sphere" in New England, 1780–1835.* New Haven: Yale University Press, 1977.

— "Passionlessness: An Interpretation of Victorian Sexual Ideology, 1790–1850." *A Heritage of Her Own*, ed. Nancy Cott and Elizabeth Pleck. New York: Simon and Schuster, 1979, 162–181.

Coultrap-Mcquin, Susan. *Doing Literary Business: American Women Writers in the Nineteenth Century.* Chapel Hill: University of North Carolina Press, 1979.

Crain, Patricia. *The Story of A: The Alphabetization of America From The New England Primer to The Scarlet Letter.* Stanford: Stanford University Press, 2000.

Culler, Jonathan. "Changes in the Study of Lyric." In Chaviva Hosek and Patricia Parker, eds. *Lyric Poetry: Beyond New Criticism.* Ithaca: Cornell University Press, 38–54.

Cushman, Stephen. *Fictions of Form in American Poetry.* Princeton: Princeton University Press, 1993.

Dayan, Joan. "Amorous Bondage: Poe, Ladies, and Slaves." In Shawn Rosenheim and Stephen Rachman, eds. *The American Face of Edgar Allan Poe.* Baltimore: Johns Hopkins University Press, 1995, 199.

— *Fables of Mind: An Inquiry into Poe's Fiction.* New York: Oxford University Press, 1987.

— "Poe's Women: A Feminist Poe?" *Poe Studies* 26: 1 and 2 (June/December 1993), 9.

De Jong, Mary. "Her Fair Fame: The Reputation of Frances Sargent Osgood, Woman Poet." *Studies in the American Renaissance*, ed. Joel Myerson. Charlottesville: University Press of Virginia, 1987, 265–283.

— "Lines From a Partly Published Drama: The Romance of Frances Sargent Osgood and Edgar Allan Poe." *Patrons and Protégées: Gender, Friendship, and Writing in Nineteenth-Century America.* New Brunswick: Rutgers University Press, 1988, 31–58.

Derby, J. C. *Fifty Years Among Authors, Books and Publishers.* New York: G. W. Carleton and Co., 1884.

Diamond, Elin. "Mimesis, Mimicry, and the 'True-Real.'" *Acting Out: Feminist Performances*, ed. Lynda Hart and Peggy Phelan. Ann Arbor: University of Michigan Press, 1993, 363–382.

Didier, Eugene. *The Poe Cult and Other Poe Papers.* New York: Broadway Publishing Co., 1909.

Dobson, Joanne. "Sex, Wit, and Sentiment: Frances Osgood and the Poetry of Love," *American Literature* 65: 4 (1993), 631–650.

Dolan, Ann Marie. *The Literary Salon in New York: 1830–1860.* Ph.D. Diss. Columbia University, 1957.

Doten, Lizzie. *Poems From the Inner Life.* Boston: William White and Co., 1864.

Douglas, Ann. *The Feminization of American Culture.* New York: Knopf, 1977.

Ellison, Julie. *Cato's Tears: The Making of Anglo-American Emotion.* Chicago: University of Chicago Press, 1999.

— *Delicate Subjects: Romanticism, Gender, and the Ethics of Understanding*. Ithaca: Cornell University Press, 1990.

— *Emerson's Romantic Style*. Princeton: Princeton University Press, 1984.

— "The Politics of Fancy in the Age of Sensibility." *Re-visioning Romanticism: British Women Writers, 1776–1837*. Philadelphia: University of Pennsylvania Press, 1994, 228–255.

Elmer, Jonathan. *Reading at the Social Limit: Affect, Mass Culture, and Edgar Allan Poe*. Stanford: Stanford University Press, 1995.

Emerson, Ralph Waldo. *Ralph Waldo Emerson*, ed. Richard Poirier. New York: Oxford University Press, 1990.

Felman, Shoshana. "On Reading Poetry: Reflections on the Limits and Possibilities of Psychoanalytic Approaches." *The Purloined Poe: Lacan, Derrida, and Psychoanalytic Reading*, ed. John P. Muller and William J. Richardson. Baltimore: Johns Hopkins University Press, 1988, 134.

Fisher, Benjamin Franklin (ed.), *Poe and His Times: The Artist and His Milieu*. Baltimore: Edgar Allan Poe Society, 1990.

Fussell, Edwin. *Lucifer in Harness: American Meter, Metaphor and Diction*. Princeton: Princeton University Press, 1973.

Gallagher, Catherine. *Nobody's Story: The Vanishing Acts of Women Writers in the Marketplace, 1670–1820*. Berkeley: University of California Press, 1994.

Gauld, Alan. *A History of Hypnotism*. Cambridge: Cambridge University Press, 1992.

Gilmore, Michael. *American Romanticism and the Marketplace*. Chicago: University of Chicago Press, 1985.

Gould, Sarah. *Asphodels*. New York: Proof Sheets, 1856.

Griswold, Rufus. "Death of Edgar Allan Poe." 1849. Reprinted in *Edgar Allan Poe: The Critical Heritage*, ed. I. M. Walker. New York: Routledge, 1986, 294–301.

— ed. *Female Poets of America*. Philadelphia: Carey and Hart, 1848.

Gruesz, Kirsten Silva. *Ambassadors of Culture: The Transamerican Origins of Latino Writing*. Princeton: Princeton University Press, 2002.

— "Feeling for the Fireside: Longfellow, Lynch, and the Topography of Poetic Power." In Mary Chapman and Glenn Hendler, eds. *Sentimental Men: Masculinity and the Politics of Affect in American Culture*. Berkeley: University of California Press, 1999, 43–63.

Haight, Gordon. *Mrs. Sigourney: The Sweet Singer of Hartford*. New Haven: Yale University Press, 1930.

Halttunen, Karen. *Confidence Men and Painted Women: A Study of Middle-Class Culture in America, 1830–1870*. New Haven: Yale University Press, 1982.

Harris, Thomas Lake. *An Epic of the Starry Heaven*. New York: Partridge and Brittan, 1854.

— *Hymns of Spiritual Devotion*. New York: New Church Publishing Associates, 1857.

— *A Lyric of the Morning Land*. New York: Partridge and Brittan, 1854.

Hart, James David. *The Popular Book; A History of America's Literary Taste*. Berkeley: University of California Press, 1950.

Hawthorne, Nathaniel. *Hawthorne's Poems*, ed. Peck and Peck. Charlottesville: University of Virginia Bibliographical Society, 1967.

Hedrick, Joan. *Harriet Beecher Stowe: A Life*. New York: Oxford University Press, 1994.

Hendler, Glenn. *Public Sentiments: Structures of Feeling in Nineteenth-Century American Literature*. Chapel Hill: University of North Carolina Press, 2001.

Hewitt, Mary, ed. *Laurel Leaves*. New York: Lamport, Blakeman and Law, 1854.

Hoffman, Daniel, *Poe Poe Poe Poe Poe Poe Poe*. Garden City: Doubleday, 1972.

Hollander, John. *Melodious Guile: Fictive Pattern in Poetic Language*. New Haven: Yale University Press, 1988.

Hosek, Chaviva and Parker, Patricia, eds. *Lyric Poetry: Beyond New Criticism*. Ithaca: Cornell University Press, 1985.

Howe, Julia Ward. "The Salon in America." *Is Polite Society Polite? And Other Essays*. New York: Lamson, Wolfe, and Co., 1895, 114–129.

Hunnewell, Fannie. *The Life and Writings of Frances Sargent Osgood*. Ph.D. Diss. University of Texas, 1924.

Irigaray, Luce. *Speculum of the Other Woman*, trans. Gillian C. Gill. Ithaca: Cornell University Press, 1985.

Jackson, Virginia and Prins, Yopie. "Lyrical Studies," *Victorian Literature and Culture* 7: 2 (2000), 521–529.

Jackson, Virginia. "Dickinson's Figure of Address." *Dickinson and Audience*, ed. Martin Orzeck and Robert Weisbuch. Ann Arbor: University of Michigan Press, 1996, 77–104.

— "Longfellow's Tradition: Or, Picture-Writing a Nation." *Modern Language Quarterly* 59 (1998), 471–496.

James, Henry. *A Small Boy and Others*. New York: Charles Scribner's and Sons, 1913.

Jehlen, Myra. "Archimedes and the Paradox of Feminist Criticism." *Feminisms: An Anthology of Literary Theory and Criticism*, ed. Robyn R. Warhol and Diane Price Herndl. New Brunswick: Rutgers University Press, 1996, 75–96.

Jones, Buford and Ljungquist, Kent. "Poe, Mrs. Osgood, and 'Annabel Lee.'" *Studies in the American Renaissance*, ed. Joel Myerson. Charlottesville: University Press of Virginia, 1983, 75–280.

Kasson, John. *Rudeness and Civility: Manners in Nineteenth-Century Urban America*. New York: Hill and Wang, 1990.

Keats, John. *The Complete Poetical Works of John Keats*. Boston: Houghton Mifflin 1899.

Kelley, Mary. *Private Woman, Public Stage: Literary Domesticity in Nineteenth-Century America*. New York: Oxford University Press, 1984.

Kennedy, J. Gerald. "Elegy For a Rebel Soul." In Benjamin Franklin Fisher (ed.), *Poe and His Times: The Artist and His Milieu*. Baltimore: Edgar Allan Poe Society, 1990, 226–234.

— *Poe, Death, and the Life of Writing*. New Haven: Yale University Press, 1987.

— "Poe, 'Ligeia,' and the Problem of Dying Women." *New Essays on Poe's Major Tales*, ed. Kenneth Silverman. New York: Cambridge University Press, 1993.

Kerr, Howard. *Mediums, and Spirit-Rappers, and Roaring Radicals: Spiritualism in American Literature 1850–1900*. Urbana: University of Illinois Press, 1972.

Kete, Mary Louise. *Sentimental Collaborations: Mourning and Middle-Class Identity in Nineteenth-Century America*. Durham: Duke University Press, 2000.

Kincaid, James. *Child Loving: The Erotic Child and Victorian Culture*. New York: Routledge, 1992.

Levander, Caroline. *Voices of the Nation: Women and Public Speech in Nineteenth-Century American Literature and Culture*. New York: Cambridge University Press, 1998.

Ljundquist, Kevin and Nickels, Cameron. "Elizabeth Oakes Smith on Poe: A Chapter in the Recovery of His Nineteenth-Century Reputation." In Benjamin Franklin Fisher (ed.), *Poe and His Times: The Artist and His Milieu*. Baltimore: Edgar Allan Poe Society, 1990, 235–246.

Loeffelholz, Mary. *From School to Salon: Reading Nineteenth-Century American Women's Poetry*. Princeton: Princeton University Press, 2004.

— "Who Killed Lucretia Davidson? Or, Poetry in the Domestic-Tutelary Complex," *The Yale Journal of Criticism* 10: 2 (1997), 271–293.

Lonsdale, Roger, ed. *The Poems of Thomas Gray, William Collins, Oliver Goldsmith*. London: Harlow, Longman, 1969.

Lootens, Tricia. *Lost Saints: Silence, Gender, and Victorian Literary Canonization*. Charlottesville: University Press of Virginia, 1996.

McGill, Meredith. *American Literature and the Culture of Reprinting*. Philadelphia: University of Pennsylvania Press, 2003.

— "The Matter of the Text: Commerce, Print Culture, and the Authority of the State in American Copyright Law," *American Literary History* 9: 1 (1997), 21–59.

— "Poe, Literary Nationalism, and Authorial Identity." In Shawn Rosenheim and Stephen Rachman, eds. *The American Face of Edgar Allan Poe*. Baltimore: Johns Hopkins University Press, 1995, 271–304.

Maslan, Mark. *Whitman Possessed*. Baltimore: Johns Hopkins University Press, 2001.

May, Caroline, ed. *The American Female Poets*. Philadelphia: Lindsay and Blakiston, 1848.

Miller, John Carl, ed. *Poe's Helen Remembers*. Charlottesville: University Press of Virginia, 1979.

— "Introduction." Ingram-Poe Collection Website, Special Collections, University of Virginia (http://www.lib.virginia.edu/speccol/colls/poemill.html).

Moon, Michael. *Disseminating Whitman: Revision and Corporeality in* Leaves of Grass. Cambridge: Harvard University Press, 1991.

Moore, R. Laurence. *In Search of White Crows: Spiritualism, Parapsychology and American Culture*. New York: Oxford University Press, 1977.

Morris, Timothy. *Becoming Canonical in American Poetry*. Urbana: University of Illinois Press, 1995.

Moss, Sidney. *Poe's Literary Battles: The Critic in the Context of His Literary Milieu*. Carbondale: Southern Illinois University Press, 1963.

Mott, Frank Luther. *A History of American Magazines 1741–1850*. Cambridge: Belknap Press of Harvard University Press, 1930.

Mulcaire, Terry. "Publishing Intimacy in *Leaves of Grass*," *ELH* 60: 2 (1993), 471–501.

Newlyn, Lucy. *Reading, Writing, and Romanticism: The Anxiety of Reception*. Oxford: Oxford University Press, 2000.

Oakes Smith, Elizabeth. *A Human Life: Being the Autobiography of Elizabeth Oakes Smith. A Critical Edition and Introduction*, ed. Leigh Kirkland. Ph.D. Diss. Georgia State University, 1994.

— *The Poetical Writings of Elizabeth Oakes Smith*, New York: J. S. Redfield, 1845.

— *Selections from the Autobiography of Elizabeth Oakes Smith*, ed. Mary Alice Wyman. Lewiston, ME: Lewiston Journal, 1924.

— *The Salamander*. New York: George P. Putnam, 1848.

— *The Sinless Child and Other Poems*, ed. John Keese. New York: Wiley and Putnam, 1843.

— *Woman and Her Needs*. New York: Fowlers and Wells, 1851.

— *Liberating the Home*, ed. Leon Stein and Annette Baxter. New York: Arno Press. 1–120.

Osgood, Frances Sargent. *The Cries of New York*. New York: John Doggett, Jr., 1846.

— *A Letter About the Lions, A Letter to Mabel in the Country*. New York: G. P. Putnam, 1849.

— *Poems*. Philadelphia: Carey and Hart, 1850.

Ostriker, Alicia. *Stealing the Language: The Emergence of Women's Poetry in America*. Boston: Beacon Press, 1986.

Pattee, Fred Lewis. *The Feminine Fifties*. New York: Appleton-Century, 1940.

Pearce, Roy Harvey. *The Continuity of American Poetry*. Princeton: Princeton University Press, 1961.

Person, Leland. *Aesthetic Headaches: Women and a Masculine Poetics in Poe, Melville, and Hawthorne*. Athens: University of Georgia Press, 1988.

Petrino, Elizabeth. *Emily Dickinson and Her Contemporaries: Women's Verse in America, 1820–1885*. Hanover: University of New England Press, 1995.

Poe, Edgar Allan. *The Complete Works of Edgar Allan Poe*. 17 vols., ed. James Harrison, 1902. Reprint, New York: AMS Press, 1965.

— *The Collected Works of Edgar Allan Poe*, ed. T. O. Mabbott. Vol. I. *Poems*. Cambridge: Belknap Press of Harvard University Press, 1969.

— *The Collected Writings of Edgar Allan Poe*, ed. Burton Pollin. Vol. 3, pt. I. *Broadway Journal Prose*. New York: Gordian Press, 1986.

— *Marginalia*, ed. John Carl Miller. Charlottesville: University Press of Virginia, 1981.

— *Essays and Reviews*. Library of America, 1984.

Pollin, Burton. "Poe and Frances Osgood, as Linked Through 'Lenore,'" *Mississippi Quarterly* 46: 2 (1993), 185–197.

Pollio, Vitruvius. *Vitruvius, the Ten Books on Architecture*, ed. and trans. Morris Hicky Morgan. Cambridge: Harvard University Press, 1914.

Prins, Yopie. "Sappho Doubled: Michael Field," *Yale Journal of Criticism* 8 (1995), 165–186.

— *Victorian Sappho*. Princeton: Princeton University Press, 1999.

Quinn, Arthur Hobson. *Edgar Allan Poe: A Critical Biography*, 1941. Reprint, introduction by Shawn Rosenheim. Baltimore: Johns Hopkins University Press, 1998.

Railton, Stephen. *Authorship and Audience: Literary Performance in the American Renaissance*. Princeton: Princeton University Press, 1991.

Read, Thomas Buchanan, ed. *The Female Poets of America*. Philadelphia: E. H. Butler and Co., 1849.

Reilly, John E. "Mrs. Osgood's 'Life Voyage' and 'Annabel Lee,'" *Poe Studies/Dark Romanticism* 17: 1 (1984), 23.

— "Sarah Helen Whitman as a Critic of Poe," *University of Mississippi Studies in English* 3 (1982), 120–127.

Reynolds, David. *Beneath the American Renaissance: The Subversive Imagination in the Age of Emerson and Melville*. New York: Knopf, 1988.

Richards, Eliza. "Women's Place in Poe Studies," *Poe Studies/Dark Romanticism* 33: 1 and 2 (2000), 10–14.

Richards, Wynola Louise. *A Review of the Life and Writings of Elizabeth Oakes Smith, Feminist, Author, and Lecturer: 1806–1893*. Ph.D. Diss. Ball State University, 1981.

Rosenheim, Shawn. *The Cryptographic Imagination: Secret Writing from Poe to the Internet*. Baltimore: Johns Hopkins University Press, 1995.

Rosenheim, Shawn and Rachman, Stephen, eds. *The American Face of Edgar Allan Poe*. Baltimore: Johns Hopkins University Press, 1995.

St. Armand, Barton Levi. *Emily Dickinson and Her Culture: The Soul's Society*. New York: Cambridge University Press, 1984.

— "Veiled Ladies: Dickinson, Bettine, and Transcendental Mediumship." *Studies in the American Renaissance*, ed. Joel Myerson. Charlottesville: University Press of Virginia, 1987, 1–52.

Sanchez-Eppler, Karen. "Then When We Clutch Hardest: On the Death of a Child and the Replication of an Image." In Mary Chapman and Glenn Hendler, eds. *Sentimental Men: Masculinity and the Politics of Affect in American Culture*. Berkeley: University of California Press, 1999, 64–87.

Schultz, Gretchen. *The Gendered Lyric: Subjectivity and Difference in Nineteenth-Century French Poetry*. West Lafayette: Purdue University Press, 1999.

Sconce, Jeffrey. *Haunted Media: Electronic Presence From Telegraphy to Television*. Durham: Duke University Press, 2000.

Sigourney, Lydia. *Letters to Mothers*. Hartford: Hudson and Skinner, 1838.

— *Select Poems*. Philadelphia: Parry and McMillan, 1857.

— *The Weeping Willow*. Hartford: H. S. Parsons, 1847.

Silverman, Kenneth. *Edgar A. Poe: A Mournful and Never-Ending Remembrance*. London: Weidenfeld, 1993.

Smith, Elizabeth Oakes. *See* Oakes Smith, Elizabeth.

Sprague, Achsa. *The Poet and Other Poems*. Boston: William White and Co., 1864.

Stewart, Susan. "Lyric Possession," *Critical Inquiry* 22: 1 (1995), 34–63.

Stoehr, Taylor. "Hawthorne and Mesmerism," *Huntington Library Quarterly* 32: 1 (1969), 33–60.

Sword, Helen. *Ghostwriting Modernism*. Ithaca: Cornell University Press, 2002.

Terada, Rei. *Derek Walcott's Poetry: American Mimicry*. Boston: Northeastern University Press, 1992.

Thomas, Dwight and Jackson, David K. *The Poe Log: A Documentary Life of Edgar Allan Poe, 1809–1849*. Boston: G. K. Hall, 1987.

Ticknor, Caroline. *Poe's Helen*. New York: Charles Scribner's Sons, 1916.

Tompkins, Jane. "Sentimental Power: Uncle Tom's Cabin and the Politics of Literary History." *Ideology and Classic American Literature*, ed. Sacvan Bercovitch and Myra Jehlen. New York: Cambridge University Press, 1986, 267–292.

Tocqueville, Alexis de. *Democracy in America*. New York: Knopf, 1972.

Todd Janet, *Sensibility: An Introduction*. New York: Methuen, 1986.

Varner, John Grier, *Sarah Helen Whitman: Seeress of Providence*. Ph.D. Diss. University of Virginia, 1940.

Walker, Cheryl, ed. *American Women Poets of the Nineteenth Century*. New Brunswick: Rutgers University Press, 1992.

— *The Nightingale's Burden: Women Poets and American Culture Before 1900*. Bloomington: Indiana University Press, 1982.

Walsh, John Evangelist. *Plumes in the Dust: The Love Affair of Edgar Allan Poe and Fanny Osgood*. Chicago: Nelson Hall, 1980.

Warner, Michael. *Letters of the Republic: Publication and the Public Sphere in Eighteenth-Century America*. Cambridge: Harvard University Press, 1990.

Watts, Emily Stipes, *The Poetry of American Women from 1632 to 1945*. Austin: University of Texas Press, 1977.

Webster, Noah. *An American Dictionary of the English Language*, 1828. Reprint, San Francisco: Foundation for an American Christian Education, 1985.

Weiss, Susan Archer. *The Home Life of Poe*. New York: Broadway Publishing Company, 1907.

Wendorff, Laura. *Race, Ethnicity, and the Voice of the "Poetess" in the Lives and Works of Four Late-Nineteenth-Century American Women Poets: Frances E. W. Harper, Emma Lazarus, Louise Guiney, and Ella Wheeler Wilcox*. Ph.D. Diss. University of Michigan, 1992.

Whalen, Terence. *Edgar Allan Poe and the Masses: The Political Economy of Literature in Antebellum America*. Princeton: Princeton University Press, 1999.

Whitman, Sarah Helen. *Edgar Poe and His Critics*, 1860. Reprint, New York: Gordian Press, 1981.

— *Poems*. Boston: Houghton, Osgood, and Co., 1979.

Whitman, Walt. *Leaves of Grass*. 1855. Reprint, New York: Library of America, 1992.

Wood, Ann Douglas Wood. "Mrs. Sigourney and the Sensibility of Inner Space," *The New England Quarterly* (June 1972), 163–181.

Woolf, Virginia. "Poe's Helen." *Granite and Rainbow*. New York: Harcourt and Brace, 1958, 225.

Wordsworth, William. *Wordsworth: Poetical Works*. New York: Oxford University Press, 1969.

Wyman, Mary Alice. *Two American Pioneers: Seba Smith and Elizabeth Oakes Smith.* New York: Columbia University Press, 1927.

Zagarell, Sandra. "Expanding 'America': Lydia Sigourney's Sketch of Connecticut, Catharine Sedgwick's Hope Leslie." *Redefining the Political Novel: American Women Writers, 1797–1901,* ed. Sharon Harris Knoxville: University of Tennessee Press, 1995, 43–65.

Zboray, Ronald. *A Fictive People: Antebellum Economic Development and the American Reading Public.* New York: Oxford University Press, 1993.

ARCHIVES

Elizabeth Oakes Smith Papers (38–707), Special Collections, University of Virginia Library.

The Elizabeth Oakes Prince Smith Papers, Manuscripts and Archives Division, The New York Public Library.

Frances Sargent Locke Osgood Papers (bMS Am). Manuscript Collections, Houghton Library, Harvard University.

Sarah Helen Whitman Papers (MS 79.11), and Hay Manuscripts (Hay MS), Brown University Library.

Sarah Helen Whitman Papers, Lilly Library, Indiana University, Bloomington, IN.

Index

abortive poetics 171–172, 184–186
Abrams, M. H. 154
Adams, John Quincy 37
Adorno, Theodore 18
Alcott, Bronson 9
Allen, Hervey 29
American Antiquarian Society 212
American Metropolitan 126
American Renaissance 207
Anthony, Susan B. 120, 155, 176
"anxiety of influence" *see* Bloom, Harold
appropriation 46–47
    Baudelaire's appropriation of Poe 55
    critical appropriation of Poe 145
    men's appropriation of women's poetry 5, 52,
        90–91, 156
    Poe's appropriation of women poets 50–52,
        94, 191–197
    women poets' appropriation of men, Poe 168
attribution 2–3, 5, 49, 75–76, 104–105, 121–122,
    147
audience *see* readers, reception
authenticity 3, 16, 19–20, 22–24, 52–53, 54, 77,
    107, 197
    of women poets 23–25, 56–58
authority *see* literary authority
authorship 2, 56, 86–88, 89–92, 138, 140–141
    female authorship 36–37, 39, 79–80
    gender of 6, 165–168
    male authorship 178–179, 193
    spiritualist forms of 120–122
    see also attribution

Bailey, William Whitman 111
Baker, Noelle 216
Barnes, Elizabeth 24
Barrett, Elizabeth *see* Browning, Elizabeth
    Barrett
Battersby, Christine 218
Baudelaire, Charles on Poe 31, 55–58, 145,
    207

Baym, Nina 12, 24, 67
Beadle's Monthly 183, 191
beauty 16–18, 37–38, 39–40, 41, 44, 56, 86, 116
Bennett, Andrew 200
Bennett, Paula 24, 25, 201, 202, 217
Berlant, Lauren and the "female complaint" 6–7,
    201, 208, 217
Bhabha, Homi 19
birds, song and poetry 49–50
Blackwell, Anna 40, 142
Blackwell, Elizabeth 142
Blasing, Mutlu 200, 205
Bloom, Harold 218
    "anxiety of influence" 20, 22, 123, 178
Bloor, A. C. 9
Bonaparte, Marie 200, 205
body 6
    female body 9, 30–31, 38–39, 45–47, 64,
        82–84, 92–93, 94–96
    male body 56–58
    see also embodiment, disembodiment
Booth, Edwin 191
borrowing *see* appropriation
Boston Lyceum 1
Boston Quarterly 110
Botta, Vincenzo
Bradley, Katherine 122
Braude, Ann 120
Bremer, Frederika 10
Broadway Journal 11, 14, 26, 92
Brodhead, Richard 210
Bronfen, Elisabeth 200, 205
Brooks, Maria 37, 150, 209
Brown, Gillian 207
Browning, Elizabeth Barrett 35, 36–37, 130, 206
    "Lady Geraldine's Courtship" 1, 39, 49–50,
        114, 170, 206
Brownson, Orestes 110
Bryant, William Cullen 9, 14, 29, 62, 77,
    117, 156
Burgett, Bruce 24